MARKETING FINANCIAL SERVICES

Marketing Financial Services

Second Edition

Colin McIver and Geoffrey Naylor

The Chartered Institute of Bankers

10 Lombard Street,   London EC3V 9AS

First published 1980
Reprinted 1984
Second edition 1986
Reprinted 1988
Copyright © 1980 & 1986 The Chartered Institute of Bankers and
Colin McIver and Geoffrey Naylor

Enquiries should be sent to the publishers at the undermentioned address:

THE CHARTERED INSTITUTE OF BANKERS
10 Lombard Street
London
EC3V 9AS

ISBN 0 85297 145 1

Typeset in 11pt on 12pt Baskerville by Staples Printers Rochester Limited
Text printed on 90gm^2 Nordset Offset, Cover on 240gm^2 Congress Art
Printed and bound by Staples Printers Rochester Limited,
Love Lane, Rochester, Kent.

Acknowledgments

As we said in the first edition, our sincere thanks are due to two groups of people; those who over the years helped us learn our craft, and those who have helped in the preparation of this book.

We are indebted to Valerie Jarvis, Lynn Lachs and Mandy Hawkins for their patient help in typing the original manuscripts, and once again to the staff of the The Institute of Bankers for their assistance.

Colin McIver and Geoffrey Naylor
May 1986

Preface

Since the first edition of this book was published by the Institute in 1980, there have been major changes both in the characteristics of the UK financial services market and in the marketing practices and philosophies of the leading UK banks. This year, which sees the 'Big Bang' in the securities market as well as the legislative changes enabling the building societies to compete more directly with the banks, is likely to prove a watershed between a relatively tranquil past and a highly competitive, highly mobile future.

UK banks (and their competitors) have responded to the challenge of a more diversified and internationalised market in a number of ways. Organisational structures have been modified to allow for a greater degree of market segmentation and specialisation. Increasing use is being made of modern technology to improve the banks' services to customers while controlling the inexorable rise in costs. And increasing attention is being paid to delivery systems – seeking the most cost-effective way of conveying our products to our customers.

Changes of this kind demand new approaches to the management of relationships between bank and customer, in other words to marketing. It becomes increasingly important that not only the members of bank marketing departments but managers and staff, at all levels, should have a sound understanding of marketing principles and practices.

The past six years have seen a substantial growth in banks' expenditure on marketing, steadily rising standards of professionalism in the specialist marketing departments and much closer co-operation between these departments and branch management in the implementation of business development projects.

This second edition of *Marketing Financial Services* has been extensively revised to take account of these developments (including entirely new or updated case studies). It is intended to provide a readable account of the present state of the marketing art in UK banking, which any banker concerned with this important subject will, we hope, find thought-provoking and informative; and which those intending to specialise will find useful as an introduction to a more intensive study of marketing technology.

Colin McIver and Geoffrey Naylor
May 1986

Contents

Part three **Marketing in action**

In this part we move from the general to the particular with a collection of case histories to illustrate the way bank marketing departments set about things in relation both to the development of traditional banking business and to the banks' incursion into related financial services.

PART ONE

The role of marketing

In this first part we define the role of marketing in management, and describe how the problems of marketing financial services differ from the marketing problems encountered in other industrial sectors.

CHAPTER ONE

Introduction

How often have you watched or participated in an argument, where the protagonists never even began to communicate, because each was using the same familiar words to describe concepts that held quite different meanings, and different associations for the one and the other?

Marketing, unhappily, is one of those chameleon words with erratic implications. In its original dictionary definition – buying and selling in the marketplace – it describes an activity that has been part of human existence since civilisation began. Because it has been around so long, we assume that at this basic level it has the same connotations for everybody. Not so. Probe a little and you will find that, for one cultural type, buying and selling in the marketplace has rather sordid associations with barrow-boys and one trickster outsmarting another; for others it will be associated with merchant venturers, braving perilous seas in search of profitable trade. One type will nourish a prejudice against marketing, the other will be prejudiced in its favour.

More recently the same word, marketing, has been used to describe the techniques, greatly elaborated during the last forty years, which producers of goods and services use, in conjunction with traditional selling, to win and retain customers and optimise profits. These are the techniques like market research, product development, advertising and promotion, which we describe in the second part of this book. These too provoke different reactions in different people. Advertising, in particular, is lauded by some because of its ability to accelerate acceptance of a new idea or a new product and distrusted by others because of its partisan habit of stressing the positive advantages of a product, rather than giving a balanced account of its pros and cons.

At another level again, marketing is used to describe that part of a general manager's job which is concerned with managing the organisation's present relationship and planning its future relationship with *customers* – that fickle and elusive body without which no business can survive. This third meaning, too, causes unnecessary misunderstanding and conflict. No advocate of marketing can have failed to meet the individual who proclaims that 'I'm a practical man, I don't hold with this marketing nonsense' – and then turns out to have spent his whole career practising the arts of marketing by the light of nature.

So we had better start this book by stating our position and saying what we mean by marketing. At least you will know what we are talking about, even though a definition never made anything happen; and the only justification for studying marketing or spending money on it, in a commercial context, is that it makes things happen which would not have happened as fast or as effectively without it.

What we mean by marketing

We believe – and those who have seriously studied the role of marketing or observed it in action seem to agree – that the definition of marketing should place it firmly in the lap of senior management with its responsibility for planning and managing the organisation's relationship with customers. As a matter of practical observation, if senior management is sceptical of the importance of marketing or hostile towards it, those who toil to apply marketing techniques at a lower level will waste a lot of energy and probably a lot of money too.

But how to put it into words when marketing takes such different forms in different countries, different industries and companies? Philip Kotler, in his monumental tome on Marketing Management (required but not always easy reading for anyone who is seriously interested in the subject), writes that 'Marketing is the set of human activities directed at facilitating and consummating exchanges'. True enough for academic purposes; and, as Kotler says, 'the definition deliberately avoids taking the point of view of either the buyer or the seller'.

But it is not a very stimulating definition for those of us in the practical world whose marketing responsibility is less concerned with buying than with selling–a responsibility that has to be exercised with proper concern for the interests of the buyer if the loyalty of the latter is to be retained. Where, for example, is the word 'profit'? Optimising long-term profit (as opposed to pursuing a quick buck) must surely be one of the most important marketing concerns in a commercial organisation; and it is not irrelevant in a public utility or non profit-making activity, now the concept of 'social profit' has been invented. Indeed, it is essential, especially given the survival of some old-fashioned get-the-order-at-any-price salesman, to distinguish Marketing from Selling.

'Profitable selling', however, though commendably brief, does not inspire us to a more detailed consideration of the marketing function. So, rather than flounder around among the innumerable definitions of marketing propounded in many text books on the subject, let us home in on the very practical, if lengthy, definiton put forward by Deryk Vander Weyer when he was responsible at senior management level for the marketing function at Barclay's Bank. The role of marketing, he wrote, is:

1 identifying the most profitable markets now and in the future;
2 assessing the present and future needs of customers;
3 setting business development goals and making plans to meet them;
4 managing the various services and promoting them to achieve the plans.

Though written several years ago (in 1969 for his Ernest Sykes Memorial Lecture), this remains a very forward-looking description of the way a genuinely marketing-orientated organisation operates in the vital area of relationships with changing customers in a changing market place; and of the direction in which most successful banks are moving. It makes a particularly sound and sensible text on which to base the main arguments of this book.

Let us briefly examine the implications of the definition's four points. The first brings the profit concept well to the fore and also highlights the concern of marketing with the future as well as the present. This last, it should be said in parenthesis, has often resulted in disappointment among managers who swallowed marketing in the belief that it would act as an instant elixir. It seldom does. Being concerned very largely with modifying people's attitudes and behaviour, something that is not done in a hurry, marketing tends to be a slow acting medicine; insisting on quick results can cause disappointment or trivialisation.

Also implicit in the first point is the concept of market segmentation, which is particularly important in banking with its wide range of retail and wholesale customers. Convenient as it would be, from a production-orientated viewpoint, to have a single product or service that pleased all the people all the time, life is not like that; so banks and other financial service institutions are having to think as seriously as the manufacturers of consumer products about concentrating their marketing efforts on those market segments which they are best equipped to serve at a profit.

Point two of the definition lies at the heart of marketing philosophy, which proclaims to all who are prepared to listen that a business is more likely to prosper if it starts by assessing present and future customer needs and from there goes on to arrange the supply (at a profit) of what is needed, than if it simply supplies what it is convenient to produce and hopes for the best. But this philosophy needs to be taken with a grain of salt. In a commercial world customers cannot have what they need unless they can afford to pay for it, so a distinction must be made between need and effective demand; and suppliers will be ill-advised to attempt to meet an identified need or even demand unless they are confident they can do so at least as efficiently as their competitors.

Point three very properly emphasises the need for setting business development goals, which is a general management responsibility, and raises the cardinal but often confusing question of planning. Practical marketing is not just a matter of bright promotional ideas and wishful thinking but involves the prediction of, and the measurement of, results and the resources required to achieve those results. Without defined goals and controlled allocation of resources, marketing becomes divorced from reality.

Business development planning, the second issue raised by point three, is sometimes a source of jurisdictional disputes between the corporate planners and the marketing planners. Where does one end and the other begin? We shall argue later, when discussing the paramount importance of planning, that one cannot be effective without the other. A corporate plan that neglects to give primary consideration to predictable changes in market conditions and customer requirements is an inadequate blueprint for action; but, equally, a business development plan that fails to spell out the physical and attitudinal demands it will make on the organisation's human and material resources is little better than a paper tiger.

Point four moves from planning to implementation or, if you prefer, from strategy to tactics. More of the readers of this book are likely to be involved in the latter than in the former, so more space will be devoted to it. But it should not be forgotten that without the strategic thinking and general management disciplines implicit in the first three points, the most vigorous marketing implementation will have very limited value.

The marketing staff function

The definition of marketing which we have discussed so far emphasises its importance in general management and suggests that any manager with executive responsibility needs to devote at least as much attention to the problems of marketing his wares and his ideas (if only within the organisation to superiors, colleagues and subordinates) as to administration, production and finance.

But in most organisations of any size, certainly in most banks and other financial service institutions, the marketing responsibilities of line management are supplemented and supported by a specialist staff function. The components of this, located either in separate pockets within the organisation or in a co-ordinated marketing services or business development department, are likely to be specialists in the various techniques described in Part II of this book, most frequently market information, business development planning, marketing communications (through advertising, public relations and other media), branch network support and new product development.

How these staff units are manned, how effectively they relate to line management and how clearly the dividing line between the two is drawn all have a lot to do with the speed at which professional marketing is accepted and the effectiveness with which it is utilised in an organisation where senior management has decided to give marketing a higher priority.

Historically, marketing research has been the most readily and widely accepted aspect of marketing, possibly because managers sincerely wanted to know more about their customers, and in a world with many links in the distribution chain from producer to consumer, this kind of research was much more reliable than hearsay 'trade reports'; possibly, it seems in moments of cynicism, because commissioning or even reading market research reports does not actually commit you to *doing* anything; and most such reports can at a pinch be selectively interpreted to reinforce existing prejudices. ('Some people', it has been said, 'use market research as a drunk uses a lamp post, more for support than illumination'). The objectivity with which market research or other forms of market data are interpreted and the frequency with which they are used as a basis for action are a more reliable indication of an organisation's commitment to 'market-led' principles than the size of the research or advertising budget.

A more analytical approach to advertising and its attendant activities – consumer and trade promotions, point of sale display, print and audio-visual sales support material – was the next major development. Thus, instead of accepting uncritically the blanket statement that it pays to advertise (sometimes it does and sometimes it doesn't) some companies, backed and often led by the more progressive advertising agencies, tried to measure the effectiveness of the various advertising media available to them and of the creative integument in which the selling message was wrapped and to evaluate the return on their total investment in sales promotional activities.

The development of new products to meet the changing needs of defined customer segments or to exploit new technology is an area in which the marketing contribution has been less readily accepted. To the dedicated marketer it seems an open-and-shut case that product development should start from an identified customer need or market opportunity and that product development should therefore be a marketing responsibility. But in practice it is often more a case of matching the demand and the resource that can satisfy it with the main motivation coming from either end. The solution most often adopted has been the appointment of a New Product Manager, usually, but not always, a marketing man, with responsibility for planning and co-ordinating the research, technological, organisational and promotional activities involved in the creation and launch of a new product. In marketing theory the product manager for either a new or an established product is profit-responsible; but since he has little authority over the departments whose contributions make most of the difference between success and failure, profit and loss, he has to discharge his responsibility by diplomatic rather than dictatorial means. Product or project management, it should be added, is one of the marketing concepts that has made less progress in banks than in manufacturing organisations, perhaps because the implications of launching a new product are more serious for a bank. Manufacturers of branded products can scrap their mistakes and suffer little loss of reputation; a bank often has to live with them.

Marketing, or business development planning, is another specialist marketing skill that is accepted more in its short-term and tactical manifestations (planning special promotions and the like) than in the contribution it can make to the organisation's long-term strategic planning.

The complete acceptance and adaptation to the financial services market of the most important marketing concepts and techniques is surely only a question of time – and there is not a lot of time to spare, with competition getting rapidly keener and profits harder to earn. The marketing specialists, who are increasingly being recruited by banks and other financial service houses to reinforce their home-grown marketers, can help to accelerate the process by demonstrating on a modest scale that marketing can produce measurable results, by building bridges with line management and by active participation in the organisation's training activities so as to develop a common language.

How does marketing financial services differ from marketing consumer or industrial products and services?

Fiduciary responsibility

A fundamental consideration which must cover the attitude of bank management to marketing and selling can be summed up in the phrase 'fiduciary responsibility'. There has always been a marketing element in banking practice throughout its recorded history, though it may not always have been described by that word. But bankers who persuade their customers to entrust personal or corporate funds to their care or to accept advice on investment or on some management matters incur a heavier responsibility than the sellers of candyfloss.

This is not to say that the manufacture of consumer products or the producer of industrial goods or services, or indeed the management of a nationalised service industry, is without responsibility. But the responsibility in these other cases is limited to the fitness of purpose, quality and value for money of the product or service concerned. It is inconvenient but seldom catastrophic if the milk is sour, the refrigerator or telephone breaks down or a manufacturer's raw material shipment is sub-standard. But a banker's failure to discharge his fiduciary responsibility for safeguarding customers' funds or to provide responsible advice on financial matters can bankrupt a company or ruin an individual's life.

For this reason the marketing style of a financial services organisation can never by as uninhibited as that of, let us say, the manufacturer of fast-moving packaged goods. The latter can say, and mean it, that 'this is a marketing company' run by marketing people; and that the production, purchasing and other departments should follow the lead and satisfy the demands of the marketing department. A responsible bank management has to say that marketing skills are important if the bank is to grow and prosper – increasingly important in an increasingly competitive environment – but that other aspects of their profession are equally important.

A corollary of this is that the qualities a bank must seek in its employees are not the same as those that cartoonists would lead us to believe belong to a typical salesman: uncaring aggression at any price. It is true that without sales no company can survive. But the bank manager, dealing with transactions which may fundamentally affect his customer's future, must be more receptive and aware of the possible consequences of a successful 'sale'.

This does not necessarily mean that he will be a less effective salesman (though he may shudder at the notion of being called a salesman); but it does mean that his selling style and the marketing programme which is built around him will be different.

Involvement in national economic policy

In the modified form of capitalism which is characteristic of developed Western nations it would be unrealistic to speak of totally free enterprise. Government economic policies, whether expressed in wages policies, price controls, credit restrictions or other rules and regulations, all make it difficult for company managements to concentrate on the textbook objective of maximising profits through customer satisfaction.

But the frustration or diversion of commercial objectives in the interest of national economic considerations is an unusually powerful factor in banking. In one year, government decisions on credit controls or interest levels may mean that banks are almost compelled to make large profits, however hard they struggle to avoid it. The next year, a shift in policy may mean that it is desperately difficult to achieve anything approaching the same profit level. This does not of course imply that the word 'profit' should be dropped from the bank marketer's vocabulary; it remains a condition of healthy growth and even survival as an independent organisation. But it does require a more flexible approach to the process of planning, targeting and monitoring marketing activities which will be dealt with later; and it does mean an acceptance of the need to make rapid changes of emphasis in a marketing programme, which is not always easy in a large organisation.

Attracting deposits

A third way in which financial services marketing differs from marketing in other industries is the involvement of marketing not only in the provision of services to customers but in the procurement of the raw material on which most of those services are based. The automobile industry does not have to *persuade* its suppliers to provide it with steel or components – though admittedly it has many other difficulties with suppliers. The banking industry can 'buy' a proportion of its raw material (money) on the money market; but an important proportion of the raw material has to be gained by persuading individuals or corporate organisations to deposit their funds with it. And persuasion is a marketing function.

The fact that the main means of persuasion in attracting deposits is the availability of services – so that the raw material supplier is at the same time a customer – adds a fascinating element of complexity to the truly fascinating business of marketing financial services. Indeed complexity is a predominant feature in this market. It involves some elements of three types of marketing: the industrial, the consumer and the retail level. It requires a range of skills and knowledge which are beyond the compass of any normal man; and it must eventually result in the progressive *segmentation* both of markets and of bank organisations to which we refer later.

The element of industrial marketing

The basic factor which in most cases distinguishes industrial marketing from the other main categories is the sale of the project or services concerned to fewer but (usually) better-informed customers. From this it follows that the element of personal selling as opposed to selling through advertising or other communications media is larger. It also follows that there is both more opportunity and more need for an understanding of the way in which the customer uses the product and of the contribution it makes to the profitability of his own business; and also of the elements in the decision-making process and their effects on the choice of your product or your competitors' – including the motivation of the individuals who contribute to the decision.

The parallel with the corporate sector of the banks' business is close. Acquiring and satisfying a corporate customer requires a range of skills which differs in degree if not in kind from those employed in attracting and satisfying personal customers. These skills range from face-to-face selling ability through the ability to assemble, analyse and interpret data from various sources about a given market and the operations of a given company within that market, to the ability to organise and apply a variety of specialist resources to satisfy the customer's requirements at an acceptable rate of return.

The consumer marketing element

In the early days of bank marketing in the UK much emphasis – possibly too much – was placed on attracting and servicing personal customers.

This was understandable since consumer marketing is much the most conspicuous category because of its extensive reliance on media advertising; and it was also the category in which marketing techniques had made the most progress. Moreover, emphasis on personal customers probably assisted the build-up of the banks' image in the corporate sector, since the decision-makers in corporate customers are individuals as well; and their attitudes to banks will inevitably be coloured by their personal experiences.

At the same time the corporate sector is more important to most banks in terms of profit contribution; and it is also more vulnerable to attack from new competition (for instance, the overseas banks which have entered the London market in such numbers during recent years). It may be that more emphasis should have been put on the industrial marketing skills, especially to help overcome the price advantage non-clearing banks can have.

However that may be, the largest proportion of bank staff is concerned with the personal customer; and there are many techniques developed in consumer marketing which can be applied or adapted to the banking scene. They include marketing and attitude research techniques, methods of new product development, 'packaging' and presentation, market segmentation and mass market communications.

Retail marketing

It would be over-dramatising the situation to say that branch banks are in a stage of transition from the equivalent of the headmaster's study – into which customers ventured with apprehension and from which they emerged with relief that the castigation for an illicitly overdrawn account had not been more serious – to a shop which invites them to enter and browse among the available goodies. Security requirements and the heavy investment in vaults and other costly hardware make it unlikely that your average branch bank will ever be as alluring as Harrods or Habitat. However, the proliferation of bank services and the acquisition of related subsidiaries such as insurance or hire purchase companies which look to the branch bank as one of their available sales outlets make it inevitable that branches should be regarded to some degree as financial services shops.

The attempt to develop this logic in the form of money shops has not been an unqualified success in the UK. But it is becoming increasingly clear that the branch structure of banks, building societies and other financial service organisations, which was built up largely to meet a pre-War pattern of demand, is no longer well suited to the demand pattern of the 'eighties and 'nineties; in particular, the trend towards planned market segmentation has raised the question whether the business customer and the private customer, the affluent and the not so well-off, can be satisfied through the same traditional 'shop'.

A possible solution that has been canvassed is the enlarged financial services supermarket. But it seems more likely that market segmentation will be reflected in branch segmentation, with business branches, personal branches, boutiques for the affluent and money shops for those of simpler needs – plus, possibly, mail order 'branches' for those who would prefer not to meet their bank manager face to face.

The implication of all this is that at least some of the marketing techniques developed by other retail trades will be relevant to financial services retailing in the future. One might instance the automated self-service selling forced on the grocery and petrol trade by the high cost of labour; the use of in-store display and merchandising techniques to whet the appetite of the casual shopper (or cheque casher); the use of store lay-out and design skills to attract the desired type of customers and made it easier for them to buy; and the use of market research to assess the business potential for a newly located outlet.

Evaluating customers' marketing skills

The main reason, we suggest, why a banker should have at least an appreciative understanding of marketing techniques used in other industries is that they can be a rich source of ideas that can be adapted and applied in the very different banking environment. But there is another reason which should be considered by those with discretionary lending powers. The lending policies of British banks are traditionally conservative and based on 'the ability to repay' backed whenever possible by tangible security. This is very right and proper, when in the last analysis it is other people's money that is being lent. But British lending policy is more conservative that that of some other countries; and it can provoke either the frivolous reaction that 'they will only lend money to people who don't need it' or the more serious if refutable criticism that bank lending policies are inimical to industrial growth and entrepreneurial initiative. If a combination of pressures should enforce a trend towards the acceptance of higher-risk loans, related less to current assets than to future prospects, the skill to discriminate between profit forecasts which are based on sound marketing planning and those which are the product of wishful thinking could become an even more important part of the bank manager's armoury.

Summary

In this chapter we have

1 discussed various definitions of marketing and agreed that the definition quoted on page 5 was a good description of the marketing function in banking and in most other industries from the *management* viewpoint;
2 made the point that in practice there is another and relevant view of marketing in the *marketing services* departments which see the same function from a different standpoint;
3 said that marketing is greatly concerned with the relationship between a changing environment and the changes in organisational structure and methods required to relate successfully and profitably to that environment;
4 suggested that the marketing of financial services differs in several important particulars from marketing in other industries; but that many of the marketing techniques and ideas developed in other sectors can be usefully adapted to the increasingly competitive financial services market;
5 suggested that marketing, while it may not be the most important part of a bank manager's skills and responsibilities, must be high on the list; and the complexities of marketing requirements, particularly in a large diversified branch banking organisation, are such that both market segmentation and segmentation of the organisation that serves the market are essential.

Now, how much of this do *you* accept, and how far does it reflect your own experience of the banking scene? You may not agree with everything we have said, but please pause and think about it.

CHAPTER TWO

Marketing in a changing environment

Recognising, reporting and adapting to change

All organisations, unless totally introverted and therefore doomed to suffer the fate of the dinosaur, must be sensitive to the environment and adapt to any relevant changes in it. This is so obvious that it hardly needs to be stated. The trouble is that most individuals and most organisations resist change. It must have been hard for the early mammals to abandon their watery environment and learn to exist on dry land. It is visibly just as difficult for Industrial Man to accept that the job he is doing, or the way he is doing it, is no longer relevant to a rapidly changing economic, social or technological environment.

To bring about change in an organisation, which involves changing the attitudes and behaviour of the people who work in it, is one of the most difficult tasks of the management team, involving all their combined skills.

Management's difficulty is seldom one of needing to take emergency action. Most changes, whether in the market place or in technology, are both predictable and relatively slow; and the process of adapting to change within the organisation is equally slow. The real problems arise from

1 the need for early recognition of impending change that will affect the organisation's activities;
2 getting the timing right. Being too far ahead of your time can have just as serious commercial consequences as being far too late;
3 the difficulties which management, reared and perhaps trained in calmer times, have in finding the opportunities amid today's crises for thinking about tomorrow and the day after;
4 the reluctance of both customers and employees to change their ways.

Marketing skills, probably embodied in a central department, have a valuable contribution to make in this area. Particularly relevant skills are

1 the ability to collect external information through market research and other means, to predict the eventual outcome of emergent changes, and to interpret their significance for the organisation;
2 techniques of planning and co-ordination, relating the speed of internal change – product development, market-related organisation, selling and distribution methods – to the rate of change in external demand and competition;
3 the skills of communication and persuasion needed, first to bring an understanding of the situation to management and others, and second, to accelerate necessary changes in the attitudes and behaviour of people involved in the company's operations, whether as customers, employees or distributors and agents;
4 techniques for pre-testing possible courses of action or reaction to change, such as market models and test markets.

Changes in customers' characteristics and related needs

The most immediately relevant environmental factor for any organisation is the customer on whose continued approval the organisation's future depends. In almost all cases the *ultimate* customer is some segment of the general public; even the industrial marketer, whose immediate customers are other organisations, is dependent in the end on the ability of those organisations to satisfy the segment of the general public which they serve.

Bankers will instantly recognise the truth of this. Indeed, when they act as lenders to industrial companies, they are one stage further removed from the general public; yet most bankers will still want to know about the ultimate sales so as to judge the soundness of a project. So we make no excuse whatsoever for talking about general marketing principles. Good bankers will see the relevance to banking, even before reading the later chapters in which specific applications of the principles to our industry are described.

For the organisation marketing goods or services (including financial services) to the general public, the changes in personal circumstances and lifestyle which have characterised the last twenty-five years in all countries have opened up many new opportunities while putting a stop to some. The UK with its 56 million population has changed less than most countries of the developed or developing world. The growth both of population and of gross national product has been relatively slow. There has been no obvious revolution in the form of government or in social structure. Industrialisation and urbanisation, the flight from the farm to the factory, from the village to the city, still taking place in many countries, had more or less run their course in Britain before the second world war.

And yet, slow economic growth or not, the income of the average British family has doubled over the quarter century in real terms. Moreover, the cumulative effect of redistributive taxation, strongly supported by the power of organised labour, has resulted in some flattening of the family income pyramid, though the flattening is not as dramatic as some would have wished or others feared. But it does mean that the producers of many products and services, not least financial services, can think in terms of a much wider potential market than they had before.

Home ownership

A wider prosperity and enlarged aspirations have led to a higher level of home ownership and an increased demand for the equipment – furniture, domestic appliances, decorating materials and so on – required to make the home comfortable and beautiful. The marketing opportunities flowing from this include not only the obvious one of making and distributing an immense variety of comsumer durables but also such satellite manifestations as home-making and do-it-yourself magazines, to say nothing of the provision of the consumer credit needed to finance purchases that could not be made out of income or savings. And now, with large investments already made in consumer durables, the way people spend their disposable incomes may well start to change; the marketers of consumer credit may have to turn more of their attention to financing other activities, like holidays, self-education and leisure activities outside the home.

Watching the banks' advertising and promotional activities will give a useful insight into the way they and their marketing departments are reacting to these trends. One quite recent manifestation has been their more aggressive attack on the house mortgage market, incidentally precipitating direct confrontation with the building societies. Another has been the development and marketing of loan 'products' or savings-and-loan schemes related to the acquisition of items (whether tangible or intangible) of current interest to the target customer segment. This is good psychology. Most people are less interested in money than in the things money can buy; talking about the latter rather than the former not only is more interesting to the audience but helps to humanise the sometimes forbidding aspect of a bank.

The motor car

After the home the most important of material possessions is the motor car. Widened car ownership again has both direct implications for the manufacturer and the provider of financial services; and indirect repercussions – some good, some bad – for other market sectors. It has created obvious problems for the marketers of public transport systems, railways and bus lines, whose monopoly position has been eroded. But at the same time the increased mobility brought about by widespread car ownership has provided innumerable opportunities for the markets of travel, leisure and other services to be exploited successfully or unsuccessfully according to the marketer's skill in predicting popular demand. Such motor-related manifestations as the drive-in quick food outlet and the drive-in bank have proved a disappointment to their promoters. But the out-of-town supermarket, totally dependent on the car and the parking lot, has flourished where local planning restrictions have been overcome.

Here again there are marketing implications for the banks. Direct loans for car purchase are usually handled by their hire purchase subsidiaries who have special skills in credit rating and, if the worst comes to the worst, in repossession; and this, together with direct loans by the banks themselves, can give an easy spin-off to their insurance brokerage subsidiaries. Awareness of commercial trends arising from wider car ownership also helps in selective lending to businesses; other things being equal, a business that is in the forefront of change will be a better credit risk than one likely to be left high and dry by changing social patterns.

Educational opportunity

Wider educational opportunities and changes in the character of employment have gone hand-in-hand to generate new forms of consumer demand. There can be more than one view (and indeed there are many impassioned views) about the practical implications of equal opportunities in education. Against the clearly ethical view that no child should be denied opportunity through an accident of birth or late developments is placed the argument that increased opportunity for the under-privileged may reduce opportunity for the well-endowed; and that the outstanding minority, as a purely practical matter, may be more important to a nation's progress than the averageness of the majority. Without taking sides in that argument, the marketing man must conclude that the widening of educational opportunity must inevitably change not only the character of consumer demand but the language of communication with the consumer market. It never was wise to assume that 'the consumer is an ass' who can easily be fooled; it will be even less wise to do so in the future.

This has implications for the communications aspect of marketing, not only just advertising but brochures, routine correspondence and face-to-face interviews. The customer is unlikely to be a banking expert and in most cases will be puzzled if addressed in banking jargon; but equally he or she will be offended if talked down to in the way some consumer product advertising talks down to that sad invention of male ego 'the housewife'. With the growing acceptance of customer segmentation in bank marketing, communication with customers can become a dialogue between equals.

Type of job

On the employment front we have said that the flight from the farm to the factory which characterised the industrial revolution was completed in the UK before the last quarter-century. But this does not imply that radical changes in the nature and location of employment are not still going on. There is the major and continuing change from employment in manufacture to employment in the service industries. There is the fact that some 30 per cent of the nation's workforce is now employed by central government, local authorities or public corporations rather than by private industry. Within industry itself (and indeed within the residual but immensely important agricultural sector) there is a progressive shift from the unskilled labourer to the skilled operative in charge of a substantial investment in capital equipment. Different types of job mean different lifestyles and different requirements for goods and services.

The working wife

From the marketing viewpoint a most important change on the employment scene has been the increased proportion of married women (about

50 per cent according to official statistics and probably more unofficially) who take full-time or part-time jobs outside the home. It would be tempting to pursue the sociological sources and ramifications of this development, such as family planning and the women's lib movement. We must confine ourselves to the more mundane marketing implications. The most obvious of these is the impact on manufacturers of demand for packaged foods and other domestic products. The realisation that a wife is not just her husband's better half, but an independent 'purchasing unit' in her own right, has changed marketing thinking in most industries, including financial services.

The additional workload taken on by wives with outside employment does not, in most cases, release them from their so-called housewifely responsibilities. The cooking and cleaning still have to be done, and husbandly co-operation still has not progressed very far beyond giving a hand with the washing up. So there is the need for convenience foods and other devices to ease the domestic burden, linked to the availability of the cash to pay for them. A second marketing implication of some importance is that total family income (particularly if there are also earning children living at home) can in many cases be substantially greater than the income of the family's main earner. At one time market researchers could feel that they had adequately established the socio-economic status of a family by finding out the income of the head of the household (who, in those not-too-far-off days was assumed to be the husband). No longer is this the case; the family's income and decisions on how to spend it can no longer be regarded as a husbandly preserve.

Another consequence of the independent working wife is a boost for the fashion and clothing industries. Independent incomes and more time spent outside the home mean independent personal purchases. Coming closer home to the subject of this book, they can also mean an increased demand by women for personal bank accounts and other financial services. The banks cannot be accused of being backward in this respect, but it is questionable whether the full marketing implications have been recognised and exploited.

The single-parent family

A variation on the working wife theme, compounded by the fact that one in three marriages now ends in divorce (and not all relationships are sanctified by marriage) is the single-parent family. Personal unhappiness apart, such families are a social problem because so many are at or below the poverty line; and they also present a problem to bank marketing strategists in reconciling their social responsibility to provide financial services to those who need them with the commercial responsibility to earn a profit. Experiments in providing a highly mechanised low cost banking service for the less well off have not so far been very successful.

The age profile

Yet another aspect of consumer characteristics which must affect the thinking of markets whose products or services are aimed at a specific age segment is the changing age profile of the population. The birthrate bulge of fifteen to twenty years ago makes this a good time for marketers with products designed for the younger generation or with an interest in establishing habits which may last a lifetime, such as the habit of using a bank account. The currently reduced birthrate makes it a correspondingly bad period for manufacturers of baby products. And in due course, as our population gets steadily older, there is a good time coming in the geriatric market. Of course against these general trends one can always find a successful company 'swimming against the tide': the Mothercare chain of shops is a good example. But the flair of individual entrepreneurs in meeting the changing market's needs more effectively and efficiently than their competitors does not invalidate the general trend.

Bank marketers, seeking to adjust their banks' products to meet changing consumer needs, will no doubt place increasing emphasis on such services as pension schemes for those anticipating retirement and financial help for those who have actually retired and must therefore adjust to a new way of life with new financial needs.

The Ethnic Group

The increasing number of unassimilated minority groups is a feature of life on our small island that neither politicians nor bankers have yet come to terms with. Some groups, like the Cypriot community in London, have their own banks linked to the national clearing system through one of the London Clearing Banks. For others it remains a question of whether ethnic branches will be a natural development of the large banks' policy of customer segmentation; or whether this would create an undesirable (and possibly uneconomic) element of segregation.

The industrial market

For the industrial market, as for the corporate sector in banking, the direction of change is rather different. Where most consumer markets are expanding, in terms of the number of individuals or families in a position to buy a given consumer product, the number of available customers for the industrial marketer is tending to shrink with the increasing concentration of company ownership. According to one study of the concentration of British industry, the 100 largest British firms in 1935 accounted for 24 per cent of total industrial production; when the 1968 census of production was carried out the 100 largest firms accounted for 42 per cent of total output. It does not always follow that central ownership means centralised buying. But it is certainly true that in many industries, not least financial services, the marketer has fewer but larger targets to aim at; and the process of negotiating a sale with powerful and sophisticated buyers or buying committees becomes a correspondingly more difficult and complex affair. It can become even more complicated when selling to the public sector, where political considerations can be superimposed on normal commercial factors.

Differential rates of growth and profitability between different industrial sectors is another element of change which imposes the need for marketing flexibility on the industrial producer. When a whole industry goes into decline, as the shipping and textile industries have in this country, its suppliers must either decline with it or find new market opportunities, in other industries or overseas, and adapt their products, services, and marketing and management methods accordingly.

A third factor among many others that might be mentioned is the growing power of labour and its involvement in management decisions. As suppliers of new equipment and new techniques to the publishing industry (among many others) have discovered to their cost, it is not enough to convince management of its economic advantages; the labour force and the unions also have to be convinced that it is in their interest to operate the new equipment.

Industrial change also brings with it the necessity for suppliers to be flexible in their choice of location. A chain of retail shops or a network of branch banks may be ideally located when it is first set up. But industrial decline in one area and industrial growth in another will make the distribution less and less ideal as time goes on. The high cost and the personal inconvenience of relocation will sooner or later have to be faced if healthy growth is to continue. And of course, as the UK banks experienced in the 1950s and 1960s, mergers bring marketing problems, especially of image, as well as organisational problems.

Changes in the economy

The fortunes of banks and other financial service institutions are even more closely related to changing economic conditions than those of other industries. Many, if not most, industries have to face the fact that demand for their products will ebb and flow more or less in step with the ups and downs of the economy; if their market forecasting is sound they can do something to mitigate the severity of the swings through planned marketing effort, diversification, the development of counter-cyclical products and so on, despite the growing inflexibility of overheads imposed by the conditions of employment and other such factors.

But financial institutions are not only exposed to the winds of economic change; they are also exposed, sometimes to the advantage sometimes to the detriment of their profitability, to the various efforts of governments to control the economy. They must accept directives about which sectors of borrowers shall have priority; about their rate of growth; even sometimes about their pricing policies (i.e. interest rate levels).

Being tied in their basic business to a sluggish and would-be managed economy has forced UK banks to adopt two major marketing initiatives. The first is to place more emphasis than hitherto on development in faster-growing economies overseas; in most banks the international division is the fastest growing part of the organisation. The second initiative is to diversify from the banking base into other financial services like insurance and hire purchase. The ultimate effect, it becomes increasingly apparent, is to convert a relatively simple business of safeguarding and lending money into a much more aggressive multi-national financial services conglomerate, with the need for much greater diversity of management and marketing skills that this involves.

The rising storm of competition

It would be misleading to suggest that the introduction by the government of 'Competition and Credit Control' in 1971 was the watershed dividing the relatively uncompetitive British banking system, which most bankers of mature years elected to join in their salad days, from the increasingly competitive scene which faces them today. Certainly this directive outlawed many previously agreed cartel arrangements and decreed that the clearing banks should compete, and be seen to compete, more vigorously against each other. But competition, even if disguised in a velvet glove, had never really been absent; managers were never uninterested in business development nor displeased at picking up a good account from the rival bank up the street. The real change in the competitive environment has come from the banks' incursions into other financial services sectors and the simultaneous invasion by other financial institutions – including overseas banks setting up in the UK – of what had previously been regarded as the traditional banker's preserve.

Just to summarise the new or enhanced competition which is battling for a share of the British financial services market, there are

1 the 400 or so US and other foreign banks which have opened branches on London and which employ around 30,000 people. In most cases their primary target has been the corporate rather than the personal customer; and their aggressive, often highly professional, marketing methods (helped to some degree by their exclusion from certain requirements imposed on their UK competitors) have necessitated greater professionalism in this sector by the indigenous banks;

2 the fringe banking operations, encouraged by over-liberal banking regulations, are less of a problem now and more of a painful memory. Here today, gone tomorrow; but could they be back again the day after tomorrow in some other guise? The answer must surely be yes. While the recent difficulties of Johnson Matthey's banking subsidiary is further evidence that banking is a dangerous game for the newcomer to play, the banking activities of American Express and Merrill Lynch in this country are presumably here to stay;

3 not long ago the local trustee savings banks could be regarded by the clearing banks as relatively insignificant competitors at the lower end of the savings market. Now that they have been united into a single Trustee Savings Bank, with a national branch network, a heavily promoted Credit Card and the imminent prospect of privatisation, the TSB must be regarded as a very direct competitor – with the different image due to its historical past, that each of the traditional clearers aspires to;

4 the National Giro system at this stage remains part of the still nationalised Post Office, with all the advantages and disadvantages that this implies. While its present range of services is limited, it does offer services such as cash collection at a cut price; and it does hold out the possibility of harmonisation with the National Savings Bank and its innumerable Post Office outlets;

5 competition with the building societies cannot fail to hot up following the government's announcement in 1984 that the banks would be required to deduct a composite rate of income tax from interest paid on deposits, like the building societies, instead of paying interest free of tax, and that building societies would be permitted, subject to various safeguards, to engage in banking activities beyond those connected with housing finance. The CRT provision will highlight the higher rate of interest offered by the building societies, thanks to their lower operating costs, and accelerate the banks' progressive loss of share in the deposit-taking market, unless effective counter-measures are taken; this wider field of competition will ... well, let's wait and see;

6 the instalment finance companies, many of them owned by banks, compete both as deposit takers to a limited extent and as providers of fixed-term or revolving credit to corporate and personal customers;

7 unit trusts, investment trusts and especially pension funds are all managed by people outside the banks, and who offer services similar to those the banks have traditionally provided;

8 finally, the insurance companies are at the same time major customers of the banks and competitors in the sense that they attract personal savings and invest them independently of the banking system, while the independent insurance brokers are direct competitors of the banks' brokerage subsidiaries.

The pressure of social responsibilities

There is a myth, still embodied in company law and in the utterances of ultra-conservative economists like Milton Friedman, that the sole responsibility of company managements is to maximise profits for their shareholders. If this theory ever could be followed in practice, it certainly cannot be today. Apart from management's obvious responsibility to its employees, the growth of consumerism and of consumerist legislation, together with the pressures from ecologists and other lobbies, make it plain that social responsibility must play a large part in corporate thinking. The commercial organisation must not only earn a profit (for without a profit it cannot survive) but must also be a good neighbour and a good citizen. It must not, for the sake of profit, pollute the environment or cause harm to the individuals or organisations with whom it comes into contact.

It is very difficult to argue with the principle of social responsibility in business or to deny its growing importance as yet another constraining factor in marketing policy. It can readily be accepted that profit opportunities must be sacrificed to some extent when there is an obvious likelihood of serious damage to the public or the environment. Toxic effluents must be purified, new drugs must be proved as nearly as possible free of dangerous side-effects, safety factors must be built into cars and other machinery, even if the resulting cost cannot be fully recovered in higher prices. Even at the lowest level of enlightened self-interest it is important not to risk public opprobrium and eventually restrictive legislation for the sake of an extra percentage point or two on the profit margin.

The trouble is that the policy decisions which must be made seldom arise in black and white terms. Certainly small profit reductions to avoid great social damage are acceptable. But what if the profit reduction is catastrophic and will throw many employees out of work, while the possible social damage is small? What, as is so often the case, if the social hazard is uncertain and the social benefit obvious – in the case, say, of a new drug which will certainly save many lives but may possibly also cause some deaths?

The decision whether or not to launch a new product or embark on a new investment project is seldom purely a marketing one. But it is a marketing responsibility to investigate and evaluate new development opportunities or to help carry out feasibility studies for new investment projects. When this is the case, consideration of social responsibility, often unquantifiable, must somehow be fed into the calculation with all the other environmental data by marketers of financial services just as much as manufacturers.

The influence of technological change

Most of the instances of change discussed so far originate outside a company or an industry, and it is marketing's task to help in bringing about the necessary internal changes. With technological change, more often than not, the situation goes into reverse. An industry or company develops more efficient systems or processes, and its marketing people have to find a way of, at worst, reconciling customers to the changes or, at best generating some positive enthusiasm for them. This can be relatively easy when the changes result in products or services which are demonstrably better or cheaper. For example, the development of transistors, printed circuits and now silicon chips has revolutionised electronics and converted bulky expensive items into new generations of very much more efficient, more reliable and *cheaper* products.

Economic pressure

But it not always the case. To take a homely example, centralised production of bread and beer since the war has resulted in changes in the quality and character of these commodities which not everybody agrees are for the better. Economic pressures in the bakery and brewing industries, made the changes inevitable; but it took a considerable effort to persuade at least a sufficient number of consumers that they were indeed fortunate to be supplied with plastic bread and fizzy beer. And now, with 'real ale' being sought after and small bakers experiencing an upturn in demand, the wheel seems to be coming full cycle. These two examples do represent the marketing principle at work – albeit slowly and belatedly. After all, plastic bread and fizzy beer were certainly not to everyone's liking and there were good marketing opportunities in catering for the variety of tastes, as the resurgence of 'good' bread and 'real' ale shows. Perhaps the economic pressures seemed so overwhelming at the time that these segments of the markets just had to be ignored. But eventually consumers vote with their feet – and a good thing too.

Similar comments could be made about retail distribution. The revolution in retailing methods from the small personal-service shop to the large self-service supermarket, which started in the food industry and has now spread to other trades, was forced on the industry by rising labour and other costs. Consumers would certainly have had to pay more for their food and other packaged goods if the revolution had not taken place. But it cannot be said to have originated in an irresistible demand from housewives that corner shops should close and supermarkets proliferate. It took considerable skill and capital expenditure by the retail chains involved – aided in this case by the powerful marketing weapon of price – to persuade housewives in sufficient numbers to adopt new shopping habits. Of course some housewives welcomed the new situation; others have yet to change. Such a differential response from different sections of the market is normal and should be acknowledged in any good marketing plan.

The versatile computer

In banking the most important technological development has of course been the increasing versatility of the computer and its various offspring. For the more excitable futurologists this opens up vistas of a cashless and chequeless society just around the corner. Such exchanges as are not handled by computer talking to computer will be effected mostly by credit card; such cash as is required by the old-fashioned and recalcitrant will be obtained from cash dispensers or automated tellers.

Much of this is already feasible. The Bankers Automated Clearing Service Limited now facilitates the processing, distribution and collection of large volumes of payments for more than 2,300 corporate customers as well as for the banks. Such payments include salaries and pensions by automated credit transfer and insurance premiums and mortgage repayments by standing order and by direct debit. The volume of payments processed in this way has grown over a ten-year period to represent about 13 per cent of all non-cash transactions involving banks. The use of credit cards also is growing, though it still accounts for less than 4 per cent of all non-cash transactions by individuals.

But the vision of a utopia when bank employees no longer have to count cash or sort pieces of paper is still a remote one. Despite the availability of automated methods of payment, the number of cheques drawn is still increasing and will probably continue to increase at least until the mid 1980s. And despite the increasing use of cheques about 98 per cent of all payments by individuals are still in cash. It will take a very long time before the psychological resistance to accepting an electric impulse in a computer's memory store as an alternative to cash in the hand is finally overcome – to say nothing of the legal considerations, such as proof of payment.

There can be no doubt that the trend towards automated, computerised banking will continue. It would be impossible otherwise to cope with the inexorably growing workload that the banks are experiencing and will continue to experience. But the rate of change will be measured in decades rather than years. The banks cannot move faster than the administrative complications will permit, without risking a catastrophic operational breakdown; it takes at least seven years, for example, to introduce a new automated communications system. Nor can the banks move faster than the customer will accept change, without incurring unjustifiable investment costs. In the US, for example, where enthusiasm for the machine is less restrained, some banks have moved faster in the direction of the automated teller and the semi-automated branch. But there is now some doubt about the charisma of the automatic teller; it seems that even allowing for the undoubted cost savings brought about, it lacks the charm to attract the additional business needed fully to justify the $20,000–$40,000 investment which it represents. Belated attempts are being made to give it a human face and persuade the public that it is a warm, friendly and instantly obliging creature. Among others the First National Bank of Atlanta has christened its under-utilised Docutel machines Tillie the Teller, painted them red and built personalised advertising campaigns around them. Results are said to have been encouraging.

Problems and opportunites
From the marketing viewpoint the economically essential trend towards automation brings in its train both problems and opportunities. The main problem is the danger of dehumanising the banks' image. The remarkably successful transition to centralised accounting by computer has not been achieved without manifestations of unease on the part of customers who have felt themselves in the grip of a machine even more implacable than the hard-faced banker of fiction. It will take more than Tillie the Teller and a lick of red paint to overcome the public's resistance to dealing on a day-to-day basis with a machine rather than a human being, however harassed. The fact that the machine is almost certainly quicker and less accident-prone is poor compensation for its inability to relax and smile.

Against this there are two potential marketing opportunities of enormous importance to marketing-minded managements. The first is the prospect that increased mechanisation of the routine back-up services, which currently absorb between 60 and 70 per cent of the banks' human and other resources, could release more management and staff time for active involvement in learning about and satisfying the less routine requirements of customers. Planned evolution in this direction will involve progressive organisational changes, the creation of new jobs and redefinition of existing jobs, and a training programme to facilitate the process of readjustment; it will also almost certainly involve reconsidering the location and layout of the banks' premises and branch network. Just how the process of adjustment will work out and how fast the evolution will be is one of the future uncertainties which will make a banking career more than usually exciting during the remaining years of this century.

The second major marketing opportunity lies in the fact that however inhuman Tillie the automated teller may be, she is prepared to work twenty-four hours a day, seven days a week; and she is quite unfussy about where she works. The bank's computer terminal, with whatever facilities are needed from cash dispensing through credit verification to money transfer, is just as comfortable, provided it earns its keep, at a supermarket check-out or in a works canteen as it is on the bank's own premises. This should give the bank's marketers a degree of freedom from the constraints of time and place which can be exploited to give an improved level of service at a profit to the bank.

Summary

In this chapter we have said that marketing has an important part to play in the process of adjustment to change, in keeping the organisation and its products or services in step with a constantly, if slowly, changing environment.

Marketing's special contribution is likely to be in the areas of

1 gathering information about the changing environment and predicting the effect of relevant changes on the demands which the organisation should satisfy;
2 planning and co-ordinating the marketing aspects of the changes in organisation, product range or distributive methods that should follow;
3 helping, by the marketing techniques of communication and persuasion, to accelerate necessary changes in the attitudes and behaviour of customers, distributors *and* employees;
4 using pre-testing techniques such as market models and test markets to assess the viability of new projects, before the commitment of major funds;
5 recognising and describing the different needs of different segments of markets served, and how they are evolving.

We have said that the aspects of a changing environment with which marketing is most immediately concerned are *customers'* characteristics and needs.

With personal customers, important areas of change include family incomes and related lifestyles, more widespread material possessions, equal opportunities in education, changing employment patterns, including more job opportunities for married women, and changing age profiles.

In the corporate sector increased concentration of ownership, growth of the nationalised and semi-nationalised sector, the greater involvement of labour in management decisions and the changing location of industry must all affect the direction of marketing policy.

For banking more than most industries, the changing fortunes of the *economy* and government efforts to control it are a major environmental factor. They have precipitated such marketing policy initiatives as development overseas and diversification into financial services other than mainstream banking.

Increasing *competition* from other banking and quasi-banking institutions is yet another factor requiring more professional and aggressive marketing action on the part of the banks.

Social responsibility is an aspect of market development planning and operations which looms ever larger. Even if managements were disposed to overlook it in the interest of single-minded profit maximisation, they would be prevented by consumerism, the ecological movement and social legislation.

Finally, *technological change* places just as heavy a burden on marketing as on production departments. In banking the computer and its derivatives have revolutionised the mechanics of the industry. Marketing has to ensure that mechanisation does not dehumanise what is, in large measure, a personal service industry.

CHAPTER THREE

Marketing management and organisation

In the very simplest form of commercial organisation, one man setting up in business for himself, there are three essential and *interdependent* functions:

make it – sell it – keep the score

For 'make it' you can substitute 'buy it' if the enterprise is a trading one rather than a manufacturing one; or 'create a service' if the new entrepreneur is entering a service industry. The selling function does not necessarily follow the making; in some types of business it is possible to secure an order before starting to make the product, which saves a certain amount of worry if you get the price right and are sure of being paid in the end. The significance of keeping the score can rapidly extend from basic accounting to raising capital and monitoring cash flow, etc. But the principle of interdependence still applies. If one of the three legs of the tripod collapses, so will the enterprise.

But of course in our complicated industrial society things are seldom that simple. There is still room for the one-man entrepreneur and for the first stage of development after the one-man stage, when the production, selling and financial functions are delegated (assuming that the entrepreneur has the none too common capacity to delegate). But in more and more industries nowadays size is essential for success. A one-man aero-engine business is inconceivable; and even the family grocer is being beaten back into the side streets and villages where it does not pay the supermarket chain to pursue him.

For many industries indeed (and banking looks like becoming one of them) a single country is too narrow a base operation, and multi-national status becomes inevitable. Entrepreneurial Man willy-nilly turns into Organisation Man, and may or may not be happy about the change.

But no matter how large the organisation becomes, no matter how many specialists are bred by the sub-division of functions, the three original legs of the tripod remain essential and inter-dependent. Indeed one of the great problems of professional management, as it struggles to cope with the complications of size, is to make it clear to as many managers as possible throughout the organisation that they are not simply cogs in a great machine but have a responsibility in their respective fields for ensuring the effective co-ordination of the three basic functions. The devices of profit centres, divisionalisation and the like have a part to play in this; and so has marketing.

Marketing in the unitary organisation

Before attemting to generalise about the way marketing management fits into the single, relatively uniform business which we call unitary, it is as well to make two points. The first is that only over the last thirty years has professional marketing gained wide acceptance in this country as an important aspect of management. The rate at which it has been accepted and incorporated in the managerial structure has varied from industry to industry and from company to company. So, for any general statement we make, it will be possible to quote a number of contradictory examples from real life – 'that does not happen in *my* company'.

The second point is the imprecision of nomenclature in the whole field of management organisation, most particularly in marketing management. A marketing manager, as we have already said, may be holding either a line management job or a staff job. Alternatively, most of the essential marketing functions may be handled by a manager carrying some other title: sales manager, commercial manager or general manager. Until you have read an individual's job specification (if he has one) you do not really know whether he is supposed to be doing a marketing management job or not; and until you have analysed the way he spends his working week you do not really know whether he is actually doing the job he is supposed to be doing.

Having admitted at the outset that for almost everything we say the contrary may also be true, we can proceed to some general statements. The first is that most typical situation where, in a small or medium-sized company whose management structure is in a state of evolution, the head of the selling function has been given wider responsibilities and has celebrated them by dropping the title 'sales manager' and adopting that of 'marketing manager'. (In this connection it is significant that the professional body which in 1950 was known as the Incorporated Sales Managers' Association is now known as the Institute of Marketing. And, to add point to this trend, in 1978 a group of senior marketing men came together as the 90th Livery Company in the City of London, the Worshipful Company of Marketors.)

These wider responsibilities derive from the realisation that there is more to selling than disposing of a business's products or service at the best price it will fetch. There is first and foremost the concept of planned *profitability*. Salesmen traditionally and temperamentally love to sell. Only too often, unless there is a proper control system, the triumph of getting a large order can override the necessity of getting the order at a price which will show an adequate profit to the company. To think in terms of profit rather than turnover as the goal requires a change in outlook which is symbolised by the change of title from sales manager to marketing manager. It can also require, particularly when there is a range of products or services to be sold rather than a single line, some addition to the organisation within the erstwhile sales (now marketing) department. This addition may well take the shape of the product manager, responsible among other things for monitoring the profitability of the product or group of products under his charge. More will be said of the product manager's role later.

Another concept which gains in importance with the transition from sales to marketing management is the traditional rule, more honoured in the breach than the observance, that *the customer is king*. This can lead in practice from the relatively uncontroversial idea that the sales function should be expanded to include a market research capability to much more revolutionary conclusions. If and when the sales side gets to the point where its market research enables it to predict with some confidence the level and character of customer demand, the logical conclusion is that production schedules should be the resultant of sales forecasts and product specifications originatating in the marketing department. This can seriously upset the balance of power within the traditional production-orientated company, though it certainly will help to ensure its long-term survival.

A third concept that marks the transition from sales management to marketing management, especially in large-scale consumer markets, is the concept of *the marketing mix*. The traditional sales manager's viewpoint is that sales are the result of heroic efforts by the salesmen, backed up by a bit of advertising and sales promotion of one kind or another. The marketing manager recognises the importance of well-directed salesmen in most situations (though quite a lot of selling is done without the intervention of salesmen as such) but recognises that they are only one of many elements to be fitted together in the right proportions. Other elements included within the general description of marketing mix are

1 product specifications;
2 packaging and product presentation;
3 pricing;
4 physical distribution;
5 point of sale display;
6 selling communications including advertising;
7 sales promotion.

A marketing department will need to have the skills, or access to the skills, required to procure all these elements. But above all, the marketing manager must have the flair and breadth of view to co-ordinate them into a single cohesive profit-orientated whole.

The final outcome can be that the marketing manager presides over an organisation along the lines of that illustrated in Fig. 1, linking the established sales force and sales office (themselves probably restructured) to specialist marketing services and a new product management function. (See overleaf).

The product manager

Most readers by now will probably have said to themselves that there's nothing so very original about the much-vaunted marketing concept. It is simply a matter of making commonsensical changes and injecting some additional professionalism to meet the demands of a changing industrial or commercial situation. We would not dispute that general conclusion.

But there is one quite important and relatively original contribution from the marketing management thinking of the past quarter-century. This is the establishment of the product manager (or project manager) as a key member of the marketing team.

Fig. 1. The marketing manager in a line management role.

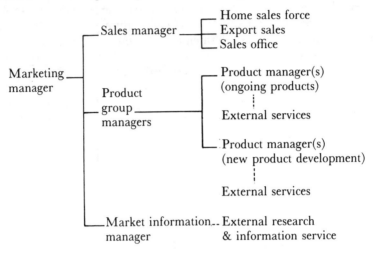

A product manager's, or product group manager's, job specification will probably read more or less as follows:

Reports to marketing manager.

Main responsibility preparing the annual marketing plan for a designated product or group of products within the context of agreed corporate objectives; ensuring that the volume and profit targets included in the plan are met.

Specific responsibilities 1 working with the production, financial and sales departments, under the overall direction of the marketing manager, to ensure that the product marketing plan is realistic and that they are committed to its successful execution;

2 preparing and securing management approval for the product marketing plan (the plan should include final and intermediate volume and profit targets together with budgeted marketing expenditure figures);

3 securing continued involvement and support for the agreed plan from the relevant departments (particularly production and sales);

4 briefing and directing the outside agencies (advertising, design, research, etc.) contributing to the execution of the plan;

5 monitoring the progress of results against intermediate targets; investigating the reasons and taking corrective action if results get seriously out of step with targets;

6 monitoring the level of customer satisfaction through attitude research, complaints letters, salesmen's reports and other means;

7 monitoring competitors' activities and recommending any counter-activity that is needed;

8 monitoring the legal framework surrounding his product(s);

9 initiating research or experimental activity aimed at improving the product, customer service or marketing methods;

10 controlling the marketing budget for the product.

Much emphasis is laid in marketing textbooks on the product manager's responsibility for the profitable development of the product or product group assigned to him. He is often described as running his own defined business within the larger business he works for. This is true only up to a point. The product manager certainly has responsibility, on paper at any rate; but seldom has the power, without which responsibility is something of a fiction. He has some degree of power over the advertising and other outside agencies from whom he commissions work, though even they can usually appeal over his head if they feel he is getting too big for his boots. But he has no power, except the power of persuasion, over the production and sales departments who can make or mar the success of his marketing plan. To some extent it can be said that his role is the mirror-image of the harlot whom Stanley Baldwin accused of exercising power without responsibility down the ages. The product manager, not yet as venerable a figure as the harlot, can be said to enjoy responsibility without power.

Nevertheless there are two very strong arguments in favour of the product manager system. The first is that it provides a framework within which detailed attention can be paid to all the inter-related activities which make for a product's success; it does not ensure success, but it makes it less likely that the product will fail simply because management is too busy to give it the necessary attention. The second argument is that it provides an opportunity for giving the bright young manager an opportunity of experiencing the many-faceted responsibilities of general management in a situation where he cannot do the company irredeemable harm.

In banking, for example, product or brand managers could be in charge of personal lending, of personal resource gathering, of an industry such as petro-chemicals, or import/export financing, and so on. Similarly, in the unit trust industry the brand management technique has been applied to different types of trust within the same 'stable'; and in the insurance business to various kinds of product, even though there are salesmen in the field who are expected to sell the full range of products.

The marketing services manager

So far we have talked about the marketing manager in the context of line management, in situations where he controls the salesforce. But it often happens that the evolution of the management organisation takes a different direction, with the sales management function separated from the marketing function; or indeed that there is no national salesforce as such – which is essentially the situation at present in branch banking organisations, though not in other financial services sectors like insurance and hire purchase, or some unit trusts.

In such situations it is more likely that the executive bearing the title of 'marketing manager' will in fact be filling a staff position, reporting perhaps to the sales director, perhaps to the managing director; and his department, though it may be described as the marketing department, would be more accurately called the marketing services department.

In this staff role the marketing manager is likely to be more closely involved with helping management to plot the future course of the organisation (a close link with the corporate planning function is likely), and concerned with current activities only to the extent of providing marketing advice and technical marketing facilities for those line managers who wish to avail themselves of them. The composition and size of his department will depend essentially on the level of demand for the department's services which he generates in line management and on building up a track record which convinces the sceptics that the advice or the services he provides produce useful, – i.e. profit-enhancing – results. (In practical terms the marketing services manager is the equivalent of an internal consultant; if in an excess of enthusiasm he builds up his departmental resources ahead of effective demand he can become a ready target for the next economy drive.)

It is likely, however, that over time some or all of the following functions will accrue to the department:

1 the provision of market information including analyses of 'own company' sales;
2 business and economic forecasting;
3 the marketing aspects of corporate planning;
4 the provision of advertising, sales promotional literature and other sales communications material;
5 the provision of promotional ideas, schemes and packages;
6 the development and testing of new products or new services;
7 feasibility studies, preparatory to entering new markets cr market sectors;
8 the marketing aspects of in-company management training.

The typical departmental organisation to which this can lead is illustrated in Fig. 2 overleaf.

The selection and direction of external marketing services

In both our organisation charts (Figs. 1 and 2), describing the 'typical' line and staff marketing departments, we have indicated that these departments are responsible for selecting and directing various external marketing services, in addition to their internal relationships. These external associations – particularly those with the providers of creative services like advertising agencies and design consultants – require a considerable amount of specialist skill and even diplomacy. Not simply because 'creative people' are involved (the legend that they are difficult and temperamental is much exaggerated) but more because everything that appears in visual or audio-visual form about an organisation or its products contributes to the image of the organisation in a particularly *noticeable* way. Its business practices or the behaviour of its employees

Fig. 2. The marketing manager in a service department role.

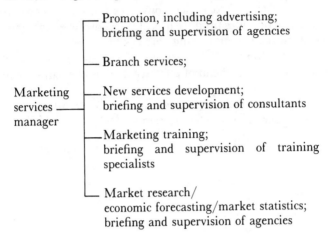

Marketing services manager

— Promotion, including advertising; briefing and supervision of agencies

— Branch services;

— New services development; briefing and supervision of consultants

— Marketing training; briefing and supervision of training specialists

— Market research/ economic forecasting/market statistics; briefing and supervision of agencies

in contact with customers or the public actually have just as important an effect. But they are seldom out in the open for *everyone* to see, including other members of the organisation. It has been said that when a banker makes an error everyone tries to cover it up; but advertising is designed to be seen, and an error is very obvious.

So marketing management often has difficult day-to-day decisions to make, in trying at the same time to keep the organisation's 'visible manifestations' in the right key without stultifying the creative skills of the outside services or embarrassing the more conservative members of the organisation. Examples of going too far in both directions are rife in the history of bank marketing and advertising.

The hazards and difficulties of using external marketing services can result in a temptation to build up internal marketing resources so as to handle as much work as possible 'in-house'. This can look like a prudent man's way of playing safe, but it is not in the long run safe at all; advertising, brochures, promotions and other external marketing activities become introverted and stale if they are all produced internally. The judicious marketing manager keeps his department small, but staffed by people of experience and judgment; and he holds his external services to very specific policy briefs, while giving them the maximum freedom of expression within those briefs. Typically, in the UK and in several

European banks, very much less than one per cent of staff would be employed in the marketing services described above. In some cases, extra jobs – virtually 'line' functions, such as school banks – may be added to the basic marketing services function and will move the percentage upwards. But of course, many many more members of staff will be carrying out marketing activities as a normal part of their own jobs.

Where does public relations fit in?

We have not attempted so far to fit PR into our marketing organisations, either as an internal or an external service. This is because the term 'public relations' is used almost as loosely as the word 'marketing' itself. In some cases PR is regarded as virtually a form of unpaid advertising – using news releases, press conferences and other devices to seek favourable mentions (or ward off unfavourable mentions) of the organisation and its products in the media. In such cases it may come under the control of the marketing manager or be bought from outside in conjunction with advertising services. At the other extreme its definition may be much wider and cover the whole range of relationships between the organisation and its customers, the general public, government, special-interest groups and society at large. It may also have an interest, alongside the personnel department, in internal attitudes and communications and in the relationships between different groups within the organisation. When this broader definition is given to the PR function (as it is in most large banks) it is likely that the PR department will operate independently from the marketing department, or even have some aspect of the marketing function under its command. (The different roles of PR, and its relationship to the marketing function, are discussed at greater length in Chapters 9 and 10.)

Marketing in the multiple organisation

It is hard enough to be precise about the position of marketing in the unitary organisation. It is even harder in the case of the multiple organisation – a phrase which we use to cover everything from the multi-national conglomerate, through the holding company with a number of specialist divisions or subsidiaries, to the chain of retail shops. Not only are there major differences between one organisation and another within these categories, but any one organisation may oscillate between different organisational structures – swinging, for example, from centralisation to decentralisation and back again – as managements strive to attain the unattainable goal of the ideally managed and effectively dynamic organisation.

We can say, however, that more often than not the multiple organisation will incorporate both staff and line marketing functions at appropriate points in its structure. It is more likely than not that the marketing function or department at headquarters will have a staff role, providing a back-up service for senior management and specialist advice or services, when required, for the operating divisions and subsidiaries. This is a pragmatic manifestation, rather than the result of strongly held theories; it becomes obvious from trial and error that effective marketing requires detailed knowledge both of the geographical area and product category involved and of the character of human and other resources available compared to the competition. A given individual may be an outstanding success at marketing apples in Germany but a total failure (until he has become acclimatised) at marketing oranges in Japan – or at telling the Japanese subsidiary how to do it. He can advise on techniques and principles, he can offer information and ideas, he can transmit central management's policy rulings, but he cannot safely issue detailed instructions on how to do it.

So it is likely that the *executive* marketing function will be positioned as close as possible to the point where the organisation meets the customer. This may be at divisional headquarters or at the level of operating units, or indeed at both levels. And at either of these operational levels it is as likely as not that the line marketing function as we have described it will be exercised by a manager who does not actually carry the title of marketing manager.

An interesting variation on this theme can be found in the case of the multiple retailing organisation. Here there are, in effect, two marketing functions to consider. There is the marketing function of maximising the turnover and profitability of each of the retail outlets in the chain, through location, layout, in-store promotion, local advertising and staff-customer relations, as well as by the total effect of the range of products displayed. And there is the complementary function of merchandising specific product categories in all the outlets by skilful buying, display and sales promotion. The two functions of shop management and merchandise management both demand other skills as well as marketing. But they both contain large marketing ingredients.

Marketing in financial service organisations

We have described the position of marketing in different types of commercial organisation before coming to grips with the financial service industry, partly because this industry was later than most in recognising marketing as a distinct managerial skill and partly because the form that marketing organisation has taken so far, in what is still a rapidly changing scene, has varied greatly according to the type and size of the financial services institution.

In the large UK clearing banks, for example, the typical marketing department is located at the centre in a marketing services role, as illustrated in Fig. 2, with tentacles extending into the divisional, regional and branch structure. General managers, regional managers and branch managers retain the line marketing responsibility (which they have always had, even if less explicitly in the past than today).

But banks in other countries, merchant banks, hire purchase and insurance companies all have different marketing problems and marketing methods; and even within the UK clearing banks, now that they are so clearly multi-national, multi-service organisations, you will find both staff and line marketing functions, elements both of 'shop management' and of retail merchandising, and both industrial and consumer marketing structures operating alongside each other.

The UK clearing banks, in fact, present a particularly complex problem for marketing organisation, since they are both vertically integrated and exposed to competition at every level.

There are marketing jobs of various kinds to be done in:

1 corporate development planning;
2 attracting deposits, the raw material for a financial services business (most manufacturing organisations can negotiate for their raw materials with a number of rival suppliers all eager to sell to them; banks must attract their raw material by competitive marketing methods, in the face of other financial institutions – building societies, trustee savings banks, insurance companies and others – all equally keen to lay their hands on available personal and corporate funds, and some of them helped by special tax advantages);
3 building good quality lending;
4 expanding internationally (in competition with financial services institutions in the countries concerned);

5 fighting off competition from foreign banks invading the home market (particularly on the corporate business front);
6 developing new banking services and packages;
7 marketing the products of specialist divisions and subsidiaries (finance houses, insurance brokers, merchant banks, trust companies, etc.);
8 building up the local businesses of branches and regional offices;
9 deciding the best location for new branches or outlets.

We must leave it to the individual reader to make up his mind where his own organisation (or the sector of the organisation in which he works) fits into the picture of different and evolving organisational structures which we have sketched. One thing he can be sure of. However it is organised today, it will be different in five years time.

Summary

In this chapter we have described in outline how marketing management fits into the organisation of different types of company; and have said that a marketing management *function* will not always carry a marketing manager *title*.

We have said that in the unitary organisation, marketing departments tend to play either a line management role, with responsibility for sales volume and profitability; or a staff role, in which they provide marketing information advice and services to line management.

We have described the 'product management' system as a device which enables managements of multi-product or multi-service companies to ensure that detailed attention is given to the co-ordination of all the elements – production, sales, and finance – which are involved in the success of a specific product or product group.

We have said that the 'multiple' organisation is likely to contain both staff and line marketing management functions or departments at different levels in the organisation; and that the staff functions are more likely to be at the centre and the line functions nearer the interface between company and customer, because of the need for detailed knowledge both of the specific product and of the market place.

We have suggested that the reader should decide for himself whether the financial services organisation (or section of the organisation) in which he works is unitary or multiple; whether the marketing functions he exercises or utilises are 'line' or staff; and which of the many different types of marketing management approach are most appropriate to his particular situation.

We have said, finally, that marketing has a contribution to make to many other functions such as corporate planning, and that the rate of change in the financial services industry is such that this year's organisation chart will probably be obsolete five years hence.

CHAPTER FOUR

The domestic market

It is tempting to write that the birth of marketing in British domestic banking took place in the 1960s, when tombstone advertising (here lieth the body of Bolger's Bank, rich in assets and good deeds) began to be replaced by advertising that sought to convey a consumer benefit; when responsibility for the development of marketing services was assigned specifically to a management team, internally appointed or occasionally recruited from outside the banking industry; and when, by the way, the present writers first became actively involved in bank marketing.

Tempting but misleading. Marketing in its basic sense of systematic development of customer relationships has always been an essential part of bank management, both at central and at branch level; banks are no more exempt than any other type of commercial activity from the inexorable rule that without a customer you haven't got a business. The post-war developments that have precipitated a more professional approach to marketing and changed its character are:

— the great increase both in the number of customers requiring banking and other financial services and the complexity of the services they require;
— the wider and fiercer competition in the financial services market with banks offering an increasing variety of specialist financial services, not previously provided by banks; and non-banking institutions offering what were previously regarded as banking services;
— the more sophisticated use of computers, not only to handle electronically transactions which were previously handled manually (encouraging arm's length, impersonal banking), but to give central management much more information and control over the details and profitability of customer transactions and commercial initiatives.

Market segmentation

The combined effect of these developments has been to force both large and small banks into more conscious acceptance of the well-established marketing concept of market segmentation. The basis of this concept is the obvious fact that the closer a producer can come to having a homogeneous group of customers, with similar needs and attitudes, the better his chances of establishing a mutually satisfactory relationship with them. This applies both to the small producer, who will be able to compete on less unequal terms with larger organisations in the same field, if he focuses his efforts on satisfying specific needs of a specific segment of the target population; and to the large diversified company, which is less likely to become an ineffectual bureaucracy, if it divides its market and to some extent its own organisation into manageable segments.

The practice of market segmentation is inevitably much less simple than the concept. Depending on the kind of business an organisation is in, or wants to be in, it may elect to segment the market by customer segment or by product segment or by both; and may find different criteria for segmentation relevant in each case. Segmentation by product category is likely to be more relevant in the case of a small high technology manufacturer, who has achieved a demonstrable, if temporary, lead in some special technological feature; and seeks to exploit it, by finding all the customers to whom this feature is important, before his lead is overtaken. Customer segmentation, which is more sympathetic to the cardinal principle of marketing that everything starts with the customer, is more relevant to producers, like bankers, grocers, and other providers of services, whose 'product range' is not very clearly differentiated from those of competitors; and who have a better chance of gaining a competitive advantage by concentrating on serving the needs of defined customer segments more sympathetically and imaginatively than by striving to invent a financial service or comestible that nobody has yet heard of.

Many large organisations manage to reconcile the alternative approaches of customer segmentation and product segmentation by adopting both, either implicitly or explicitly, with the customer service side of the organisation thinking primarily in terms of delivering the requirements of targeted customer segments; and the production or banking side concerned primarily with the development and efficient management of the 'products' needed to satisfy customer requirements. Most banks, with their tradition of all-round managers, responsible both for winning customers and for administering the branch or other organisation that looks after the 'product' are some way from making the clear-cut distinction between marketing and production that is commonplace among manufacturers; and the different characteristics of a service industry make it unlikely, and perhaps undesirable, that they will ever make the drastic organisational changes that this would involve. But the increasing frequency of account managers and thinly disguised sales forces on the one hand, and product managers and other technicians on the other suggests a significant trend in this direction.

Customer segmentation

The most basic form of market segmentation in banking is between the personal or retail sector and the institutional or wholesale sector. These two sectors clearly need different types of service and different methods of delivery. But even here there is a fuzzy area. (Market segmentation is an imprecise science). A small shop, a one-man farm or a proprietorial business can sensibly be consigned to the retail sector, since personal and business affairs are likely to be closely intertwined. But at what point do you decide that Laura Ashley the person has become Laura Ashley the business and adjust classifications and delivery method accordingly?

The traditional methods of personal segmentation are those used over the years by market researchers in classifying and analysing their respondents, namely age, sex, occupation, geographical location and that bastard classification, socio-economic status. Age is clearly important, particularly in relation to the banks' competitive desire to 'catch 'em young and never let 'em go'; hence the proliferation of products aimed at young savers, school-leavers, college entrants and the like. Sex is an interesting segment, even for bankers. It could plausibly be argued that banks, in common with H.M. Inspector of Taxes, have been slow to recognise the independent economic status of women and to serve them in their own right, not just as 'housewives'. But any attempt at sex differentiation is in danger of turning into sexual discrimination. The simplistic notion, for example, of women's branches staffed by women for women, much discussed in banking circles some years back, was very sensibly abandoned. Occupation can be relevant both as an indication of likely income and life-style, and as a guide to the fuzzy area between personal and business customers; a farmer, a doctor, a partner in a firm of accountants or solicitors may be of interest both as a personal and a business customer. Location again, is important both for a bank which wants to regionalise its business, and for purposes of ensuring that the type and location of branches corresponds as closely as possible to the distribution of customers; bank premises are expensive and inflexible investments, not easily shifted when the economic fortunes of different areas rise or fall.

Socio-economic status, encoded by the market researchers as Groups A, B, C1, C2 and D/E, is widely regarded as an unsatisfactory form of segmentation; but endless learned committee meetings, extending over many years, have so far failed to come up with any more satisfactory means of distinguishing between the haves and the have-nots, with the intermediate gradations of have-quite-a-lot and have-just-a-little. The trouble lies in the assumption implicit in the word socio-economic, that there is a close correlation between wealth and life-style. There is, of course, a connection. But when you hear socio-economic group A described as the top 5% of the population you can never be quite sure whether this includes the impoverished lordling camped in the gardener's cottage of his ancestral mansion and excludes the affluent pop-singer or vice versa. However, until a more satisfactory system of classification is devised, it is better than nothing to accept that people's financial service needs are derived both from their inherited way of life and from their accumulated wealth or current income; and for business development initiatives to be targeted at Group A/B – the 'top' 10% or so of the population; Group C-1, the next 30%, mostly in white collar jobs; Group C-2, the next 30%, mostly in blue collar jobs; and the bottom Group D/E, made up mostly of the unemployed, retired, single-parent families and other under-privileged groups, whose lack of purchasing power makes them a more suitable target for sympathy than for commercial enterprise.

The 'life-cycle' approach to segmentation has also been useful in bank marketing. A lineal descendant, no doubt, of Shakespeare's seven ages of man, this concept distinguishes six stages in an individual's life, each with its particular financial needs. The childhood stage suffers from limited purchasing power – more appropriate to the sweet shop than to the investment bank – but is still of interest to bank marketers who believe that banking habits established then will last a lifetime. The first main customer segment consists of the young independent earners who are likely, while they remain free of domestic responsibilities, to have more money to spend on themselves than they will again till much later in life. Next come the young couples, still without children but struggling to get a home together with all the material and financial problems that this involves. Next the harassing stage of raising a family, when budgets are still tight and expenditure directed towards necessities rather than lux-

uries. Then a second period of relative affluence when the earning
capacity of one or both partners (assuming the partnership has survived)
is likely to be at its peak and children have departed. Finally, retirement – not as impoverished for some as dismissive terms like OAP and
Group D/E would imply – and involving for the more affluent special
financial problems such as the maximisation of income and the minim-
isation of Inheritance Tax liabilities.

Like any form of segmentation, the life cycle concept is pretty crude;
the single-parent family and the two-earner family at the same stage in
the life cycle are poles apart in life style. But, used imaginatively, it can
stimulate the marketing planner's thinking about the financial service
needs of real people leading real lives.

Rather less common personal classifications used by some bank
marketers rejoice in the titles of demographic and psychographic. The
demographic approach to segmentation is straightforward enough. Foreign banks setting up branches in this country find it easier, in the early
stages at any rate, to attract business from their own nationals; and are
disposed to open branches in areas where there is a relatively heavy
concentration of their countrymen and to promote their special facilities
for remittances to the home country and so on. Branches of the Bank of
Cyprus in London, for example, still deal almost exclusively with the
banking needs of resident Cypriots and their families; while the UK
branches of Irish banks got their start with patrials, though soon attracting
a less discriminatory circle of customers.

Psychographic segmentation depends on the identification and pur-
suit of customer groups distinguished by psychological characteristics or
prejudices relevant to the marketer's business. For a food manufacturer
this could take the form of exceptional concern with the nutritional or
vitamin content of the family diet and willingness to pay a premium for
products with the right credentials; for a bank it could take the form of
a pre-disposition to make full use of a bank account and the financial
services linked to it, together with the willingness to pay for services
rendered: or a different set of attitudes towards savings. Research has
shown wide variations in psychological attitudes in these respects, not
always directly correlated with such factors as income level. It makes
sense to focus marketing effort on them, though there are practical
difficulties in finding the right way of identifying and reaching them.

There are two main ways of segmenting corporate (wholesale)
customers. The first is by size, which in turn is likely to affect the services

demanded, the nature of the customer-bank relationship and credit-worthiness. The second is by industrial classification – most conveniently the Bank of England's Standard Classifications, since banks have to make regular returns under these headings. But neither way is completely satisfactory for marketing purposes. If you decide, for example, to concentrate marketing effort on one or other of the Bank of England's industrial classifications, you run into problems in your approach to the increasingly frequent case of the large, diversified organisation, with an involvement in several classifications; if you decide that organisations with a high proportion of international business are particularly interesting, this is not necessarily a function either of size or of industrial classification.

Product segmentation

The 'products', alias financial services, which a modern bank offers its customers can be classified broadly into:

— Lending (still the major source of income)
— Deposit-taking and safekeeping
— Money transmission (essential but not always profitable)
— International
— Specialist fee-earning services.

Each category, including the last catch-all classification, obviously includes a number of sub-categories each requiring specialist treatment; and one of the major innovative activities of bank marketing departments nowadays is to devise, package and promote differentiated products to fit into these sub-categories. The occasion for this may be the identification of a reasonably homogeneous group of customers with a common need – within the lending category, for example, the home-buyers looking for mortgages, the holiday-makers looking for travel money, the small businessman looking for start-up finance all constitute separate though sometimes overlapping subsegments with products to match. Or the occasion may be some technological development, like the electronic communications revolution which makes possible faster and more convenient forms of money transmission.

From a marketing viewpoint it is evident that customer segmentation and product segmentation inter-act. You cannot get far with developing a new product without visualising the customer segment or segments to whom it will appeal; you cannot get far with attacking a target customer segment, without defining the range of products required to satisfy their needs. A given product, with variations, will probably reach several different customer segments; a given customer segment will certainly require a number of different products to establish a durable relationship. The inter-action can be illustrated by a simple matrix – see opposite.

Implications of market segmentation

We have discussed market segmentation at some length because it lies at the heart not just of banks' specific marketing activities, such as product development, research and promotion, but also of wider issues such as strategic planning, organisational structure, the systems of infrastructure and the whole question of training, motivating and deploying *people* to be as productive as they can. Opinions may differ about the extent to which marketing should be involved in these wider issues (jurisdictional disputes are no less frequent in banks than in other organisations). But there can be no doubt that expenditure on marketing departments, advertising, sales promotion and so on will be limited in its effectiveness if the wider issues – which might be described as macro-marketing to distinguish them from the micro-marketing activities which are customarily entrusted to a marketing department – have been thought through and acted on.

In the macro-marketing area a bank's thinking about market segmentation affects first of all the organisation's business development *strategy*. If it is small it will be well advised not to rely simply on the assumption that small is beautiful (which it probably isn't in the financial services market where solvency is of paramount importance) but to find a market niche appropriate to its particular skills where it can make itself as important as its larger competitors. If it is large, offering a complete range of services, it will have to debate the relative advantages of presenting itself to the public as a one-stop financial services supermarket, where everything can be bought under one roof; or as an interactive group of specialist businesses: at present the second strategy seems to be prevailing.

Market segmentation also affects thinking about the number and nature of the 'shops' or branches through which the financial services are sold. All the big English clearing banks are now reviewing the question

Simplified product/personal customer matrix

Customer Segment

Products	Children	Young Singles	Young Couples	Mature Couples	Retired
Savings Schemes	✔	✔		✔	
Personal Loans		✔	✔		
Travel facilities		✔		✔	
Credit Card		✔	✔	✔	✔
Mortgage		✔	✔	✔	
Insurance			✔	✔	
Tax Advice			✔	✔	✔
Asset management				✔	✔
Trustee/executorship				✔	✔

whether the traditional branch network inherited from pre-war days is appropriate to the very different conditions of to-day. Most have concluded that it is not and are reorganising their networks to include, within what is likely to be a diminishing total, fullscale business branches catering to the needs of corporate customers, personal branches serving mainly private customers and sub-branches providing a restricted range of largely automated services. For smaller or foreign banks and specialised financial service institutions, peering into a technological future pregnant with home banking and other 'hands-off' facilities, it becomes a debatable question whether the expensive process of opening branches around the country is essential to the development of a national business.

Thinking about the systems infrastructure is affected as well. If you are going to provide different levels of service and different varieties of product for different customer segments – and if you hope to persuade some customers to dispense entirely with personal service – a single central computer system, however powerful, will become too inflexible. In banking, as in many other service industries, there is a degree of tension between the desire to supply in bulk and the individual customer's demand for a bespoke service, which is not found in the market place for packaged food-stuffs, for example. The trend towards separately programmed minis and micros linked together as necessary, which is already apparent, will inevitably gather pace.

Inevitably, too, the training motivation and career patterns of people working in the banks and other financial service institutions is bound to be affected. Specialists, starting with data processing experts and going on to researchers both operational and marketing, advertising and P.R. experts and marketing people from other industries, are infiltrating the ranks of generalist career bankers. The tradition of cradle to grave employment is being eroded by willingness on the part of banks to recruit at more senior level than school leavers and to find early retirement or other means of shedding non-performers; and a parallel willingness on the part of employees to consider the merits of a change of occupation. Within banks also it is becoming more usual for individuals to acquire a special expertise and settle permanently in the relevant department instead of pursuing the traditionally mobile course up the banking ladder. And remuneration is beginning to be related rather more to performance, rather less to seniority, despite Union pressures to the contrary.

Such macro-marketing developments, all related to the fact that the banking industry is no longer a simple and homogeneous business, but a diversified collection of assorted financial services, has far more to do with making companies within the industry more marketing-oriented than the micro-marketing activities with which this book is more directly concerned. But the implications of market segmentation certainly permeate all the micro-marketing techniques that we shall be discussing. In planning market research it is essential to focus on the market, product or customer segment that management has in mind; or in the case of general studies, to include in the survey key particulars of informants which will enable segments likely to be of special interest to be separately broken out and analysed. In creating new services or products it is essential to recognise that you can't please all the people all the time, and to have a clear picture of the main target customer segments and of the particular benefits they will derive from the new services. In planning advertising, sales promotional and P.R. campaigns it is equally essential, while attempting to create a consistent image for the whole bank, to think in terms of the customer segments at which individual campaigns are aimed; and to use the media which reach them with the least waste, and with the selling copy most likely to arouse their interest. In organising a marketing department it is essential to supplement the specialists in advertising research and so on with experienced market segment specialists, responsible for co-ordinating and focusing the totality of business development activities on designated market segments.

Summary

It is difficult to make a clear pattern out of the highly mobile and competitive domestic market for financial services (described in some detail in Chapter 7). It looks like an unthinking free-for-all, with English and Scottish banks, foreign banks, merchant banks, building societies, finance houses and para-banking institutions all frenetically taking in each other's washing and changing their character in order to do so.

A pattern begins to emerge when you start from the customer end (in true marketing fashion) and consider the different types of customer, with their different needs, and how they can be segmented. Then it is possible to see how banks and other financial service institutions are evolving – either deliberately or by force of circumstance – so as to provide individual customers or customer segments with a choice of services tailored more or less skilfully to fit their particular needs.

The main contribution of marketing, on both the macro and the micro level, is to make that fit as close as possible, aiming both to maximise customer satisfaction and produce profit.

CHAPTER FIVE

The international market

The shrinking world created by modern communications is nowhere more apparent than in the financial services market. Whereas people can travel halfway round the world in a matter of hours, money can do so in seconds. The value of funds sloshing around the world in purely financial transactions far exceeds the funds needed to finance conventional trade, with corresponding consequences for currency exchange rates. Moreover, multinational corporations demand a worldwide service and an informed world outlook from their bankers – and threaten to make their own financial arrangements if these are not forthcoming. Business travellers and holiday makers alike require the financial aspects of their peregrinations to be made as painless as possible.

We do not aspire in a single chapter to describe all the ramifications of international banking. But for anybody interested in the marketing problems and policies of British banks and other financial institutions it is important to understand how they have coped with the formidable challenge of a rapidly expanding but highly competitive and hazardous international market. The UK, personified in the City of London, has a reputation for expertise and reliability in the provision of financial services which has outlived the reputation of the majority of manufacturing industries; and it has the fortuitous advantage of spanning the time zone between bedtime in Tokyo and breakfast in New York. But it has not been helped, in competing with the other leading financial centres, by the fragility of the UK economy nor, until the government removed them in 1979, by the constraints of exchange control.

Both the importance and the hazards of the international market are manifest in the accounts of the 'Big Four' English clearing banks. In all of them, international activities have accounted for a steadily increasing proportion of total business and in normal circumstances a contribution of a quarter to a third of total profits. But in the latest year, bad debt provisions have substantially reduced the international profit contribution, in one case turning it into a heavy loss; and the value of a stable domestic business, to balance the ups and downs of the international market, has been made clear.

Organisation

Since the war the principle of market segmentation has been recognised, implicitly at any rate, in the way British banks and other organisations have deployed their resources in the international field. In the case of the large clearing banks, for example, three distinct market opportunities have been tackled in quite different ways.

— The opportunity to provide UK exporters and importers with trade-related facilities and individuals with travel-related facilities has continued, as it was in the past, to be largely a function of domestic branch banking.
— The opportunity to earn profits from participation in the borrowing, investment and fund transfer activities of multinational corporations, international investors, sovereign countries, correspondent banks and other 'big ticket' customers is too complex to treat just as an extension of domestic banking. Such highly specialised and competitive activities are usually the province of separate International Divisions, or of the Merchant Banks that now form part of most major banking groups.
— The opportunity to invade the domestic banking market of foreign countries, where legislative and other considerations permit, is different again. Successful invasion of a country with its own customer attitudes, banking legislation and competitive marketing methods requires a high degree of local knowledge and operational autonomy. If they are to be more than representative offices for UK customers, the overseas branches of UK banks (like the branches of overseas banks in the UK) need to be staffed at all levels, except possibly at the very top, with local people and to be given sufficient independence to become part of the local scene.

For other financial service businesses the organisational consequences of an internationalised marketplace are equally profound. With competition no longer confined to our tight little island, the range of products and services on offer, the methods used to market them and the question of optimal size all need to be reviewed. Some of the consequences can be seen in the current upheavals at the Stock Exchange and at Lloyds of

London. In the early 1980s it became clear to the regulatory authorities and to the more farsighted of the participants in these two historic organisations that the brokers and underwriters trading and providing customer services based on them needed to become much larger and more versatile; otherwise from being historic they would become simply quaint survivals, with business progressively shifting to more modern and dynamic centres or being handled direct between large erstwhile customers.

The immediate result of this conclusion was deregulation, allowing outside organisations like banks to join or buy into the charmed circle of underwriters and brokers, breaking down the arbitrary distinction between the two and otherwise exploding what had been a tightly controlled oligopoly, increasingly dwarfed by the scale of international business. The proximate result, which cannot be consummated until promised legislation has been passed, is the flurry of mergers and acquisitions, some of which no doubt will flourish while others end in tears. The ultimate result, from our marketing viewpoint, will be a new specialist international market segment, offering the marketers fortunate enough to be involved in it both the problems and the opportunities associated with free competition and rapid change.

How this specialist market segment will develop organisationally remains to be seen. The main runners in a highly competitive race will be the non-banking financial service organisations, mostly merged into larger units; the investment and merchant banks, which already advise their customers on investments in these sectors; the foreign banks and para-banking institutions invading the UK market; and the clearing banks taking yet another step in the direction of providing a total financial services range by the acquisition and absorption of brokers, underwriters and other sectoral specialists. Whether victory goes to the specialists or the generalists, the foreigners or the home team is a matter in the end of consumer choice – not uninfluenced by the competitive marketing efforts of the participants.

Marketing international products and services

Segmented marketing goes naturally with segmented organisation. Target customer groups, products and services required to satisfy their needs, selling and promotional methods and bank-customer relationships all differ radically between the three organisational segments described above and the subsegments contained in each.

The UK-based individuals and small or medium-sized corporate customers, whose international requirements the clearing banks usually service through their domestic divisions, represent in effect subsegments of the banks' mass market – for example those individuals who travel abroad especially on holidays and those companies that do business abroad. So holiday money can be marketed to the former and export/import facilities to the latter as specific products in the total range of products and services that add up to a customer relationship.

Individual holidaymakers or travellers need in the first instance the wherewithal to go abroad at all – hence the marketer's opportunity to package and promote travel-related savings and loan products. They also need spending money when they are abroad in a form which exposes them neither to the risk of loss through theft nor to the inconvenience of wasting, queuing in banks, hours that would have been more agreeably spent on the beach. Travellers' cheques were the original answer to this need – having the convenient feature for the bank that issued them of the 'float' (the free use of the money between the time the cheques were bought and the time they had to be redeemed from the foreign banks cashing them). Then, with exchange control removed, there was the alternative of the credit card that can be used overseas – Access through its membership of the international Mastercard chain, Barclaycard through its membership of Visa. The latest development is the uniform Eurocheque which can be made out in various local currencies in countries which have joined the scheme and can be used for cash advances or direct payments to retailers, and is backed by an identifying Eurocard which itself is becoming acceptable in cash-dispensers. The extent to which these various credit instruments are recognised and accepted varies between countries depending on the overall effectiveness of their marketing campaigns. (American Express is said to have suffered some embarrassment when its upmarket Gold Card was rejected here and there for not being the familiar green colour.) It is something of a test of marketing orientation when a foreign-desk teller decides whether to offer a travelling customer the credit instrument that is most convenient and profitable for the bank or the one that is most easily used in the destination country.

For the small and medium-sized corporate customer the product range will include help with export/import credit, including negotiations with ECGD; foreign exchange, including forward purchase of currency options to avoid the risk of loss through exchange fluctuations; the collection of moneys due from overseas customers (a service which banks could perform with greater efficiency, to judge from responses to customer research) information about business opportunities and credit risks in relation both to countries and to individual firms; guidance on documentation; and introduction, when needed, to overseas branches and correspondent banks. Here again marketing orientation on the foreign desk is indicated both by the level of product knowledge and by the extent to which the bank executive is able to put himself in the customer's shoes and understand his problems.

The market segment represented by the 'big ticket' customers – the multinationals, sovereign borrowers and so on – serviced by the international divisions of clearing banks demands an entirely different approach, more akin to industrial marketing than to the mass marketing techniques of 'consumer product' companies. Because the target customers are large, they need to be studied and handled individually rather than *en masse*. Because their financial direction is sophisticated, they need to be serviced by bank executives with equal or superior expertise. Because they are operating in a worldwide market they will probably work with a number of banks, with bases in a number of different countries – and may well be ruthless in playing off one against another. Because their size and creditworthiness (in most cases) makes them such attractive customers for so many banks, they can command very keen prices for loans, deposits and services: it may require some ingenuity for a bank to earn a profit from doing business with them.

(It should be observed in passing that creditworthiness is not a word that applies to all sovereign borrowers, particularly in the Developing World. The myth that a country cannot go bust, which was an excuse for much overlending by banks to these countries, has been overtaken by the realisation that national debts can be repudiated; one of the necessary skills of the international banker nowadays is to negotiate the re-scheduling of such loans to avoid default.)

A fundamental strategic question in industrial marketing is whether to adopt a relationship approach or a transaction approach to business development. The same question arises in marketing financial services to 'big ticket' international customers. Should a bank attempt to build a long-term relationship with such customers, seeking to become its lead bank and satisfy the lion's share of its banking needs; or should it seek simply to carry out short-term transactions, where it has special skills and can anticipate earning a profit? As in many such conundrums, the practical answer is 'both', depending on customer demand; the same customer may very well want a long-term relationship with a versatile lead bank that understands its business; but also want to shop around on a day-to-day basis to find the bank that will offer, say, the best rate on a foreign exchange deal.

When the relationship strategy predominates, it brings with it the need to develop relationship-enhancing products like Cash Management (described in Chapter 6); and to instal internal management information and control systems, ensuring that the services provided to the various customer branches and subsidiaries by the various bank branches and departments are of uniformly high quality, that total exposure is not excessive – and that a fair profit is made overall.

A relationship strategy, at least in theory, gives the large banking group an advantage, when it comes to competing for business from large customers in the increasingly internationalised markets for investment, insurance and other specialist financial services. Customers who have developed a close understanding with their bankers should be pleased, it is argued, to buy their non-banking requirements from the same organisation. But the theory does not always work out in practice, either because the banking group's skills in cross-selling are inadequate or because (as some research suggests) customers are not yet convinced that the bank subsidiaries are as expert in these specialist services as the traditional providers of them. It may be, also, that customers feel more firmly in the saddle, when they buy the services they need from a number of different suppliers. Whatever the motivation, it raises the fundamental marketing question whether the investment, insurance and other specialist subsidiaries of banking groups competing in the international market are better advised to emphasise or de-emphasise their membership of the group: opinions clearly differ on this question – and indeed on the question whether such subsidiaries are better run by bankers or non-bankers. Moreover, the banking-customer relationship is a 'people business'. It is never just a question of a bank and a customer, but rather a number of bank executives dealing with a number of customer executives. To expect and demand a consistent relationship among so many participants is unrealistic. To a greater or lesser degree this fact militates against the total relationship strategy, giving opportunities for the 'horses for courses' approach.

Probably the best way for a British student of bank marketing to appreciate the problems of attacking the third major international market segment – retail markets overseas – is by observing the successes and failures of American and other banks invading the UK retail market. Apart from the ethnic banks, dealing largely with the affairs of their own patrials, very few of the 400-odd foreign banks represented in London have attempted to build up even small branch networks or attract substantial numbers of personal customers; most have confined themselves to the corporate market, where their more aggressive marketing methods have been successful to the extent of gaining a share in excess of 30% of all advances to UK corporate customers.

In the retail sector the two main Irish banks have successfully opened a few branches, extending beyond the heaviest concentrations of Irish residents; and Citibank of New York, having failed in an earlier attempt to establish a chain of moneyshops, is now showing signs of becoming a serious competitive threat to the British clearing banks by alternative means. Banking or para-banking organisations like American Express and Merrill Lynch have chosen to attack the retail market on a strictly segmented basis, offering various financial services packages to the affluent.

But the approach most likely to make a serious impact on a national scale is through acquisition or joint venture, combined with the introduction of new products and marketing methods. The Hong Kong and Shanghai Bank's attempt in 1982 to take over Royal Bank of Scotland Group, with its Williams & Glyn's subsidiary, was frustrated only by what some regarded as a questionable decision on the part of the Mergers & Monopolies Commission; and various foreign banks are currently embarking on joint ventures with building societies and others to introduce innovative marketing concepts like home banking and plastic banking, which side-step the need for an expensive branch network. It looks as though the stir-up in international banking caused by more efficient communications, technological advances, deregulation and the like will facilitate the entry of foreign organisations into the UK domestic market – and, by analogy, of British financial service organisations into those foreign markets which have similarly open structures.

How international marketing differs from domestic

It can be argued that the principles and techniques of marketing are constant. No matter what the industrial sector, the marketing skills of information collection and analysis, persuasive communication, new product development, project planning and control are needed for successful business development, as is an effective marketing element in management training. This is true enough. But the ways in which these skills are applied are so different that the tradition of serving a stint in the international division before returning to a domestic banking career is likely to give way to permanent specialisation.

The fundamental truth, which many multi-national companies as well as banks have been slow to learn, is that the marketing strategies of a small organisation with a small market share have to be quite different from those of a market leader; and a bank which is dominant in its domestic market will almost always be a small bank in a foreign market. So a centralised strategy of reproducing without modification in a foreign country a product or marketing approach that succeeded at home is likely to end in disaster (even if it does not run foul of local regulations). Even more than in the domestic market, the marketing initiative and responsibility need to be concentrated at the sharp end.

This need to decentralise marketing is compounded by the 'big ticket' nature of much international banking. Dealing with large numbers of relatively small customers in the domestic market, it is possible to devise a new product or service in a central marketing department and sell it largely (or, if need be entirely) by media advertising and direct mail. This is not possible when dealing with a relatively small number of large customers, doing business in all quarters of the globe and exposed to political as well as commercial hazards. Policy in this situation still needs to be controlled centrally; but the marketing activities of selling, servicing and creating relationships with individual customers need to be handled up front; you cannot handle negotiations with what are often equals in financial strength and expertise on an armslength or mass production basis.

This raises the question, to which different banks have found different answers, whether the intermediary between bank and customer should be primarily an account manager or primarily a salesman. The American banks have tended to adopt the salesman alternative, with bright young MBAs, equipped with all the presentation paraphernalia of the modern industrial salesman, competing for the favours of corporate treasurers and financial directors. They have had considerable success in winning business from the softer-selling British banks; but there are signs of a backlash with prospective customers complaining that they are tired of sitting at the receiving end of a succession of highly polished and almost identical sales pitches and would welcome a more informed discussion of their actual financial problems.

On the other hand, the British banks which have adopted the account manager alternative have not always equipped their intermediaries with the sales and marketing expertise or provided them with the marketing back-up needed to succeed in an immensely competitive environment.

The differences in the necessary marketing back-up between the domestic and the international scene are mainly matters of *selectivity*. Marketing information, communication, product development and training all need to be selectively targeted to cope with the international marketplace – it is, by definition, so much wider and more varied than the domestic scene.

Where information is concerned, decision-making management needs first of all enough general information about relative creditworthiness, political and economic prospects, comparative growth and profit potential in different countries and industries to select the target sectors for business development; and then more detailed information about the needs and idiosyncrasies of the selected targets. Account managers or sales people require to be equipped not only with comprehensive product knowledge, but with enough information about current business conditions in the specific target industries and companies with which they are concerned, to anticipate their banking needs and discuss them intelligently. Since it is not feasible in an international context to know everything that needs to be known about every industry and every country, the market information flow needs to be segmented by region and industry.

Marketing communications, through media advertising, print, P.R., direct mail and so on also need to be more selective and segmented in the international context than in the domestic market, where a case can be argued for saturation coverage. Internationally a bank which has achieved a position among, say, the world's top 100 banks and is represented in all the leading financial centres can justify some investment in image-building background advertising placed in media read by the international financial community. But most of its communications effort, and certainly that of smaller banks will be better directed into 'rifle-shot' communications, aimed to convey specific messages to specific target companies; and personal contact, supported when necessary by promotional and informational material, will be the core of the effort.

It may seem contradictory to write of product development in the international field after emphasising the importance of building flexible service relationships with large customers; the marketer's role in developing packaged products would seem more relevant to the mass consumers of the domestic market. True enough. But in a very competitive market, if you want to get away from the unprofitable constraint of competing on price alone, if you want to escape from the flatness of commodity dealing and create a raised profile based on a distinction which is uniquely yours, it is helpful to offer some facility which others cannot provide in exactly the same form; and modern electronic technology with its facilities for the rapid transmission of information and instructions opens the door to the development of products like Cash Management offering a demonstrable benefit to the international customer.

As for marketing training there can be little doubt that the international market demands special skills both from account managers and sales people in the field and from their marketing support teams; or that competition in this sector is exceptionally fierce; or indeed that it is exceedingly important for British banking to hold its own in the international arena. The need for specialist training with a strong marketing element seems clear.

Summary

The international market for financial services demands a segmented approach. It includes three distinct types of customer need – the needs of UK exporters and importers for trade-related facilities and of individuals for travel-related facilities; the borrowing, investment and fund transfer requirements of multi-nationals and other international operators; and the local banking needs of countries willing to admit branches of foreign banks. Within each type there is a wide variety of marketing opportunities and hazards; and a large assortment of competitors.

With London now one of the two or three leading international banking centres in the world, it is possible to be an international banker without having a permanent office or home outside this country. But while the basic marketing skills required for international banking – information collection and analysis, persuasive communication, new product development, project planning and control do not differ in principle from domestic banking – the specific expertise and competitive situations are very different indeed. Increasing specialisation in the international field, and in specific sectors of that field, seems inevitable.

This is as true of marketing strategy and organisation as it is of people. In the domestic market centralised control is possible, even if not always desirable; in the international arena decentralisation is essential.

CHAPTER SIX

Plastic and electronic banking

It is a commonplace observation that few people living through a peaceful revolution are fully aware that it is going on. The new electronics technology – stretching from the computer with its constantly increasing capabilities through vastly more powerful systems for the storage, access, analysis and dissemination of information to communications facilities that enable information and instructions to be flashed around the world in seconds rather than weeks – is bringing about a revolution in the banking industry, the consequences of which are far from complete. Yet for the bank customer and the bank employee it remains true that a bank is a bank is a bank. The customer may sometimes find it exasperating that the computer, which now seems to manage his affairs, is so reluctant to see reason or make exceptions; the employee may regret the erosion of individual discretion and the personal touch. But the reality of a revolution even more profound than the change from the personal service neighbourhood store to the self-service hypermarket is seldom fully appreciated.

It is only necessary, however, to describe some of the electronically-inspired developments of the past twenty years and reflect on their long-term potentialities to recognise that a revolution is happening here and now, which cannot fail to affect the careers of bank employees as profoundly as it is affecting the thrust of marketing strategy. Already in 1986, with technology still advancing by leaps and bounds, there is no technological reason why a bank customer should ever go inside a branch to draw or deposit cash – or indeed should use cash at all except for very small purchases; nor is there any insuperable obstacle to abandoning the use of cheques in favour of plastic cards and electronic impulses.

There are, of course, practical and psychological barriers. The capital investment required for the installation of a nationwide network of enhanced ATM's, an EFTPOS or home banking system is stupendous; and banks and their collaborators hesitate to make it because electronic equipment continues to get better and cheaper; and because customers' willingness to accept plastic cards and computer terminals in place of cash and cashiers remains doubtful. There can be no doubt, however, that by the end of the next decade a much larger proportion of financial transactions will be handled impersonally; nor that marketing and promotional skills will have had an important part to play in winning acceptance for the change.

T & E charge and credit cards

For personal customers the first conspicuous move towards cashless and chequeless banking came through plastic credit cards rather than through electronics – though, in fact, no major credit card system could be developed without a highly developed computer system to support it behind the scenes; and the still dormant magnetic strip incorporated in modern credit cards has major electronic implications for the future.

Though today's major credit card systems are all owned and operated by banks, they were not actually originated by banks. Charge cards issued by individual store, car rental and other chains pre-dated them, as did Travel and Entertainment (T & E) cards of which Diners is the best known. The first UK 'plastic card' with an extended credit facility was Barclaycard, launched by Barclays Bank in June 1966 – with an initial base of 1 million card-holders and 30,000 retail outlets. Barclaycard was in fact a naturalised version of the blue, white and gold card scheme of Bank Americard, now called VISA worldwide. The sophisticated marketing planning and execution needed to make Barclaycard a success undoubtedly had a profound effect on the marketing outlook of all banks. Indeed in many ways it can now be seen as the most public expression of the changes in this area in the last twenty years. It is a good example if the interaction between factors in a rapidly changing environment where one development begets another.

By about 1970 the other clearing banks, having watched Barclaycard survive its early struggles, began to be alarmed by the competitive threat it posed – particularly since their research showed that a credit card was a potential moneyspinner for the bank owning it; and that some 20% of Barclaycard holders were customers of other banks. Their research also showed strong resistance by retailers to the idea of handling a separate credit card for every major bank. Consequently NatWest, Lloyds and Midland – joined later by Williams & Glyn's – decided to co-operate in the planning and launch of a second nationally recognised credit card. The Joint Credit Card Company Ltd., staffed by individuals from the participating banks was established in Southend with a massive computer installation to handle administration and marketing; and the Access Card was launched in the Autumn of 1972.

Since then both cards have steadily increased the number of cardholders (holders who make little use of their cards have been a problem) and the number of co-operating retailers. Public acceptance of a credit card as a convenient method of borrowing money (though for all but very short term borrowing, at a higher rate of interest than an overdraft or bank loan) over a longer period than the monthly credit cycle has increased – to an extent that on at least one occasion has caused Government, concerned with the money supply, to ask for restraint.

Nor has the Joint Credit Card Company's conclusion in the early 1970s that retailers would refuse to recognise more than two national credit cards proved correct in the longer term. The American Express Company has widened UK usage of its card with an upmarket bias. The TSB and even overseas operators have successfully introduced and obtained significant retailer acceptance of their credit cards for their own benefit and that of their own customers. And the super-imposition of Gold Cards on top of recognised credit cards has provided additional facilities for the sought-after affluent personal customer segment, as well as causing more recognition problems for retailer staffs. On top of this retailers have introduced their own credit card service, and have extended the provision of credit outside their own province, just as Marks & Spencer's recently introduced charge card is unlikely to be confined for ever to their own branches, but to be just the opening shot in a plan to emulate Sears Roebuck in the States as a national provider of financial services. And its own credit card is likely to be one of the tools used by the American Citicorp in its latest drive to penetrate the UK retail market.

The five immediate marketing tasks for credit card operators are the competitive ones of recruiting creditworthy cardholders (any pretence of limiting usage to a bank's own customers has been abandoned); securing full co-operation from retailers; the co-operative one of avoiding fraudulent use; finding ways of enhancing the benefit to cardholders, for instance by offering a consolidated accounting system to companies issuing cards to their employees; and utilising what is, in effect, a captive, credit-rated mailing list to promote other products or services. (So far UK banks, but not all other operators in this market have resisted the temptation to sell their lists to third parties.)

Longer-term tasks are those of widening acceptance of the UK cards in other countries – likely to be achieved through participation in the major international card systems – Visa in the case of Barclaycard and Mastercard in the case of Access, and activation of the 'smart card' potential represented by the so far largely unused magnetic strips on the back of the cards. (Some credit cards issued by some banks can however already be used in their ATM's to draw cash from the credit card account.) Technically a magnetic strip or silicon chip on a card could carry an identifying code, details of the card-holder's balance and other information. Based on this the futurologist will rhapsodise about the day when card-holders can carry their bank statements in their pockets, to be instantly updated by on-line terminals and printed out when required by a home computer; and when one multi-purpose card can substitute for today's pocketful of plastic. The more down-to-earth marketing planner will consider how and how fast the transition can be achieved; and how the benefit to card-holders, co-operating retailers and issuing banks can be made to match the enormous cost of a compatible, on-line computerised national communications system. And indeed whether or not a separate market niche might not be better.

ATMs, servicetills, cashpoints etc

Of course, the universal plastic card, if it ever materialises, may develop out of the cards that bank and building society customers now carry to obtain access to Automated Teller Machines, Servicetills or other brand-names. By early 1985 the number of on- and off-line ATMs in the UK had reached 5,000, allowing some 12 million card-holder customers to obtain virtually 24-hour, 7-day access to cash and to account details (so long as their friendly neighbourhood ATM was not out of order). ATMs were located in the walls of banks and building societies, in entrance lobbies (Lloyd's Bank, the protagonists of ATMs in lobbies, found that their Lobby Service tills outperformed their through-the-wall tills when both were available on the same site) and although still in small numbers, in department stores, offices and factories, and other 'off-branch' sites.

Now that the mechanical difficulties which plagued them in the early days have been largely overcome, an acceleration in the rate of increase in this facility can be anticipated. Questions which remain to be answered are whether systems can or should be made compatible, so as to increase the number of sites available to the customer of any one bank (Natwest and Midland have made a start in this direction by making the ATMs of each available to the customers of the other and, at the time this was written, Barclays, Lloyds and The Royal Bank of Scotland have announced plans to couple their on-line systems); whether or not the cost of having ATMs on-line to the central computer is justified by the immediate availability of account information and instantaneous debiting; and how the time saved in branches by the automation of routine transactions can or should be diverted to more productive customer services.

EFTPOS

Electronic Funds Transfer at Point of Sale, known by the inelegant acronym of EFTPOS, is a further manifestation of the plastic/electronic revolution that is not just on the horizon but already with us. The theory is simple. The procedure of totting up a customer's purchases on a supermarket till, then processing a cheque or credit card and despatching the resulting forms for further processing by the bank's or the credit card company's computer is laborious and time-consuming; why not short-circuit it by arranging for the till to communicate direct with the central computer holding the customer's bank account and at the same time – if the customer's card is sufficiently smart – adjusting the balance on it?

Why not, indeed? As with all technically feasible concepts, there are problems and questions to be answered, which working parties set up in the 1970's by the Committee of London Clearing Bankers struggled with long and hard. Would it be all that attractive for the card-holder to have his account debited instantaneously instead of benefiting from the month's free credit now offered by a credit card? What system of new generation cash registers and communications links should be adopted and who should pay the bill, the retailer or the bank? Would the savings resulting from faster processing and cash transmission be sufficient to cover the costs? And could the ideal, from the card-holder's and the retailer's viewpoint of a single compatible system, recognising every brand of card, be achieved in a climate of growing competition between banks, building societies and other financial service organisations? While the discussions were still in progress, one bank set up an independent experimental scheme in Scotland; and others showed signs of breaking ranks.

Home banking

Like EFTPOS, banking at home through a personal computer, linked by an inter-active cable system to the bank's computer is already not only technically feasible but actually happening in test areas. And to judge from some of the more excited reports on the subject, it will not be long before the clearing banks can all cut down their postal departments, convert their branches to massage parlours and leave their customers to conduct their financial transactions, check their balances, make and receive payments electronically without leaving the shelter of their own homes.

Visions of the future like this tend to telescope the time taken for changes that are feasible, even desirable, to be brought about and the practical obstacles that must be overcome on the way. Looked at through the sceptical eye of a marketing planner, the first question to be asked is whether and when the consumer – who one way or another has to pay for every service received – will see enough benefit in a home banking facility to pay for it. Certainly the attractions of home banking in itself will be insufficient to justify the cost of a dedicated transmission system. Any viable service will need to be combined, as now with Prestel, with home shopping, entertainment, information and advertising before large scale take-off is achieved. Then there is the question who is to make the capital investment in the extra communications infrastructure (British Telecom, a competitor or a consortium of interests?) and who will devise and market the consumer proposition? And of course, who will carry the risk and pocket the eventual profit (or loss)?

Probably the whole system will not develop as one co-ordinated grand plan but take shape piecemeal, over a long period, with local and regional experiments sorting out the winners from the losers. The banks will inevitably be involved in whatever develops, if only as organisers of finance; and bank marketers will need to be alert in order to seize the opportunities that are always inherent in change – provided that you don't miss the boat.

The corporate sector

Electronic, if not plastic, technology also enables banks to develop and market new services for their corporate customers, mainly through the facilities of detailed information collection, analysis and distribution and of rapid communication. As one experienced international banker remarked (he had seen it all and didn't altogether like it): 'We don't do anything very different from my early days, we just do it very comprehensively and frighteningly fast'. The frightening part was not just nostalgia for the good old days when it took three weeks for a banker's draft drawn in London to be cleared in Hong Kong; it is frightening when a false rumour that an American President has had a stroke can destabilise exchange rates and share values around the world within minutes. And the reduced 'float' in the banking system resulting from faster fund transmission, while giving customers more immediate use of their funds, also represents a loss of profit to the banks which needs to be made up in some other way.

Within the UK the recently inaugurated CHAPS service (Clearing House Automated Payments System) set up by the 13 English and Scottish clearing banks makes possible same day value payments nationwide of large sterling transactions (the minimum is £10,000 and the average payment around £650,000) between the member banks and their customers. CHAPS, a 1980s version of the Town Clearings system which dates back to Victorian days, had some early problems in recruiting users. Non-member banks were less happy than the founding clearers because they could only gain indirect access to the system and because there was no standard interface between the computers of the 250 or so other banks who might be interested in participating and the clearers' computers. But technologically the system works and will undoubtedly grow from handling an average of 6,000 transactions a day in 1984 towards its rated capacity of 16,000 transactions an hour.

The older established UK transmission system, BACS (Bankers Automated Clearing Services) offers more general facilities for replacing manual by electronic handling and circumventing the three-day time-lag in clearance. For example, customers can send their payrolls to BACS on tape or discette – though they have to get there on Tuesday for payment on Friday; and a few very large companies have direct on-line access to the BACS computer. BACS is owned by Interbank Computer Access, a non-profit organisation set up by a group of UK clearing banks, and other banks with branches in the UK can use its facilities. As competition between the banks and the building societies warmed up, the question whether the latter should be allowed direct access to BACS became a burning issue, not yet resolved; on the banking side there is some reluctance to share a facility that gives the banks a competitive advantage and would be very expensive to match.

In the international sector there is a variety of competing electronic systems, offering instantaneous financial information and dealing facilities to banks and other customers. Reuter's Monitor system originally introduced in 1973 to offer constantly updated information to dealers on foreign exchange and money market rates, Eurobonds, equities, commodity rates and so on was extended in 1981 to provide a direct communication and dealing facility for subscribers on a confidential basis. Other financial information services are offered by Dow Jones, ADP Comtrend, Commodity News Service, Quotron, Telekurs and Quick. Private communications networks available to bankers include GEISCO and ADP Network Services.

The bankers' own entrant in this overcrowded field is SWIFT (the Society of Worldwide Interbank Financial Telecommunication). Established in 1973 by 239 banks in 15 countries as a non-profit bank-owned co-operative society, SWIFT had 1084 member banks in 54 countries by 1984 when a daily total of some 500,000 transactions, including customer transfers, foreign exchange confirmations, bank transfers and documentary credits and collections were handled by regional processing centres in London, Belgium, Holland and the US. The system's information transmission facilities, not yet fully exploited, can carry foreign exchange, stock market, interest rate and other data or special messages between correspondent banks and their customers; special payments mechanisms, based on credit cards, can be organised, and there is no technical obstacle to linking the system with local ATM or POS networks.

The most elaborate, though by no means most profitable, electronic service offered to large corporate customers is Cash Management. This, like many innovative financial services, originated in the US and can be traced back to the old lock box system, introduced by RCA in the 1950s, when most American banks were local or confined within state boundaries; to help rationalise RCA's cash flow and cash control, receipts were consolidated through post office boxes strategically placed near the mailing addresses of major customer bases.

Chemical Bank is credited with taking the initiative twenty years later in converting a customer-controlled manual system into a bank-controlled electronic system for the daily consolidation of receipts and payments through the first version of its BankLink service, gaining a substantial amount of large corporate business in the process. In its early versions Cash Management was confined to the US. But before very long the scope of the various services was widened to include the rest of the world; at which point, UK and other European banks, finding themselves in receipt of requests from multi-national customers to furnish account information to Chemical Bank, Citibank, Chase or whoever, sat up and took notice. Setting up a cash management system for a large customer was not very attractive in itself; after the initial installation fees it was unlikely to generate enough revenue to compensate for the loss of float. But letting customers do it for themselves or commission a rival bank, which might build on the relationship to acquire the lead bank position, were even less attractive options. Reluctantly and defensively every major bank with international aspirations developed its own cash management product.

Cash management in its widest international application cannot be regarded as an instant success; by the end of 1984 there were probably no more than 200 multinational companies buying the full international service. But scaled down to meet the needs of smaller companies or rich individuals it could have considerable appeal; given the flexibility and development potential of modern electronic systems, a tailor-made installation is capable of incorporating a variety of special features, such as:

— timely forecasting of receipts and disbursement;
— tight control over disbursement;
— mobilisation of funds for investment of surplus;
— transaction and balance information;
— analysis of cash costs and investment information.

In short, cash management has a lot to offer in addition to the quick collection and concentration of funds to companies or individuals that want to exercise a tighter control over their financial affairs; how the banks that provide the service are to earn a profit from it is less clear.

Marketing implications of plastic and electronic technology

Technological change is always a challenge to marketing strategists who have to recognise an opportunity for creating a new benefit for existing and prospective customers, while earning an additional profit for their companies; and to get the timing right, so as to be ahead of competitors, but not too far ahead of arousable consumer demand. (A new product or service that fails through being before its time, while its successors and imitators succeed, is high on the list of marketing nightmares.)

Financial marketing strategists pursuing innovation in the fields discussed in this chapter – particularly the plastic cards that serve as instruments for the creation of consumer credit – have the additional complication of needing to keep a weather eye open for government reaction. How far the banks' successes in marketing credit are responsible for the change in social attitudes from 'save now, spend later' to 'spend now, pay later' must be a matter of opinion. But all governments, whether vocally monetarist or not, are bound to be concerned with the effect on the money supply of the increasing availability of consumer credit.

The marketing voice cannot expect to predominate in the major strategic decisions, involving not only massive investments and redeployment of people but ultimately the structure of the whole banking industry – though it could well make itself heard more authoritatively than in the past, when it comes to predicting the future. But while senior management will make the basic decisions, marketing skills will unquestionably be needed in accelerating consumer acceptance of new technology-based services, many of which need to be developed on an industry-wide basis; and in extracting the maximum competitive benefit for individual banks and their customers from these services.

If EFTPOS is to take off, for example, it will be necessary for the industry to construct a marketing proposition that will clearly benefit the customers who are invited to use the facility, the retailers who will have to instal the specialised hardware and the banks that will make the major investment in the communications and processing network; it will be necessary also to gain acceptance of the proposition modified if necessary in the light of experience, fast enough and widely enough to secure a return on the investment.

And always there will be the challenge for the marketers of individual banks, of finding ways to quarry proportionately more customers or more business from existing customers or enhanced profits out of innovations that are available to all. Every bank can offer a credit card and a cash dispenser card, subscribe to SWIFT or offer some form of cash management service. The winners will be those that succeed in creating a difference, probably quite minor, in product formulation or presentation; and communicating it more effectively to their customers – plus any customers of competitive institutions who happen to be listening.

Summary

The encoded plastic card and the electronic feats of Information Technology have combined to revolutionise the character of retail banking, at least in prospect. The cashless society could be with us by the end of the century, individual customers by then need never visit their banks in person – if it were not for certain practical difficulties.

The most substantial of these difficulties are the enormous capital investment involved for the banks and their collaborators, together with the uncertain return on the investment; the need for co-operation in the installation of basic systems; and the reluctance of people, both customers and bankers to change engrained habits.

In wholesale and international banking the facilities provided by modern Information Technology for transmitting funds and information instantaneously around the country or around the globe open up both new opportunities and new risks for financial institutions. At best there is the opportunity to earn additional profits through new customer services; at worst there is the risk, if the new facilities are not soundly managed, of destroying the world's precarious economic structure.

Professional marketers claim special skill in forecasting the speed and direction of change; in persuading customers (and staff) to recognise the need to change; and in finding ways of earning *profits* from a changing market, without taking undue risks. The next decade will offer marketers of financial services exceptional opportunities to justify these claims.

CHAPTER SEVEN

The clearing banks and their competitors

Traditionally, the 13 English and Scottish clearing banks, particularly the 'Big Four' in England and Wales and the 'Big Two' in Scotland, have regarded each other as the competitors to watch; and have watched with a jealous eye shares of advances, deposits and customers from data published by the authorities or recorded by syndicated research. A shift of a percentage point or two from one bank to another was grounds for jubilation in one camp and anxious self-examination in another.

This is, of course, a manifestation of the shift from a *de facto* cartel to the more active competition enjoined by the Bank of England's Competition and Credit Control paper of 1971. It should not be treated lightly. One percentage point gained or lost in as large a market as this represents a lot of customers; and it is demonstrably possible, through some marketing action such as the introduction of 'free' banking (so long as it is not immediately followed by competitors) to bring about significant changes in market share. Inter-bank competition is certainly increasing; but a long tradition of interbank co-operation (which needs to continue in many areas, such as clearings and funds transmission, in order to give the public a satisfactory banking service) together with the public's not unjustifiable belief that all the big banks are much of a muchness, make it unlikely that the battle will ever be fought to the death.

From the strategic marketing viewpoint, a much more serious competitive threat than the still relatively friendly rivalry between the clearers comes from foreign banks attacking the UK market and from specialist financial service organisations. In the long run the most absorbing conflict will be between the holistic approach of the big UK clearing bank groups, capable of offering any one customer, personal or corporate, a complete range of financial services; and the specialist attack of the invaders from other countries or other financial disciplines. The main battle will be fought in and around the Square Mile of the City of London, which is striving to maintain its position as one of the world's two or three leading international financial centres, making the conflict of more than parochial interest.

Foreign banks in the UK

At the last count well over 400 foreign banks, as well as a number of other financial service institutions, had branches in London. Their objectives in coming here – some within the last decade, some as long ago as the last century – have clearly been different, and in some cases have changed over the years. The ethnic banks, like the Bank of Cyprus, have London branches mainly in order to supply the banking needs of their own nationals resident in this country. Others find London a convenient base for servicing their international customers, dealing in Eurocurrency and other world markets. Others again deliberately confine their activities to corporate business or to the upmarket personal sector. And just a few clearly intend to attack the UK retail market – which looks exceedingly attractive in terms of profitability, until you calculate the cost of building a branch network from scratch.

Not being encumbered with the overheads of a national branch network, the foreign banks can adopt a segmented marketing strategy, picking off the segments where the margin between revenue and cost is likely to be most favourable; and while individually they may not constitute a major threat to the established British banks, their combined attack can siphon off large chunks of the more readily accessible market segments. Corporate borrowers, for example, particularly the large companies with good credit ratings, can and will shop around for the most favourable terms; and foreign banks whose executive time can be occupied in selling rather than managing branches, are well placed to compete.

The absence of branch overheads also enables the more aggressive foreign banks to consider, in the light of today's market and today's communications technology (and what can be predicted about tomorrow's) whether a dedicated branch network – and if so what type of network – is needed to establish an efficient and profitable UK retail business. With cash dispensers, point of sale terminals and home banking all in existence or on the near horizon – and building societies interested in developing more banking business, if need be co-operatively, through their retail sites – does a newcomer need to invest in strongrooms, counters, security screens and expensive High Street sites?

Citicorp, America's leading banking group, is a conspicuous example of this considered, flexible – even experimental – approach to market penetration. Citicorp (or Citibank) has been represented in the UK since 1902 and has made various innovative attempts to build its market share; one attempt that looked promising but failed in the 1970s was to penetrate the savings and loan market through a chain of moneyshops. The bank has now committed itself publicly to expanding from its traditional base in the multinational corporate sector, and becoming a major force in British domestic banking. With an openness that is more frequent in America than in British marketing, it has announced its development strategy as based on market segmentation, reflected in a divisionalised organisation, and profit-related business selectivity. Separate divisions will handle its traditional core business with other financial institutions and large international companies; its commercial banking activities, based in 1985 on ten branches; its retail banking activity, based on Citibank Savings, with 37 branches in 1985 (destined to grow to 250); a number of charge card schemes, operated for leading retail chains; and a Treasury Division, handling foreign exchange and other currency dealing operations.

Citicorp's intention to enter the financial services arena has been signalled by the acquisition of a leading London stockbroker; and its intention to join the select company of British clearing banks by its application for direct entry to the London clearing system. Its majority holding in Diners Club International and its membership of a bank and building society ATM consortium make it clear that it will not be laggardly in applying its American plastic banking expertise to the British market.

No doubt some of Citicorp's ventures – and those of other progressive US financial service businesses, like American Express and Merrill Lynch – will be less successful in Britain than others. But their competition will most certainly enliven the British marketing scene.

TSB and National Girobank

Further direct competition in the retail banking sector will result from the Trustee Savings Banks' decision to relinquish their friendly society status and become a fully commercial national bank. They will have the advantages of a sound capital base, resulting from their public flotation in 1986, a large number of exceptionally loyal customers (more down-market than the established clearing banks' customer profiles but with a warmer, less apprehensive attitude towards the bank); and – to stimulate the creativity of their marketing people – a virtually clean sheet for introducing their own version of many of the more sophisticated services offered by the clearers.

To complete the picture on the clearing bank front, the National Girobank offers an economical money transmission service through the 21,000 branch post offices up and down the country, together with simple banking services; as a publicly owned concern it was spared the obligation imposed on the clearing banks in 1984, to deduct the composite rate of tax from the interest paid on customer deposits, giving it a competitive advantage with small savers who are not liable to income tax. Traditionally National Girobank's appeal, since it was opened in 1968, has been to the less sophisticated members of the public who found banks intimidating. But its transmission facilities are increasingly being used by cost conscious customers of the commercial clearers, as a low cost element in their total banking requirements – in much the same way as some shoppers will buy their dresses from Harrods but their underclothes from Marks and Spencer.

Building societies

While foreign banks have provided the most formidable competition for the clearing banks in the wholesale (corporate) sector, the most formidable competition in the retail (personal) sector has come from the building societies. The Building Society movement has had a long and honourable history beginning in the late 18th century, when groups of ten to twenty people, transplanted by the industrial revolution from the country to the towns, would get together to pool their savings for the purchase of building land; once the land was bought and the members' houses built the societies would usually terminate. But some were permanent and in due course were recognised by the Building Societies Act of 1874 as friendly societies with a privileged tax position, specialising in attracting deposits from savers and lending them to prospective house purchasers. Over time, the 2,000 mostly local or regional societies which existed at the turn of the century were reduced by merger or closure to the 206 which existed in 1983, of which the largest five – now national in coverage – held 55.7% of the movement's total assets of almost £86 billion and the largest twenty held 87.0%.

The growing strength of the building societies was largely a post-war phenomenon, related to the growth of home ownership. In 1938, 32.5% of all dwellings in England and Wales were owner-occupied and 38% of the owners had building society mortgages. By 1982 the number of houses had nearly doubled and increased immensely in value; nearly 60% were owner-occupied and nearly 45% of owners had building society mortgages.

For the banks the competitive threat to their personal deposit-taking and lending activities was masked by the rapid growth in the societies' total assets (from £1.25 billion in 1950 to £10.8 billion in 1970, £53.8 billion in 1980 and £85.9 billion in 1983; and by the fact that every building society was a bank customer. But by the 1980s the threat could not be ignored. The building societies were attracting a steadily growing proportion of personal savings to the detriment of the banks; and they were also doing the lion's share of the financing of what for most people is the largest single purchase in their lives.

On the lending front the banks reacted to some effect, as shown below, by introducing and havily promoting their own house mortgage schemes:

Mortgage loans for house purchase 1979–83

Net advances during:	Total £m	%	Building Societies %	Monetary Sector %	Local Authorities %	Other Sources %
1979	5,271	100.0	81.6	9.2	4.5	4.6
1980	5,722	100.0	78.5	8.1	6.3	7.0
1981	6,331	100.0	66.8	25.8	2.8	4.5
1982	8,147	100.0	57.7	36.0	3.9	2.3
1983	11,041	100.0	75.0	24.5	−2.0	2.5

(Source: Government Green Paper on Building Societies, July 1984)

On the deposit-taking front the banks also reacted by introducing high interest deposit accounts and a variety of savings schemes. But here they were less successful. The building societies' 'shareholders' continued to increase – from 30.6 million, including those with deposits in more than one society, in 1980 to 37.7 million in 1983; and the societies' share of personal savings also continued to increase:

Selected liquid assets of the personal sector 1979–83

Amount outstanding at end year:	Total		Building Societies	Monetary sector deposits	National Savings	Other
	£billion	%	%	%	%	%
1979	91.4	100.0	46.4	41.3	11.7	0.6
1980	107.4	100.0	46.2	42.0	11.3	0.6
1981	122.9	100.0	46.1	38.8	14.8	0.3
1982	140.7	100.0	47.6	36.7	15.4	0.3
1983	157.3	100.0	49.3	34.8	15.6	0.3

(Source: Government Green Paper on Building Societies)

In 1984 the government announced their decision, in line with their policy of encouraging competition in the financial services market, to allow building societies 'to offer a fuller range of personal banking and money transmission services to their members, if they so wish'; and also to provide additional services, related to their basic home loan business, such as conveyancing and structural surveys. While the necessary legislation has yet to be passed, the largest societies – which are the most likely to elect to compete more directly with the banks in such market segments as small loans for purposes other than house purchase and the issue of credit cards – are already laying their plans; and strengthening their competitive position by yet more mergers.

Meanwhile, the banks are taking preventive marketing action. The most interesting development is the decision by Lloyds Bank to put together a national chain of estate agencies designed eventually to provide a complete one-stop home transfer service, so pre-empting anything the building societies can offer (see Chapter 18).

The direct confrontation between the banks and the building societies should provide a fascinating spectacle for aficionados of marketing. The building societies will start with the advantage of a lower cost structure and operating systems that in some respects are more advanced; in most large building societies, for example, unlike most banks, counter staff have personal electronic work stations on line to the central computer. But this is largely a function of a very simple, streamlined business, which may be compromised if the societies are too ambitious in their diversifications. The banks on the other hand have the advantages of a national money transmission system and a much wider range of established services and managerial skills. No doubt the consumer will benefit through keener prices and more imaginative services, from the enhanced competition – that, at least, is what 'O' Level Economics would assert. But there will be another possible consequence of enhanced competition, that the weaker societies and even the weaker banks may find themselves in unexpected financial difficulties.

Retailers as bankers

In the United States, one of the largest retail 'banks' is the banking subsidiary of Sears Roebuck, the giant retailing and direct mail house, which developed out of the normal retailing practice of offering credit to customers into full-blown banking. It requires no great effort of imagination to foresee similar developments in the UK. So far the retail chains have made only modest inroads into the banks' personal credit business, mainly through proliferating their own charge cards in competition with the banks' credit cards. But the increasing concentration of ownership in food and drink, clothing, department stores and other forms of retailing must open the way to more serious competition. If you have a healthy cash flow, a substantial customer base and a large number of High Street outlets already paid for, the temptation to diversify into the simpler forms of banking must be considerable. Marks and Spencer for one have made it plain that their successful introduction of charge cards in 1984 can be expected to lead in due course to more ambitious banking initiatives.

Related banking services

So far we have discussed competition in the context of the core banking business of generating deposits, loans and money transmission. But in recent years the banks, eager to supplement their interest revenue with more income from fees and commissions, have been much more vigorous in attacking such related financial services sectors as insurance broking, investment management, merchant banking, unit trusts, trusteeships and executorships and tax advice. Most recently, de-regulation of the Stock Exchange (and the fear that foreign interests would move in to dominate the market) has led to a sharply increased interest in direct participation in dealing in stocks and shares, financial futures and other forms of security; and most large banks have hastened to acquire stockbroking subsidiaries.

All of these initiatives have led the clearing banks into competition with specialists in the sectors concerned – all of them, of course, bank customers – such as insurance brokers, solicitors, stockbrokers, merchant bankers and investment houses. There have been, and will continue to be, major organisational and marketing problems. The early days are long past, when neophyte marketing departments were instructed to concentrate their efforts on pushing a variety of related services through the branches and tried to do it by circulating innumerable leaflets and point of sale posters. This resulted simply in a lot of waste paper and much resentment on the part of branch managers, who were far too busy looking after customers and branch administration to join the flavour of the month club – last month insurance, this month will appointments, next month you name it. It soon became clear that competing casually with specialists, each ensconced in his traditional niche, was a formidable task for the generalist banker. A more serious approach was needed.

But what was the best way to mobilise the massive strengths of the large clearing banks in attacking the relatively small and nimble specialists – rather like an armoured division attacking an assortment of guerrilla bands? The answer is beginning to emerge in the form of customer segmentation and organisational segmentation, tied together by a more efficient internal communications system.

The principles of customer segmentation are applied by recognising in the approach to product development and promotion the fact that large, medium and small businesses and the various personal customer segments all require different products and different methods of servicing. Its organisational equivalent in the clearing bank groups is the restructuring of branch networks to include business branches, upmarket personal branches and so on; and the increasing dependence on merchant banking, trust company, insurance and other semi-autonomous subsidiaries to handle the related banking services.

It looks as though the bankers and their competitors will divide into two streams – the generalists seeking to understand and satisfy all the financial service needs of defined customer segments; and the specialists offering highly developed expertise in particular product areas. Which approach will prove more attractive to customers – and how the two will relate to each other in groups offering both – remains to be seen. What is certain is that organisations in which the marketing principle of starting with customers and their needs is disregarded are unlikely to have a bright future.

Summary

The large UK clearing banks are coming increasingly to recognise that the most important competition they face comes not from each other but from foreign banks and from other financial services institutions both foreign and domestic. On the one flank there are the foreign banks that have identified the UK and London in particular as an attractive market together with the specialist financial service companies; both for the most part are pursuing a niche strategy, directing their marketing effort at corporate customers and relatively affluent individuals. On the other flank are the building societies, which have already mopped up nearly half the total savings of the personal sector, and – now that the banks have successfully invaded their mortgage lending base – have been freed by government legislation to offer a wider range of personal banking and money transmission services.

The clearing banks, attacked in this way on both flanks (and briskly counter-attacking), face an interesting marketing strategy dilemma. Should they continue to present themselves as generalists, capable of handling all the financial needs of all their customers, from the richest to the poorest? Or as specialists, offering their specialised services from separate profit centres linked only by their common ownership? Or are there ways, with the new resource of instant communications, of getting the best of both worlds?

And how will the customers, who ultimately decide which strategist has got it right, choose between all the competitors for their favours.

CHAPTER EIGHT

The marketing plan

Nobody – not even Cassandra, and she came to a sticky end – can predict the future with any certainty. Even when the direction of change seems clear, the speed of change may yet be uncertain; and a sharp change of direction may be precipitated by a quite unanticipated event. The ability of people, however powerful or managerial their position, to control the behaviour of other people is conspicuously limited. So why does marketing, which claims to deal with the future, with change and with people, make such a big thing out of the marketing *plan*? Surely it is unrealistic even to attempt to produce a detailed plan of action, including a quantified prediction of its results, for the next twelve months, let alone for three, four or five years ahead?

Good questions, which require the thorough answers we hope to give them in this chapter. The short answer is that planning can be valuable or futile, depending on the nature of the plan and the planning procedures, and on the way the plan is integrated into the process of management. It is certainly not unknown for companies to adopt the procedures of planning without accepting its implications, and thus for the marketing plan – *prepared at some considerable cost in executive time* – to become simply a statement of good intentions which is only fit to be buried in some file shortly after publication and disinterred nine months later to provide a basis for next year's essay.

But when planning is taken seriously, the marketing plan can make an essential contribution to the methodical development of a company's business by

1 providing a clear statement of marketing objectives (within the framework of corporate policy) to which every department of the organisation which has accepted the plan is committed;
2 compelling the responsible manager to think through in advance all the assumptions and all the conditions which must be met if the plan

is to succeed; and perhaps to face up in time to the realisation that some of the assumptions or conditions are unrealistic;

3 providing a yardstick against which progress will be measured, with provision for appropriate action if achievement is seriously above or below target.

In short, a living, flexible plan for action, about which considerable thought has been given as to how it can best be modified in the light of events, is a vital tool for management. A rigid, ritualistic plan is a waste of time and money. In any large organisation which has accepted the planning principle there will be all sizes and shapes of marketing plans: plans for on-going products and services and for new products or services, plans for increasing business with defined customers or customer segments, group plans, regional plans, divisional plans and unit plans. In theory they should all reflect different aspects of corporate strategy and fit neatly, like pieces in a jigsaw puzzle, into the master plan for the organisation. But even if they fit together neatly at the beginning of the planning period they will begin to reflect the normal untidiness of human affairs before the period is far advanced. Total, inhuman neatness is less important in practice than a level of commitment which will ensure that those plans, or elements of plans, which 'fail' do so for better reasons than managerial inertia.

In enumerating, as we propose to do, the main ingredients of the 'ideal' marketing plan, we risk advocating by implication long, detailed documents which could have diminished impact because busy managers have no time to read them. We should say at the outset that a plan should be no longer than is needed to ensure the right course of action by those involved in implementing it, and to gain acceptance of the reasons for adopting one course of action rather than another. Like bikinis, marketing plans should be brief enough to be interesting but still cover the subject adequately.

Subject headings for the marketing plan

We now turn to the various ideas and topics which everyone who writes a marketing plan should consider, even though he will sometimes write little or nothing under a particular heading. Equally, there will usually be one or more points to be made that are highly specific to any given plan, and obviously these cannot be included here. (For example, the heading 'Distribution methods' obviously needs to be interpreted in a very special way by those who seek to provide a real-time computer-based information retrieval system.)

Conventionally, the first section of a marketing plan is devoted to a description of relevant factors in the market place, a short or long description depending on the amount of explanation required to ensure conviction. The factors which may need to be described are listed below. (Writing the market description for the first time can be a considerable chore, but updating it in subsequent planning periods should not be too difficult.)

1 Overall market characteristics

Total size and value and expected evolution. If it is a growth market, for example, it will look more attractive than if it is static or declining; though a large static market can sometimes offer better opportunities than a small growth one.

Product/market segments. A very important heading. A company which identifies the product or market segment which it is best equipped to supply, and focuses its marketing effort on it, is more likely to succeed than one which looses-off in the general direction of the total market. (We use the words 'product' and 'service' interchangeably in this chapter, recognising that the range of financial services can extend from a standardised and essentially inflexible 'package', at one extreme, to a completely flexible individual service at the other.)

Relative importance of segments. Obviously, the size of the selected segment should be compatible with the company's strength and sales objectives; and a growth sector is preferable to a declining one.

Seasonal fluctuations. These can be important to profit planning. A product or service with pronounced seasonal peaks – for example, making Christmas toys or providing surrogate Father Christmases for department stores – can raise serious problems of financing stocks or finding alternative uses for the relevant resource in off-peak periods.

Regional differences. If the plan involves, as it should, detailed targeting of individual sales areas or sales offices, an understanding of regional differences and their causes is essential. A demand for the same *per capita* sales or percentage sales increase in every case can be both unjust and demotivating for individuals who know very well how the situation in their territory or catchment area differs from that of their colleagues.

Existing distribution networks. You can have the most delectable product or service in the world to sell, and get nowhere if the channel of distribution to the customer breaks down. The motivation of distributors if you do not own them, the location of outlets if you do, are vital considerations in an effective marketing plan.

2 The position of your products or services in the market

Names of your products and those of the leading competitors. Names oddly enough can be important, particularly in the case of a range of competitive products with little but their names and packaging to differentiate them.

Description of products. Obviously if you have a product plus, so much the better. But in most highly competitive markets a clear-cut product advantage is seldom maintained for very long and often carries a penalty in higher production costs. Skilful marketing is more often than not the real reason why one product outsells another.

User benefits. The virtues of a product are often, in the eyes of the beholder, more obvious to the producer than to the customer. It is necessary to be realistic about just what are the advantages *to the user* of your product compared with its competitors.

Positioning of products. In a segmented market a producer may opt to attack the high-priced 'quality' segment of the market, or to go after a share of the lower-priced mass market; or he may decide to have an entrant in each segment.

Alternative packages. The producer of packaged goods will probably need to offer a range of several sizes or flavours. In the same way the producer of financial services will probably want to develop a range of services all satisfying the same basic need; for example, a range of unit trusts may be built around a variety of different investment policies; or institutions may offer a range of saving schemes for shorter or longer periods.

Sales history. Analysis of sales and market shares by units, value, region, package type, etc., as a basis for directing future marketing efforts.

Market gap or problem areas. Identification of areas where product improvement is needed or where there is an opening for a new or modified product.

Planned developments. Any new products or product improvement now on the stocks or under consideration.

3 The company and its competitors

Relative strengths and weaknesses. It is sometimes difficult to be entirely objective about this; your own strengths or your own weaknesses can loom larger than those of your competitors. Evidence from a third party (for instance, a market research company carrying out a sample survey of customers) can be enlightening.

Market shares. Sometimes difficult and expensive to establish exactly. An informed guess may be good enough for the practical purpose of planning marketing tactics.

Marketing methods of competitors. If a competitor is using a different marketing tactic from your own the results should be monitored; it may be an initiative that should be followed, or he may be driving up a dead end.

Expected developments. What is in the wind in the way of new marketing initiatives, pricing policies or product developments?

4 Customers and potential customers

Main customers/customer categories. Description, number, actual and potential value of target customers or customer categories.

Relative importance of individual customer segments. Another aspect of the segmentation of markets and marketing effort which is so important a part of effective marketing.

Customer characteristics, motivation, loyalty, etc. In the financial services industry, which depends so heavily on personal relations, it is especially important to obey the old marketing maxim about knowing your customer; the level of customer loyalty is particularly important, since loyal customers are likely to be the most prolific source of new business.

Purchasing methods and decision making. In an impulse-buying situation, like a self-service grocery store, it is a fairly simple matter to determine what combination of packaging, positioning, labelling, etc., will maximise the chances of a favourable purchasing decision; in the case of the more considered purchase of financial services, particularly by corporate as opposed to individual customers, some understanding of the how, when and where of purchasing decisions, and of the events leading up to them, is more difficult to come by, but is just as important for planning a marketing campaign.

5 Institutional and environmental constraints

Government directives and guidelines. The importance of these in banking and other financial services need not be underlined!

Consumer protection legislation. Increasingly tough in the area of lending, but also present in resource-gathering activities.

Restrictive practices legislation. Again particularly tough in the financial area.

Professional ethics. Sometimes apparently in conflict with restrictive practices legislation, to judge from the periodic government investigations of professional associations.

Labour relations. It cannot be taken for granted that marketing recommendations – for example, for longer opening hours – will be acceptable to the representatives of organised labour, even on an experimental basis.

Tax considerations. In a number of cases a tax advantage may be the major selling point for a financial services package.

Contractual arrangements. Are there any existing contractual requirements which inhibit the penetration of a new market or the launch of a new financial service?

6 Summary of problems and opportunities

The sections of the plan reviewing *relevant* aspects of the market situation are not an end in themselves (though in a ritualistic planning situation they may come to be one). Their purpose is to give background information leading up to a statement of the identified problems and opportunities which the marketing plan sets out to deal with.

As a point of presentation it can be a good idea to relegate the background market data into appendices and plunge the reader straight into a statement of the problems and opportunities created for the company by developing market trends and changes.

The important thing is to state the problem and opportunities as clearly and simply as possible, so as to ensure that those who must approve or implement the plan recognise that it is designed to deal with real-life situations.

7 Marketing objectives

Sales and profit targets. This is at the very core of the whole marketing exercise. There will be other marketing objectives, some of them defensive, some of them designed to improve the long-term health of the organisation at the expense possibly of short-term profits. But they should all be designed to contribute sooner or later to the improvement or greater certainty of profits and turnover (in that order).

Target number and value of purchases. Whether you are aiming for a large number of small purchases or a small number of large purchases has an important bearing on marketing and sales tactics.

Penetration and value of usage. Given the size of the market or its segment, and given the sales target, what is implied about the proportions of potential customers who will choose to use it, at what value? Are these proportions reasonable?

Exports, foreign operations. This will apply only in cases where the foreign operation is managed from the centre. More and more foreign operations are becoming profit centres in their own right, with their own marketing plans.

Enhancement of corporate or product name recognition and reputation. Another marketing objective which has an indirect but often important effect on turnover and profit.

8 Distribution methods

Sales outlets. How will the necessary number of sales outlets, whether owned by the company or independent, be achieved? How will they be made into effective selling outlets, rather than nominal stockists who half the time do not push or display your product?

Agents and associated companies. Should they be involved and how can they be motivated to make the contribution required of them? (In some cases a company with an established distributive network may decide that it is better to provide certain services or look after certain customers direct, in which case the question of agents will not arise.)

9 Pricing policy

Price segments. Which price segment in the market is to be attacked, and why?

Discount structure. What standard or negotiated discounts from the recommended price are envisaged?

Agents' commission, outlets' mark-up. When agents or distributors are used, what will be the gap between the recommended price to the final customer and the net return to the producer?

Average revenue predictions. When the price structure is complicated by quantity discounts, agents' commissions, special offers, and so on, what will be the average revenue per unit sold?

10 The selling plan and sales support activities

Targets for individual areas, salesmen or branch offices. These need both to be calculated theoretically from data about the sales potential of the areas concerned and agreed to in advance by sales management as being fair and reasonable; otherwise the necessary commitment will be lacking.

Relationships with the distribution network. How can the best value be got out of the existing distribution network, whether it consists of the company's own retail outlets or independent distributors? Should only some of the available distribution points be included in the plan on a 'horses for courses' policy? Do the existing distributors (in the company's own outlets or elsewhere) need to be supplemented by others if sales targets are to be achieved? If so, how should they be motivated?

Merchandising through distributive outlets. For example, training and motivating outlet staff, point of purchase display material, leaflets, educational and publicity material, stationery supplies, audio-visual sales promotional devices.

Direct selling to end-users. Should some or all of the potential customers be approached direct rather than through branches, agents or distributors? What should be the method of establishing initial contact with them and generating enquiries? What should be the method of converting enquiries into sales?

Salesforce. Who will be involved in the actual selling? Will this be a full-time job or just a part of their responsibilities? How will they be organised, trained, directed and motivated? What back-up services will they need? How will they be targeted, and what provision will there be for checking results against target? What will be total selling cost, to be set against gross sales revenue?

Sales control and information systems. What provision will be made for management to monitor the performance of individual salesmen, outlets, regions, customer categories and end-products? What provision for salesmen to report back and for their reports to be analysed? What provision for identifying potential customers and keeping track of efforts made to convert them into customers? What provision for an in-flow of relevant information about competitive activity, customer requirements and developments in the market place? What will be the cost of the control and information system to be charged against gross sales revenue?

Sales accounting. What will be the billing procedure? What credit policy and what provision against bad debts? How will customer accounts be kept and how will they be analysed for purposes of market and profit planning? What sales accounting costs should be charged against gross sales revenue?

11 Marketing communications, sales promotion and advertising

Media advertising. How much should be spent on advertising the products or services to be marketed through press, television, posters or other public media? What should be the objective of the advertising? Should it be concentrated on promoting the company name as an 'umbrella' under which the individual services can be marketed? Or should the key services be advertised individually, with the minor services riding on their backs? What should be the advertising message and target audience? Which are the most cost-effective media for conveying the required message to the target audience? What advertising agency or agencies should be used? What form of management control should be imposed to ensure maximum value for money?

Direct mail. How much, if any, of the available marketing funds should be spent on direct mailings to target customers or customer categories? What should be the content of the mailings? How should they be designed to ensure maximum attention and response? What criteria should be used in compiling the mailing list? What provision should be made for evaluating results?

Public relations. Should public relations or editorial publicity techniques be used to help achieve sales targets? What message should be conveyed, how and to whom? What should be the budgeted expenditure and how should results be evaluated?

Special promotions. What types of special promotion – for example, special offers to customers or distributors, conferences, exhibitions, educational courses and seminars – should be included in the marketing communications effort? What will be their objectives, frequency and location? What message will they convey to what target audiences? What will be the budgetary appropriation for them and how will results be evaluated?

Measurement of marketing communications effectiveness. What standards will be used to measure the *overall* effectiveness of the marketing communications effort? What will be the method of measurement – for example, customer attitude and awareness research?

12 Legal considerations

Trade names, patents, etc. Have all possible objections to the use of proposed trade names, or the possibility of patent infringements been cleared?

Forms of contract. Are any proposed contract forms both watertight and within the terms of existing or anticipated legislation?

Consumer protection legislation. Are the products or services to be marketed within both the letter and the spirit of the law? Do the advertising claims that will be made conform with the Code of Advertising Practice?

13 Market information and research

Market information. What provision should be made for providing a continuous in-flow of market information and for presenting it to management in easily usable form?

Market research. What special market investigations are planned, with what objective – for example, discovery of gaps in the market or investigating possible new markets or market segments?

Consumer-attitude research. What provision is to be made for periodically checking consumer needs and habits, their attitude to the company and its products and the extent to which these products satisfy their needs?

New-product testing. What provision is planned for testing new or improved products, services and packages?

Cost-effectiveness. What total market research budget is recommended and how will its spending contribute to long-term profitability?

14 Marketing timetable

Synchronisation. How will the proposed selling and sales promotional activities be linked to product availability so as to ensure maximum impact?

Seasonality. Has the selling and sales promotional plan been timed to exploit seasonal buying peaks?

Build-up. Has sufficient time been allowed for all the preparatory work that is needed before a fully effective marketing plan can swing into action?

15 Marketing budget and revenue forecast

Sales revenue forecast. What will be the total sales revenue before and after commissions to agents, discounts, etc.?

Gross margin. What will be the gross profit on sales after all production costs?

Selling costs. What is the budgeted cost of selling, sales accounting and sales administration?

Marketing communications. What is the budgeted cost of marketing communications, incuding market research?

Marketing administration. What is the budgeted cost of marketing administration and other marketing overheads?

Net profit. What estimated net profit or contribution to company over-heads will result from the efficient implementation of the marketing plan?

Follow-up

So much for the structure of the marketing plan. But the plan, as we keep insisting, is not an end but a beginning. It is only when the plan is implemented and works that it justifies the time, money and effort that went into its composition.

If the plan is to be implemented and have a good chance of succeeding, three things listed below are essential.

1 Securing commitment by all those involved

This means 'selling' the plan both up and down the management line. It needs to be sold up the line to senior management, because the marketing manager or executive who writes the plan is asking for resources of money, material and people to be allocated to its execution, and he is promising that those resources will be productively employed; and, to put it in down-to-earth terms, because it will help him to secure co-operation from departments not under his direct control if he is able to say that the boss is backing the plan.

It is just as important to sell the plan down the line because successful implementation is ultimately in the hands of the men and women in the front line. This applies with particular force to the marketing of financial services, where to a large degree *the service is built around or wrapped up in the person who has direct contact with the customer.* If that person has no confidence in the product he or she is selling, how can the customer be convinced?

2 Plotting and checking progress

We referred earlier to the importance of timing and of having a number of individual and intermediate targets against which progress can be measured. These individual checkpoints may be worked out in the form of a PERT network or critical path analysis (to which we shall refer to later) when the plan is a complicated one; or it may be a simpler matter of a list saying that so and so must have done this or that by such and such a date. But unless the checkpoints exist, and people are constantly nagged to observe them, the best of plans is unlikely to succeed.

3 Providing for change

We have also referred to the need for marketing plans to be flexible and subject to change when unforeseen circumstances arise. The sound principle of flexibility can of course be carried to excess; it is not good practice when things fail to go according to plan simply to revise the plan to conform with the actual outcome. But predicting the future is an uncertain art, and it must be accepted that sometimes assumptions which seemed sound at the time they were made are disproved by events. The financial services environment is more vulnerable than most to invasion by uncontrollable factors like radical changes in government economic policy or the effects of any one of a number of overseas events. When this happens it is pointless to plod on with an unchanged plan as though nothing had happened.

But in saying that provision for change should be implicit in any plan – more so of course in the case of long-term than of short-term plans – we should emphasise the difference between the objectives, the strategic and the tactical aspects of the plan. Objectives may need to be modified or the time-scale of achievement adjusted if developing circumstances make them clearly unrealistic; but they should be abandoned only as a last resort. Strategy, with its roots in long-term policy, should certainly not be changed because of problems which may be only short-term. But tactics – the methods used to achieve objectives within the framework of strategic policy – should be adapted to changing circumstances.

Even tactical changes should not be made lightheartedly; in large organisations, particularly, quite minor changes of direction can be difficult and costly. But a readiness to adapt tactics to suit particular circumstances needs to be built in at all levels of a dynamic marketing organisation. Moreover, it is possible to study the likely consequences of at least limited changes by calculating in advance the sensitivity of the end result to alterations in the assumptions made. For example, it is simple in theory (but perhaps time-consuming in practice) to calculate the effect on bank profits of changes in various interest rates. Such predictive calculations not only forecast the resultant outcomes, they usually also lead to a much clearer insight into the internal relationships in the 'model' or budget or plan being studied.

Finally, wherever possible, and wherever it can be done economically, it is a good idea to build on to the plan some deliberate experiments. Such ploys could include extra advertising in a selected town, area or region and the measurement of its effect; or the use of four or five different direct mailing shots, each to a representative sub-section of the target audience, again measuring results. (One such test in a bank's Access operation revealed a near 3:1 difference in response, with the marketing executive's favoured version doing worst!) Building in such tests is not easy and is seldom willingly accepted by those concerned, but it is an excellent way to learn about market behaviour.

Summary

We started this chapter by emphasising the importance of brevity, and ended by writing one of the longest chapters in the book. To make amends we have briefly listed the main headings of the 'model' marketing plan below.

The main headings for a marketing plan
  1 Overall market characteristics
  2 The position of your products or services in the market
  3 The company and its competitors
  4 Customers and potential customers
  5 Institutional and environmental constraints
  6 Summary of problems and opportunities
  7 Marketing objectives
  8 Distribution methods
  9 Pricing policy
 10 The selling plan and sales support activities
 11 Marketing communications, sales promotion and advertising
 12 Legal considerations
 13 Market information and research
 14 Marketing timetable
 15 Marketing budget and revenue forecast

The plan writer should regard the headings (particularly the first five) as a checklist of points to be considered, but not necessarily to be covered exhaustively in the final plan presented to management. The main objectives of acceptance, commitment and a yardstick against which to measure progress may be obscured rather than assisted by excessive detail or repetition of known facts.

PART TWO

The tools of marketing

In this second part we describe the 'toolkit' of marketing techniques introduced initially in the consumer goods industry, but used nowadays in all 'industries' from capital goods to charities, and suggest how the appropriate tools and techniques can be applied.

CHAPTER NINE

The marketing mix

In the first part of this book we concentrated on the management aspects of marketing, describing the elements of the marketing plan and the way marketing management fits in with the general management structure. In this second part we describe some of the tools and techniques which the marketing specialist will need and which the general manager should understand and utilise in furthering his marketing objectives.

Before describing the individual tools and techniques we should emphasise that none is very useful or effective in isolation. There is a tendency for established organisations, which embrace the marketing concept in their maturity, to mistake the part for the whole. They fall in love with market research, which has the attraction of providing management with interesting information, but not committing them to doing anything about it; or they embark on a costly advertising campaign without ensuring the executive or sales follow-through which makes the advertising claims credible and converts them into profitable sales. The cost of market research is justified only if it leads to a considered marketing decision, even if the decision is to do nothing. Image-building advertising, when reality is not made to conform to the advertising image, can do positive harm by generating cynicism and disbelief.

It is important, therefore, to think from the outset in terms of the 'marketing mix', the balanced blend of marketing ingredients best calculated to achieve a defined marketing objective as economically as possible. There is no standard all-purpose mix, or even a 'right' mix for a given situation; it is not uncommon to find two organisations pursuing similar objectives in the same market sector allocating their marketing budgets to a quite different mix of ingredients. Table 1 gives a simplified indication of the relative importance likely to be attached to the different marketing mix ingredients in typical situations. But this should not be taken too literally. The most important of marketing skills is not exhaustive knowledge of a single marketing technique, but the ability to devise a cost-effective mix for a given situation with the touch of originality which distinguishes an organisation from its competitors.

The starting point

In the medical field the starting point for compounding a prescription is the diagnosis and definition of objectives. The doctor defines, if he can, the root of the problem facing his patient, decides what changes he needs to bring about in the patient's condition, and prescribes the appropriate combination of treatments. A similar procedure is followed, or should be followed, by the compounder of the marketing mix. With the aid of market research and other sources of market information he will diagnose the problem or opportunity to be dealt with, including definition of the specific market segments needing attention; he will analyse the various changes of attitude and/or behaviour needed to achieve his objective; and from his analysis he will arrive at a first idea of the ingredients which should go into the marketing mix, and an idea of their relative importance in relation to his defined marketing objectives.

Almost always he will find that to do a thorough job on each of the subsidiary objectives will cost considerably more than the value of the whole objective justifies. Then comes the process of deciding where it is feasible to reduce effort or expenditure or to postpone a desirable initiative in favour of some more urgent action. Since the ingredients of an effective marketing mix are inter-dependent it may in the end be better to lower targets or lengthen the time-scale of achievement than to eliminate some marketing element entirely. The latter course could jeopardise the whole plan. In other words, successful marketing is more likely to come from a properly balanced set of activities than from one or two actions carried out intensively.

To take simple examples from branch banking: it would be foolish to have a strong sales drive without adequate back-up in the branch; to have a strong local advertising campaign without adequate follow-up literature (including the inevitable forms); to have smart new premises but poorly motivated staff; to have a great new service to sell but little help in identifying the precise people to whom it will appeal; and so on. How does one achieve the correct balance? By careful analysis of customers' needs as well as our own; by experience; and by an element of creativity which suggests ways in which to bolster weakness without either undue cost or causing a further lack of balance.

The active ingredients

The seven most important active ingredients from which the marketing

Table 1. The marketing mix in typical financial services situations

	Corporate image-building	Regional development	Branch development	International development	New product development	Personal business development	Corporate business development	Business-related services
Preliminary								
Definition of objectives	●	●	●	●	●	●	●	●
Market research	●	●				●	●	●
Market segmentation				●	●	●	●	
Active ingredients								
Product/service design					●	●	●	●
Shop/branch design				●			●	
Pricing					●	●	●	●
Selling			●	●	●		●	●
Marketing communications	●	●	●				●	●
PR	●	●			●		●	●
Merchandising				●			●	
Internal communications	●	●	●		●			●
Catalysts								
Market models						●		
Critical path networks						●		
Accounting controls		●			●		●	●
Management information	●	●	●	●	●	●	●	●
Measurement	●	●	●	●	●	●	●	●
Sales/marketing training		●	●				●	●

● = more important for each situation

mix is usually compounded in the financial services market are listed below, but not necessarily in either order of importance nor of sequence.

1 Product/service design and packaging

For the man in the street or even the average businessman there is a great sameness about the services offered by competitive financial institutions. Putting together a package of financial services, and then presenting it in such a way that it catches the interest of the customer segment at which it is aimed, is an ingredient in the marketing mix that can do more to create sales than heavy advertising expenditure on an uninteresting or indistinct product. The presentation is often regarded as 'mere window dressing', but most customers are not experts and they cannot be blamed for wanting the benefits of a product or service explained to them in terms they can readily understand. And bankers should certainly not feel they are reducing the importance of what they may offer, or their own status in offering it, by making their offering as easy as possible for a particular customer-type to understand.

2 Shop/branch design

Most financial services organisations are retailers as well as producers of their services. It is not easy to display a range of financial services (or to display the readiness to help and explain of the people who provide them) in a way that encourages 'shoppers' to come inside; and security requirements make it no easier. Nonetheless, going as far as possible towards making the office or branch attractive to the target customer groups who want to do business face-to-face is an important element in the marketing mix. A marketing-oriented international bank, for example, is likely to have types of branch related to its different target customer segments in its home country and to adapt its branch style to the local environment when it goes abroad.

3 Pricing

Most marketing people would agree that pricing is one of the more crucial ingredients in the marketing mix, with much more to it than the classical economists' theory of the perfect market would imply. It is of course a help, usually, if you can charge less than your competitors for the same quality of product or service and still make an adequate profit. But in market segments where consumers are not very price-conscious it does not necessarily mean that you will sell more. Moreover a relatively high price can be regarded as an indication of quality and attract buyers, particularly when it is allied to effective presentation and promotion. The marketing manager compounding his marketing mix has to regard price as a variable to be traded off against product quality and promotion, rather than as an absolute where the lowest price is the most desirable. Whether he opts for a relatively high price, high-quality product and heavy promotional expenditure or sets his price as low as he can manage (with quality and promotion to match) will depend on the position in the market which he wants to establish for his service or product. If he is aiming for the top segment of the market he will be inclined to price high; if he is aiming for the mass market he will probably, but not necessarily, price low.

4 Selling

For the marketing manager of a manufactured product the cost of the salesforce, or that part of its total cost which is attributable to the product he manages, is a defined expenditure to be included in his total marketing mix. In marketing financial services, the face-to-face selling resource is at the same time even more important and rather less easily defined; and it is harder to apportion the total cost of 'multi-purpose' staff fairly between selling and administrative activities. It is more important because the banker or other purveyor of financial services is himself a major part of the service he has to offer. He has a 'product' in the shape either of specialised access to financial resources or of investment opportunities to match the customer's own resources; but the customer's acceptance of the product's value will be greatly affected, for better or worse, by his confidence in the reliability of the 'salesman's' advice and his personal probity and expertise. So the personal selling element in the marketing mix will be of crucial importance and will merit more detailed attention from the marketer than it does in, say, the grocery trade, where the product, with its backing of advertising, can be expected to sell itself, once the salesman has ensured that it is properly displayed in the right outlets.

But, important as it is, the selling element is much harder for the financial services marketer to control, because the 'salesmen' are seldom simply salesmen. The corporate business development manager, the manager of a branch bank, or even of an insurance company's branch office, has important administrative responsibilities and some 'buying' functions as well as his selling tasks. These components certainly cannot be neglected, and they may well be a more congenial use of the individual manager's time than what is sometimes thought to be the 'distasteful business of selling'. It is not an easy task for the marketer to activate a reluctant part-time salesman; but unless he solves the problem the rest of his marketing mix will very likely be negated.

5 Marketing communications

We use this blanket term to cover advertising, direct mail, brochures and all methods of informing or persuading target customers other than face-to-face selling. Some financial services may be sold entirely by such methods. For example, a bank may be able to 'sell' a new credit card to a selected number of its existing customers largely through direct mail; though securing acceptance of the card by hoteliers, shopkeepers and restaurateurs will probably require a personal selling campaign. Or investors in a new unit trust may be solicited primarily by couponed advertising in financial journals or newspapers.

But in the majority of financial services marketing campaigns the marketing communications element – which is sometimes regarded as virtually the whole marketing story – will be only a part of the total marketing mix. And in many cases it will be, or should be, subsidiary to the main thrust of personal selling. The purpose of the advertising, printed literature, demonstration films, exhibitions, conferences and so on will be to make it easier for the personal salesmen to reach the right customer 'prospects' and persuade them to become customers, rather than to do the complete job on their own.

6 Public relations

An important part of the PR function, as we have said before, is to inform target customer groups about the company and help to persuade them to try its products, through means other than paid advertising, direct mail or direct selling. In this capacity it could well be regarded as just another form of marketing communications. However, it also has a wider responsibility for safeguarding and improving the relationship between the organisation and relevant environmental factors, such as government and society at large. Because of this wider responsibility it cannot be regarded as just another marketing tool, and indeed in many financial services organisations its line to senior management is separate from that of marketing. This wider role should not be under-estimated. As one distinguished banker has said, 'Opinion-formers, MPs or journalists, for example, *will* have an opinion. Without information it will be an uninformed opinion. The job of public affairs people is to give the information which enables them to have informed opinions.'

7 Merchandising

In marketing manufactured products through distributors or retail outlets, merchandising is the term used to describe that part of the marketing mix which is allocated to expediting movement of the manufacturer's products *out* of the distributors' shops or other premises. It includes a variety of items, often lumped together under the general heading of 'below the line' expenditure, such as the provision of in-store display material, the organisation of dealer or consumer competitions and other incentives, and reduced price or other special transient offers. In highly competitive market sectors these items may well account for as much as half the total marketing appropriation.

In relation to the total marketing mix, merchandising can be characterised as an often essential *stimulant,* sometimes dramatic in its effects but ultimately debilitating if over-indulged in. For the packaged goods manufacturer, selling through very powerful multiple retailers in highly competitive market sectors, it is usually an indispensable activity; his product will be squeezed out by more compliant competitors if he does not provide the distributors with a succession of special offers and other merchandising schemes. But he runs the risk, particularly if he is forced to reduce his image-building advertising, that his product eventually will be brought just because it is on special offer this week, not for its intrinsic merits. Once the point is reached where the brand name is meaningless and the product indistinguishable from its competitors, the manufacturer is at the mercy of his distributors, who are free to handle his product – on their terms – or not, as it suits them. It will have become a commodity not a branded product and sold on price alone.

In the financial services industry, where confidence is so important, the use of merchandising techniques borrowed from other industries is a particularly delicate matter. The financial services organisation which operates through a number of branches cannot escape the fact that it has a shopkeeping role, with an ever-widening range of products to sell through its 'shops'. To sell them and to cover the cost per outlet it must attract more customers into its shops, and/or increase its average sales per customer. Any merchandising device which will help to do that deserves serious consideration. On the other hand the long-term value of the financial service packages on offer, so largely dependent on confidence, needs to be considered. The offer of a hamper of groceries or a package holiday in Majorca may bring customers into the money shops and sell the financial services on offer. But will it in the end persuade the customers that the services cannot in themselves be worth very much if such devices are needed to sell them?

The catalysts

We use the term 'catalyst' to denote those elements in the marketing mix which are not 'active'. Unlike the active ingredients discussed above, the catalysts do not have a direct impact on the prospective customers. But they do contribute to our understanding of the marketing process, to our ability to establish sensible and realistic controls, and also to the total effectiveness of the mix. The most important of these 'catalyst' elements are listed below.

1 Market models

Marketing, as a relative latecomer to the field of management sciences, has been somewhat shameless in borrowing useful techniques from other sectors. One such technique is that of 'models', more familiar in the context of operational research. In the marketing context it is used to describe a manipulable representation – based partly on theory and partly on such data as are available – of the sector (economic, behavioural, psychological and competitive information can all be relevant) with which the marketer is concerned and of the market influences which affect its behaviour. To be of maximum practical use, especially when there are a lot of data, models need to be incorporated in a computer program. Such models can be useful in helping to establish in advance the likely effect on net sales revenue of different levels of marketing expenditure and marketing mixes. The technique, which is described more fully in Appendix II, is of practical value only in large markets where substantial amounts of reliable research data already exists. But the logical approach which it implies – trying to think through, if only on a commonsense basis, the likely joint and several effects on an existing market situation of a variety of complementary marketing initiatives – is to be commended to all those concerned with market development planning.

2 Planning networks

Another borrowed technique, this time developed by the wartime necessity to organise the rapid production of new armaments and equipment, is that of network planning, variously described as critical path analysis or PERT (Production Evaluation and Review Technique). This also is described in more detail in Appendix II. Briefly, this technique is based on charting as a sort of elongated Spaghetti Junction the way in which the various elements in a marketing project must fit together, and the deadlines involved at each stage, if the project is to get off the ground on time. It can be as complicated as the complexity of the situation demands. But simple versions can provide a useful discipline in keeping a project up to time and can help to ensure that a planned explosion of marketing activity really explodes instead of going off in a series of splutters.

3 Accounting and management controls

Here we get back from the type of catalyst that is useful on occasions to one that is patently essential for any properly controlled marketing project; but it is one that is frequently neglected. It should be superfluous to argue that, before a marketing project of any importance is launched, provision should be made for regularly checking its progress and its cost; otherwise the marketer will come to resemble the fabled general launching his troops into battle with little hope of seeing them return, or earn a return. Yet every day there are fresh examples in industry of business development projects where costs escalate out of control, or progress grinds to a halt, because nobody in authority is regularly informed of any departures from budgets or time schedules. Indeed a well prepared budget is itself a model of much of what we expect to see, and when we expect to see it, expressed in monetary terms. To good managers it is an ally and an aid, certainly *not* something to be hidden away. It should be the basis for actions not excuses.

4 External measurement

Unlike product development or organisational projects, for which internal controls are usually adequate, marketing projects require the responsible managers to measure the impact of the project on those aspects of the external world that the project is designed to influence. Part of the management control information system, the part most likely to trigger off adjustments to marketing tactics and consequent changes in the marketing mix, has to be data on changes in customer or distributor attitudes and behaviour related to the project. So we come back full circle to market research, which provided the data for initiating the marketing project in the first place and should also provide key data for measuring and speeding its progress and its ultimate success or failure.

Adapting the marketing mix to the market situation

In the chart at the beginning of this chapter we indicated in very broad terms the elements in the marketing mix which could be considered in a variety of financial service marketing situations. It goes without saying that the actual mix employed must depend initially on the marketing resources controlled by the manager concerned, or available from a central marketing department. In a large structured organisation the discretionary authority and the marketing budget available to the majority of local managers are likely to be limited; more often than not the individual manager will need, within his own sphere of authority, to ride on the back of centralised marketing campaigns initiated by others.

Nevertheless at any level a manager will have at his disposal two essential ingredients: his own capacity to gather and analyse market information, and the proportion of his own time and energy that is not devoted to higher-priority activities. He can clarify in his own mind the objectives of the marketing project on which he is embarking; he can carry out at least basic market research from published data and customer records; and he can analyse the market research so as to identify the market segment on which his efforts can most productively be focused.

As for the active ingredients of the mix, the basic design of the service being marketed may be outside the individual manager's control; but he can at least adapt the way he presents it, in writing or face-to-face, to the individual customer. The layout of the branch or office from which the service is marketed may well be pre-determined; but the way it is adapted or exploited to draw attention to the service package being marketed, together with any supporting merchandising material, can offer scope for imaginative action. Discretionary power to use the tool of price is probably very limited; but other selling methods and the optimum use of available selling time offer ample scope for individual initiative.

How many of the techniques included under the heading 'Marketing communications' are available to the manager with a marketing problem, who is not a marketing specialist, will vary from situation to situation. Few are likely to command the discretionary budget needed to finance a major advertising campaign. But advertisements in local media, *extending and localising* the message of the main advertising campaign may be feasible; local small-scale conferences can be organised at modest cost; and a direct mail 'campaign' taking the form of a few personal letters to carefully selected individuals may well be more effective than a massive but unselective mail-out. In the same way PR and merchandising activities can be adapted to almost any situation; and the important element of internal communications will apply whenever more than one individual is involved in executing a marketing project.

As for the catalysts, market models and critical path networks, even when simplified, are probably too elaborate for local marketing projects; but the discipline they embody will always help to get one's thinking straight. And making provision for accounting controls and some feedback of management information is essential to the successful management of all projects, as is the principle of measurement. Measurement, in fact, should be inherent in all marketing projects from the outset. (Measurement does not need to be precise for this purpose – a good estimate will do, or even a jotted down guess at a pinch. The important principles are those of feedback and of learning, and both are enhanced if some prior, written-down measure can be compared with a similar measure after the event.) Measure at the beginning the value of the objectives to be pursued; measure the likely cost of attaining them – and abandon the project if the cost is likely to exceed the net return; measure during the course of the operation and at the end of the project, to check whether or not your calculations were valid. Ultimately the only sound criterion of a successful marketing project is a measurable surplus of directly or indirectly related income over outgo.

Summary

In this chapter we have said that effective marketing must be based on a co-ordinated mix of activities. Reliance on a single unsupported marketing activity, whether it is advertising, personal selling or some other tool, is unlikely to give a good return for the effort and expenditure involved. We have outlined the main tools and techniques likely to be useful in one or other of the many different situations in which financial services are marketed. We have suggested the tools which could be most appropriate in the different situations, but have emphasised that the individual manager must make his choice in the light of prevailing circumstances. No marketing rule of thumb is an adequate substitute for the creative thinking of the individual.

Finally, we have pointed out that local managers have the same duties and opportunities, even though 'writ small', as central managers *to get the facts, to plan, and to act.*

CHAPTER TEN

Marketing information

The need for information

'Information is the ever-moving, mighty river on which the marketing craft is floated.' The origin of this pretentious quotation is obscure (we rather think we made it up ourselves). But the principle that a flow of information is essential for a well-managed business will not be unfamiliar to those repsonsible for managing financial services enterprises. Prudent lending, efficient investment and responsible financial advice all depend on adequate and reliable information.

If marketing information differs from the general information used to manage a business, it is essentially a matter of degree rather than fundamental principles. First of all, marketing is concerned so very much with the future; by the time a marketing decision has been taken and implemented, time will have moved on and circumstances may have changed. So an element of prediction is inherent in all worthwhile marketing information: 'this is the situation today, whence it can be predicted that the situation when the marketing action bites will be . . . .'

Marketing is also concerned more directly with people – people as individuals and people as the decision makers in corporate organisations – and less immediately with figures than are the more technical aspects of financial services. The marketing man is constantly asking himself two questions, 'What are my competitors doing and is it paying off?' and 'Supposing I do *this*, how will my target customers react?' Figures remain of vital importance in establishing the parameters for marketing action, and in measuring the level of success or failure, but always they are the outcome of interaction between people.

It was symptomatic of this difference in priority that when the British clearing banks first embraced the marketing concept their marketing specialists began to ask questions about customers; not just the military formula of name, rank and number, but the more three-dimensional questions, about needs, attitudes and lifestyles, which a financial services organisation should understand if it is to provide a high standard of personal service. In the old days of decentralised and personalised banking it would have been time-consuming but not very difficult to come by the information; it would simply have involved asking the branch managers, most of whom would have spent many years in the same branch, to describe their customers as fully as possible without breaching professional confidences.

But in a more centralised, computerised era it became very much harder to collect and analyse the relevant information. In theory it should have been much easier and much faster; a computer can sort out the predominant characteristics of a very large customer file in a matter of minutes *if* it has been programmed to do so. But the first generation bank computers were programmed in such a way as to deal with the *accounts* of customers rather than the customers as such. Partly because of a commendable reluctance to infringe personal privacy, and partly because nobody had anticipated the questions which could arise in the search to provide a higher standard of service; the personal data which could answer the marketer's questions had not been included.

Schematically, the way the 'moving river' of marketing information relates to marketing activities is illustrated in Fig. 3.

Out of the information, marketing ideas are dredged up; the ideas, if they stand up to rigorous analysis and review, are incorporated in marketing plans; these in turn lead to marketing actions, the results of which are checked against the now possibly changed marketing information scene. As a result of this fresh immersion, modified ideas re-emerge, and the cycle begins again.

Fig. 3.

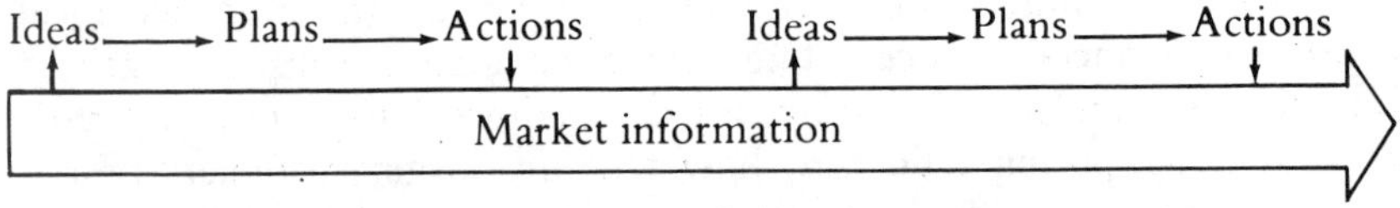

Ideas ⟶ Plans ⟶ Actions   Ideas ⟶ Plans ⟶ Actions

Market information ⟶

As a simple, and quite improbable, example let us suppose that information reaches Our Hero, a branch manager, to the effect that old J.B. has left his wife and is setting up home with his secretary. The information gives rise to a number of ideas, some of a marketing nature. Perhaps J.B. will need advice on taxation or financial matters. Or perhaps a personal loan or a bridging loan to deal with his new housing problem.

Or a new will appointment could be a possibility. The obvious plan is to write to J.B., or better still find an excuse to go and see him. Action – picking up the telephone – follows almost immediately after the plan.

But then further information emerges. The lady was certainly his secretary, but she is also the daughter of a Greek shipping magnate, so the idea of a personal loan seems inappropriate. But what is her relationship to the shipping business, and indeed how long will her *new* relationship last? A revised plan, to find out whether the bank's corporate finance department is interested in an introduction to the shipping industry, begins to take shape.

The intention of this frivolous example was not to suggest that the type of information needed for marketing purposes is mainly of a gossip column variety. While in any financial services business there will be some customers of sufficient importance to be given extensive individual attention, practical marketing economics require a large measure of generalisation on the personal side of the business. Customers and potential customers will have to be divided into more-or-less homogeneous *segments* for business development purposes.

Basic marketing information is then needed to answer the following questions in relation to each of the financial services being marketed and to each of the catchment areas from which the company hopes to draw its business.

1 What are the characteristics of those segments of the public who
   (a) buy the service from the marketer's company;
   (b) buy it from competitive sources;
   (c) do not buy it?
2 Why do they behave in this way?
3 How satisfied are users with the service provided by the company and its competitors? Does the service satisfy all or only some of the relevant users' needs? Is it generating repeat or 'once only' business?
4 Which of the customer and non-customer categories are, or are likely to be, the most profitable for the company over a reasonable time-span?
5 What can the company do to encourage customers or potential customers to modify their behaviour to the company's advantage; or prevent them from modifying it to the company's disadvantage?
6 What recent or predictable changes in the situation of customers or

potential customers are likely to create new needs which the company can satisfy?

7 What changes in the economic, legislative or social environment are likely to create new problems or opportunities with which the company can assist its customers?

The type of information needed in relation to a corporate customer is similar but rather more complex. It is necessary, or at least desirable, to know about the industry in which he is engaged, its growth trend, its significant features, its dependence on key resources – and whether they are imported or not – about your customer's place in it, about *his* customer relationships, about his corporate structure, about his financial history and prospects. And since the part of a business which counts in the end is not its customers and premises or even its products, but the people who run it, it is important to have as much information as possible about the key people in the business who make the decisions that really matter.

The nature and sources of information

While information is essential for effective marketing it must be recognised that information which involves people and their predicted behaviour can never be either fully comprehensive or wholly reliable. Even those endowed with the rare gift of self-knowledge are seldom certain in advance of how they will react to a particular set of circumstances, or willing to reveal the whole truth to inquisitors. So the seeker after market information has to be satisfied with information of varying reliability from a number of different sources; and he has to lean heavily on the law of averages, thanks to which it is usually possible to predict not what a single individual will do but how many on average out of a large number will turn left, turn right, or march straight ahead. The danger is that when the proportions are written down in a well-presented document, whether a market research report or a government white paper, the figures may be accepted as the whole truth rather than a reasonable approximation.

Marketing-information sources are customarily divided into two categories: primary and secondary. A secondary source, as the adjective implies, comprises data collected by other people for other purposes. Its great advantage is that it is either free, or a great deal less expensive, than specially commissioned research. For this reason first consideration should always be given to the collection and analysis of relevant secondary information before special studies are commissioned. Its disadvantage is that the information collected in this way, through desk research, seldom answers exactly those questions which the decision-making manager had in mind; and it is not always easy to establish exactly how much reliance should be placed on the figures themselves.

So it is prudent when using secondary information to collect it from as many different sources as possible, and to cross-check. It is prudent also to obtain skilled advice on the degree of reliance which should be placed on the various sources. This is particularly important in the case of research into foreign markets. The need to relate the cost of marketing research to the benefit likely to accrue from it usually leads to a basic dependence on secondary information in the less important markets; and in these markets it takes local knowledge to indicate which of the available facts and figures are relatively reliable and which may be misleading.

Secondary information sources

The main secondary sources worth investigating in the UK are listed below.

1 *Government statistics.* The publications of the Central Statistical Office and the various government departments provide an increasing variety of information both about economic and industrial trends and about the characteristics, lifestyle and spending habits of the various segments of the population. The sources of the information should always be checked. Census information for example is entirely reliable within the limits of human error; but there is a lot of published information based on relatively small samples or on voluntary returns from businesses which is accurate enough as a basis for broad commercial policy, but will not support any notions of fine tuning. It is worth checking, incidentally, with the statisticians concerned; quite often they can provide unpublished figures relevant to a particular marketing problem. (HMSO can supply a list of government statistical sources including the topics covered.)

2 *Local authority statistics.* For the manager of a localised business interested in identifying target customers or in finding a suitable site for a new branch, local authority rating lists, electoral registers and development plans are important sources. It is always worthwhile, in the

context of forward planning, to establish contact with the local planning department.

3 *Trade associations.* In theory, trade associations should be a valuable source of information for marketers focusing their business development plans on specific industries. But more often than not what they can offer is somewhat disappointing, partly because many do not in fact represent all the firms within the industry they purport to cover, and partly because their statistics are often based on voluntary returns from member companies who are not always as conscientious in their form filling as they might be.

4 *Chambers of commerce or trade.* Some can be very helpful, other less so.

5 *Financial and trade publications.* Again, some can be very informative, others less so; only experience can tell which is which.

6 *Trade directories.* By the nature of things in a mobile economy any trade directory is likely to be somewhat out of date by the time it is published. The best of them can be a useful starting point for listing prospective corporate customers; but they usually need to be supplmented by investigation on the ground: and note carefully whether the firms included have paid to appear. If they have, coverage is likely to be far less complete.

7 *Media research studies.* Many of the studies sponsored and published by media proprietors or television contractors have a wider usefulness in describing the region or population group they serve than the primary intention of the research – to provide reasons for using their advertising facilities – would suggest.

8 *Syndicated market studies.* A number of market studies, for instance those carried out by NEDO working parties, by the Economist Intelligence Unit and by MINTEL, are offered for sale on a subscription basis to companies interested in the market sector covered by the study. These usually state their degree of reliability – where they don't, ask; otherwise, *caveat emptor.*

9 *Economic forecasting services.* Marketers of financial services cannot fail to be as interested in the publications of the economic forecasters as the ancients were in the pronouncements of the Delphic Oracle. But the ancient view that it is not given to mortals to know the future continues to be borne out. Even the most professional of economic forecasts cannot be swallowed whole, but needs to be incorporated as another piece of evidence in the manager's own essential but frustrating task of foreseeing the future of the particular business sectors with which he is concerned.

10 *Other companies' information.* Other companies interested in the same business sector, even friendly competitors, can be a very helpful source of secondary information. This can be particularly true for newcomers to a foreign market, where they are welcomed to the club by their compatriots or existing associates. But – be Grecian in your attitude to unexpected gifts of information!

11 *Commercial attachés and consular officials.* Again, in foreign markets official national representatives can be exceedingly helpful. It is also not unknown for them to be exceedingly unhelpful.

To anyone who wishes to become more familiar with secondary sources of data, a visit to a good library is a must. Most librarians are only too willing to help and will respond very readily to requests for information – indeed they seem to enjoy the challenge. It is obviously best to pose a question as near to the real core of your quest as possible; even if the answer is not forthcoming you will be sure to get as close to it as the data available will allow; whereas if you ask what you think is as near a question *as is likely to be answerable* you are, of course, substituting your guess for the librarian's years of training and experience.

Primary information sources

The main primary sources of information can be categorised as follows:

1 personal enquiry (the most primary of all);
2 the various types of market research described later in this chapter;
3 the less formal collection of market information from a variety of first-hand sources, best described as market intelligence;
4 advertising research; again, described later in this chapter;

5 analysis of internal records. It is surprising how much information, quite apart from that of a confidential nature, accumulates in the records of a large organisation like a bank and would be exceedingly useful for marketing purposes but is simply never used. And the sampling techniques of market research can be applied to internal records very effectively.

The collection and interpretation of information

The effective use of secondary marketing information sources depends eventually on knowing your sources, being able to assess their reliability, and having some talent for lateral thinking – perceiving a not-always-obvious connection between the data and the profitable business development opportunities which are sought. The collection and interpretation of primary information requires rather more technical skill. There is no reason why a generalist manager should acquire those skills; but he should be sufficiently aware of them to know what research can and cannot do, to be able to brief the research technicians adequately, and to be able to assess the value of their findings.

Most formal market research falls into one or other of the following five categories:

1 consumer behaviour or attitude research;
2 consumer product acceptance research;
3 trade research;
4 advertising research;
5 consumer or trade panels.

All of them are exceedingly simple in concept. Leaving aside the technical hardware of 'black boxes' attached to TV sets, and the more esoteric examples of the art, such as 'dustbin research' (in which consumption is estimated by packages and tins discarded by a household), market research consists of posing questions. The researcher simply asks (whether in personal interviews, by telephone or by mail) about people's opinions and behaviour, about their habits and experience, about their reactions to samples of new products, about their readership or television viewing habits.

The technical skill is in asking the right people the right questions and producing reliable results at affordable cost. Do you, for example, insist on personal interviews, or do you use the telephone or the post? Personal interviews are expensive, because they involve travel, time and money. Telephone interviews are usually a good deal cheaper, but not everybody has a telephone so you may not reach the poorer groups of the population; and those approached by telephone find it easier to hang up on you than respondents in a face-to-face interview. Postal surveys are the cheapest of all, but you cannot ask many questions if you want a good response rate; and you are never quite sure whether those who go to the trouble of replying are typical of the whole group to whom the original mailing was addressed, nor, when the research is carried out among companies, whether the person who does reply is the best respondent.

Since it is usually impossible to interview everyone who is relevant, practically all formal market research must depend on sampling, in order to produce reliable results at affordable cost. That this can produce such results derives from the fact, observable by the layman and embodied by the mathematician in algebraic equations, that if you go on choosing units *entirely at random* from a collection of known characteristics your sample after a while will conform very closely to those characteristics. For example, if you pick balls at random from a large well-mixed bag filled half with white balls and half with black balls, you may start with a run of whites or blacks, but after you have picked out 100 or so you probably will not have more than fifty-five in either colour; and as you come up to the thousand mark you will very probably be not more than 2 per cent away from a fifty/fifty split. Similarly, if you pick human beings at random out of the total population you will come closer and closer, as the sample gets larger, to reproducing in the sample the characteristics of the total population; not just age, sex and class, but other characteristics such as home ownership or the possession of a bank account. The mathematician's probability theory can tell you how close you are likely to come at different sample sizes. In principle the probable margin of error is reduced only slowly as the sample gets larger; its size is, in fact, in proportion to the square root of the sample size. So it is usually better to be content with a reasonable sample size than to add expensive interviews in the hopeless search for complete accuracy. (The crucial test usually is how small will the smallest sub-group be? For example, if we are interested in bank account holders in the UK about three in four adults would qualify; but if we were interested in a characteristic ten times as rare then obviously the number we would need to interview to get the same number of 'useful' respondents will be ten times as great. It is this rarity factor which usually determines the basic sample size.)

The main snag in applying pure probability sampling theory to commercial market research arises from the words 'entirely at random'. If you were to pick a sample of, say, 2,000 people to interview out of the entire population of the United Kingdom you could find your interviewers travelling at great cost from one end of these islands to the other, pursuing widely scattered individuals. So for practical purposes it is more usual to concentrate the interviewing through a two-stage sampling technique; first dividing the country into a number of blocks and taking a sample of these blocks, secondly picking a random sample within each sampled block.

When cost is more important, and a calculable standard of precision less essential, market researchers commonly resort to quota sampling. This means giving interviewers a list of individuals to find – so many men, so many women, so many in each age group, so many in each economic group – which roughly corresponds to the structure of the total population.

The trouble with the quota-sampling method is that the less conscientious interviewers may stretch the definition of interviewees in order to fit into the required quota; and assessing the reliability of the results is much harder.

But, unhappily, deficiencies in sampling method are not the only cause of unreliability in market research results. An equally important cause derives from the old tag which starts, 'Ask a stupid question . . .'. Stupid questions can take many different forms. They can be quite simply unanswerable, like the traditional 'Have you stopped beating your wife?' conundrum. Or they can be questions to which most people probably do not know the answer, such as, 'What will you be doing at 3.15 p.m. next Thursday fortnight?' Or they can be questions which tempt people to give a misleading answer for reasons of self-respect or prestige, such as, 'How often do you clean your teeth?' Or it can be very easy to prejudice people's answers to the later questions you wish to ask by indicating in the earlier questions what response you are looking for (people have a tendency to give the answer they think will please on a point which doesn't matter greatly to them one way or another). Questionnaire construction, in fact, is just as essential a skill for the professional market researcher – and a working knowledge of it just as essential for those evaluating their work – as sampling technique. (It is usual, indeed it is required by the constitution of the Market Research Society, both to include details of the sample achieved, together with a description of the sampling method, and to attach a copy of the questionnaire to every full report of a market research study.)

The manager in a position to commission a market research study, who wants to get full value and reliable results out of it, should put a lot of thought and effort into briefing the researchers. Only too often researchers are told simply that, for instance, more information is needed on the attitudes and behaviour of school leavers in relation to bank accounts. The result of this is likely to be a report which is comprehensive and largely irrelevant. The manager ends up saying, 'This is interesting, but what in the world do I do about it?' or, 'Well there's not much in all this that we didn't already know.'

If on the other hand the commissioning manager takes the trouble to think through for himself and discuss with the market researchers the hypotheses which he has in mind, and the marketing actions which might result from their confirmation or denial, a far more relevant study is possible: for example, 'We rather think that school leavers find our branches a bit intimidating, and are thinking of doing thus and so to make them seem more welcoming', or, 'We rather think that the parents are the main influence on whether or not, and with what bank, school leavers open an account; if this is so should we direct our promotional effort towards the parents?' Taking the market researchers into your confidence to this extent will enable them to apply their technical skills and experience in a more constructive, practical and profitable way.

Internal information

It has often been said that the best prospects for new business are the customers you already have. This is certainly true when marketing a steadily growing range of financial services. The confidence built on mutually satisfactory (let us hope) relationships is a better launching pad for a new service than cold canvassing or broadscale advertising. Few financial service companies, however disorganised, can fail to know, one way or another, about the characteristics and needs of, as well as about the financial status of, their more important customers. But much of the knowledge, as we have said, is likely to be inaccessible – either filed away in widely scattered branch records or locked up in the heads of individual managers and executives. (Of course for individual branch managers this information *is* accessible – his own records are a mine of information which can be of real use. But only if the body of customers is considered as a whole can he expect to see patterns. Customer-by-customer analysis will help him to understand each customer but general marketing guidance can only come from a broader perspective.)

But from the central management's point of view, the great practical problem is how to make the relevant information readily available when it is needed for marketing planning or operational purposes. Logically the first step in overcoming this problem is to have an organised system for reporting and recording marketing information that is relevant either to immediate marketing problems or to problems that may be expected to arise in the future. This requires the facility to analyse sales and customer records in a way which is relevant to future business development, including an organised feedback of information from salesmen and others in contact with customers or prospective customers; and also the ability to relate current information both to past information (so as to establish trends) and to external market data (so as to establish how far the company's own experience is typical of the whole market). This is more easily said than done. In theory a well-planned computer system will make it all possible. But there are practical problems.

The first problem derives from the computer expert's favourite acronym GIGO – meaning garbage in, garbage out. The amount of useful marketing information which can be extracted from a computer system depends firstly on anticipating the questions which management is likely to ask of it and ensuring that the computer staff make it possible to extract the relevant information; and secondly on ensuring that the right information in the right form is input in the first place. This in its turn gets back to the human factor; for example, persuading managers and salesmen to overcome their notorious reluctance to fill in standardised forms after sales trips or information-gathering interviews.

But, difficult or not, if information is to be interpreted into marketing action, availability and compatibility of marketing information is vital, and completeness an important goal. Given that practically all information is more or less inaccurate, it is dangerous to rely simply on a single piece of information or market study as a basis for an important marketing decision; information from a variety of sources, including the managers' personal experience, should be collected, collated and evaluated before a decision is made.

The presentation and use of information

If market information is not well and clearly presented, it probably will not be used by management as a basis for decisions and actions; if it is not used, the cost of collecting and analysing it will have beenwasted. But how to ensure, when managers are constantly bombarded with information, only a fraction of which can possibly be absorbed (has anyone ever tried to read every single word in a daily newspaper?), that the research report which you have toiled to compose will be absorbed and used – assuming of course that it has something useful to say?

It is impossible ever to be sure of commanding an audience. A lot depends both on the importance and topicality of the subject matter and on the reputation the report writer has built up for having something worthwhile to say. But there are a number of quite simple rules (summarised in Appendix I) for presenting facts and figures in a written report which should make it quicker and easier for the reader to absorb the gist of it. The essential points are listed here.

1 To remember that your readers are much less interested in your subject matter than you are. So keep it brief. Even the title, like a good advertisement headline, can enliven a report; for example, 'Should we increase prices? Yes' or, 'Three reasons why prices should be increased.'
2 To remember that some readers are even less interested than others. So have a summary section at the beginning. It should always be possible to summarise into a couple of pages the main findings of a report of a score or so pages. The very busy and only marginally interested reader can stop at the end of those pages; the more interested can read on if they choose.
3 To tabulate figures in a format which helps the eye to fasten quickly on the exception. It is the exceptional figures which precipitate action, not the predictable, usually.
4 To illustrate the more significant figures by charts. Most people find it easier to draw conclusions from spatial relationships than from numerical relationships.
5 'Keep it simple, stupid.' Like most other technicians, market research specialists can be exhibitionists and parade their expertise in pretentious jargon. The harassed manager cannot be bothered with this. He is interested simply in what the research means, how reliable it is, and what he should do about it.

A written report is of course not the only way of communicating the results of a research study. A personal presentation, either face-to-face or, if need be, in the form of an audio-visual cassette can be a much more effective way of getting the message across and avoiding misconceptions.

Towards an information system

The effective use of information will always be an active rather than a passive affair. The ideal starting point is for the decision-making manager to analyse marketing problems within his own area of authority, determine what information is needed to solve them and then ask for the information to be produced. The passive receipt of a quantity of unsolicited information may prompt the initiating ideas but is unlikely by itself to provide the complete answer.

However, with the present state of computer technology, there is no insuperable reason why most of the information a manager needs to make marketing decisions should not be available on tap, whether it is current information, historical information, or more hazardous predictions about the future. The essential elements for the ideal information system are

1 the input of reliable and relevant information already discussed;
2 a readily accessible, probably computerised, data bank or storage system;
3 a system of regular reports which enables managers to keep track of the routine information they need for control purposes;
4 an information retrieval system which enables managers to ask specific questions of the central data bank and get prompt replies;
5 a clear picture of the information each individual manager needs or is likely to need in the course of his job.

It is this last element, together of course with cost, which creates the greatest practical problem. The constantly repeated experience of experts trying to devise information systems for large organisations is that managers find it very difficult to specify in advance precisely what information in what form they are likely to need and be able to use. The tendency is either to ask for too much, and then be appalled by the flood of paper which in due course descends on their desks, or to regret, when it is too late, that they have failed to ask for this and this and this. Notoriously, over the whole field of information, the basic problem is not finding the right answers but asking the right questions. Nevertheless, information systems are improving and will continue to improve; cynics might say that there is only too much room for them to do so.

Summary

In this chapter we have said that information about people and companies as a basis for predictions about their future behaviour underlies all effective marketing management; and because information is constantly changing, it needs to be continuous and continuously revised and referred to.

We have divided information sources into two categories, primary and secondary, stressing that data from both sources are almost always no better than approximations; so it is prudent to check the reliability of your sources and to cross-check, whenever possible, against other independent sources.

We have listed the main UK sources of secondary information, saying that this category has the advantage of being inexpensive, but the disadvantage of seldom answering exactly the right questions.

We have also listed the main methods of primary information collection, saying that the reliability of most market research studies depends on the techniques of sampling and questionnaire construction, which involve professional expertise. But the manager who commissions the studies can contribute greatly to their usefulness by comprehensive briefing and explanation of the expected use of the results.

We have said that the marketing researcher or manager can also do much to ensure the usefulness of his work by putting himself in the place of his readers, and presenting his reports in a way which they will find easy to understand and act on.

We have said, finally, that efficient marketing information *systems*, based on a computerised data bank, are a practical possibility for the medium term, provided that the information users can be induced to anticipate the main categories of information they are likely to need and the form in which they will need it.

CHAPTER ELEVEN

The product range

In the early missionary days, when marketing was the new religion which would revolutionise Western industry, its apostles liked to draw black and white contrasts between production-oriented and consumer-oriented companies. The old-fashioned production-oriented manufacturer, they would claim, churned out on his obsolescent machinery whatever product caught his personal fancy, added what he regarded as an adequate profit to his production costs, and then despatched his hard-driven salesmen to foist the results on the consuming public, or suffer the consequences. The virtuous modern consumer-oriented manufacturer would start by ascertaining what consumers want and what they are prepared to pay for it, and would then arrange to produce a range of products to meet those specifications.

Perhaps this exaggerated approach was necessary to get across the point that in the end the customer decides whether the company will flourish or collapse (unless, that is, a benevolent government steps in and elects to preserve it as an ancient monument). But putting the case in such black and white terms now seems rather naive. The fact is that most companies were not born yesterday but have a history, a reputation, substantial resources of capital, expertise and above all people – and an established product range. The product range certainly needs to be constantly modified in the light of changing consumer needs and environmental developments; new products need to be introduced, to ensure maximum customer satisfaction not to say growth for the company; obsolescent products, which have ceased to pay their way or justify the demands they make on management and selling time, need to be discontinued, often to the great grief of some minority groups inside or outside the company who continue to cherish them. Existing products, which continue to satisfy a basic consumer need but have become a trifle old-fashioned, need to be improved or modernised; but there is no sense at all in the marketing man insisting that an identified consumer need must be satisfied when his company lacks the skills or the resources to do the job, profitably, at least as well as its competitors. Nor, when the company has under-utilised capacity of one kind or another, can he stand aside, saying it is none of his business. Unless a market is found for the idle capacity or, if totally unusable, it is disposed of, it will just be an added burden, increasing the overheads chargeable against the successful products.

Ultimately, of course, it is the marketing man's responsibility to press for change, to identify emerging consumer demands which it is within the company's capacity to satisfy, to protest loudly on the customer's behalf when there is evidence of some remediable dissatisfaction. He must perforce adopt this somewhat unpopular role because he is more closely in touch with the customer's needs than some of his management colleagues. But as a marketing man he should not emulate the over-enthusiastic salesman who is prepared to risk bankruptcy for his company in order to get the order. His task is to achieve a proper balance between customer satisfaction and company profitability, always remembering that governmental consumer protection agencies and other outside bodies are liable to intervene in the buyer-seller relationship. This is not to suggest that customer satisfaction and company profitability cannot go hand in hand – indeed, without the former there will be no long-term profit – but that there can be short-sighted managements, pursuing the proverbial 'quick buck', who preach the antithesis of good marketing practice under the marketing banner.

Of the three main categories of marketing activity related to the product range – developing new products, killing off old products, and modifying existing products – the first is much the most glamorous. But it is also the most costly and the most risky. In most industries, whether manufacturing or service, experienced marketing managers looking back over their careers will be forced to admit that thought and effort spent on the relatively unglamorous activities of product improvement and range extension produced more profit and growth for their companies than fundamental new product development. There are of course situations when the advent of radical new technology makes the last essential; but as a rule organisations are more successful at doing rather better what they already know than at learning entirely new tricks.

In banking, as in other industries, it is the *successful* new ideas that are remembered: cheques long ago; personal loans and unit trusts more recently. Readers will have their own views about which of the many new services launched in the 1970s, following the introduction of Competition and Credit Control, will survive, and for how long. Will credit cards run beyond the nineties? Will cash dispensers be made obsolete before they have been fully depreciated in banks' books, if society moves more quickly than expected into a low-cash era, helped along by cheap point-of-sale terminals? These sorts of questions can at least be approached rationally. But at what point in the life cycle of tax-related services – for example, those which include life assurance as a means of gaining tax relief – will the law be changed? The 'at a stroke' syndrome for curing our ills is now widely discredited, but the scope for creating change at a stroke remains very wide in the field of tax legislation. Nevertheless marketing must go on, and must attempt to take such facts of life into account. So we turn now to consider some possible approaches to the development of a banking product range.

Analysing the company's product position in relation to its resources and corporate objectives

The logical starting point for any product range policy, whether of product improvement or of new product development, is an analysis of the company's existing product range, including the extent to which it satisfies the company's vision of itself and the degree to which it is adequate as a base for the achievement of long-term corporate objectives. The familiar question, 'What business are we in?', can elicit a different answer from decade to decade in financial services as in other industries. A couple of decades ago the traditional banker's answer to this question might have been to the effect that our business is borrowing and lending money, preferably borrowing long and lending short, with an adequate spread between the two rates. Today the answer would more probably be to the effect that, 'We aim to provide a complete range of financial services and advice to both our personal and our corporate customers and to achieve a sufficient rate of return on capital employed to keep shareholders happy.' (And, in parenthesis, in print, but not in our minds, we would add that creating careers for staff by offering satisfying jobs at various levels is also a most proper aim – especially in a personal service industry such as ours.) At the same time the concept of long-range planning has gained sufficient acceptance for managements to take a view of the size and shape of business to be aimed for in five or ten year's time.

In this situation the product range planner can begin to identify market gaps, areas of customer or potential customer demand which the company is either failing to satisfy at all or satisfying less efficiently than its competitors; and he can begin also to quantify an emergent profit gap, a widening discrepancy between the revenue that can be anticipated from normal growth in the existing product range and the profit targets which management has set for future years. An improved or extended product range, and eventually (if the gaps are very wide) diversification into totally new product areas will almost always be needed, though this is not to deny that the classical routes of extra sales efforts and cost-reduction exercises on existing products will also have their place.

A product development methodology

The starting point for any innovation or product improvement is an idea. But where ideas come from is a mystery that has never been fully explained. Anecdotes of Archimedes leaping out of his bath and rushing naked into the street crying, 'Eureka, I've got it!', or of the apple bouncing off Newton's cranium are all very well. But it is clear that a lot must have gone on – the study of other men's ideas, discussion, creative incubation, exploration of dead ends – before the final illuminating moment arrived. The marketing man whose job requires him to produce successful new product ideas to order cannot afford to wait for inspiration to strike; he must somehow find a way of systematising the creative process.

The first principle in doing that is to recognise that for every good idea which finally makes the grade and earns a profit as a successful new product or product improvement, perhaps 100 have to be investigated and eventually discarded. So it is important at the outset to collect as many constructive ideas from as many different sources as possible, and then to screen out those which do not stand up to serious examination.

Sources of ideas for new or improved products and services

The most frequent external sources for new ideas are listed below (see also Fig. 4 overleaf).

1 Customers (including prospective customers), making informal suggestions either spontaneously or when stimulated by formal market research.

Fig. 4. A product development programme.

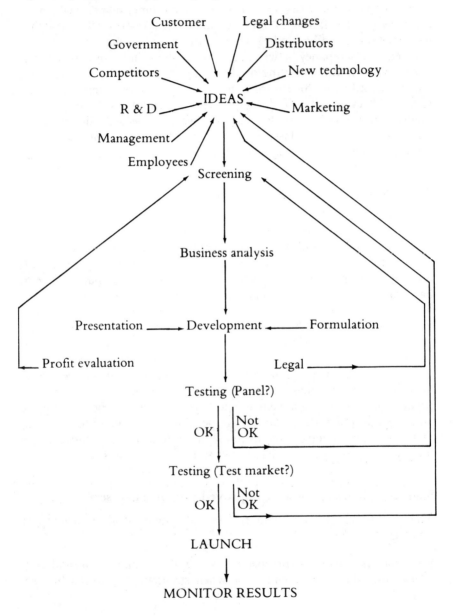

2 Distributors and associated companies. One of the benefits of an international organisation is the opportunity for an exchange of new product ideas between companies serving different markets at different stages of development.
3 Knowledge of government needs. As the largest single 'consumer' in most countries the government, with its changing requirements and ample purse, merits special study.
4 Competitors. Allowing a competitor to make the running with a new product, learning from his mistakes, and then launching an improved version is a favourite marketing ploy. But there is of course the risk that if you give him too long a lead you may never catch up.
5 Academic research or other outside technological developments. Formal links with external think-tanks, prepared to work to a client's brief, can introduce a useful element of lateral thinking, free from the constraints of tradition.

Internal sources can include:

1 the research and development department, or in a financial services context the specialists in devising new methods of corporate finance, personal savings or insurance schemes and so on, to meet changing economic or fiscal circumstances;
2 the marketing department, whose job it is to monitor customer needs and the market place through the research methods described in the previous chapter;
3 experienced company executives (experience is not necessarily synonymous with conservatism);
4 employee suggestions. Often junior employees, in daily touch with customers, have a closer understanding of customer attitudes and needs than senior managers who have climbed up the promotional ladder into the stratosphere.

The more communication there is between all these sources, and the more comparison and discussion of ideas, the greater the likelihood of worthwhile innovation. From this viewpoint the device of brainstorming sessions is a useful one. When individuals from a variety of backgrounds and different levels of seniority are brought together and induced by a stimulating chairman to discuss new product ideas without inhibition and without fear of embarrassment if any of their ideas are unworkable, the results can be surprising. A great number of ideas will certainly emerge, and individuals are likely to go away having learned something as well as contributed something, which can be at least a minor amelioration of the ever-present problem of internal communications. But such sessions need to be carefully handled; early criticism will quickly stifle the flow of ideas.

From product idea to product launch

Producing ideas is fun – a slightly more organised version of day-dreaming. Turning the ideas into marketable new products or services is hard work. Very hard work. Success can never be guaranteed, but is more likely if a nominated individual is assigned the task of making the product or group of products succeed, and if he

1 has the task as a sole or major responsibility, not as an afterthought to other more important charges;
2 has working with him on a part-time basis a multi-disciplinary team of executives who have a talent for innovation (a talent not always associated with a successful record in line management);
3 is empowered to co-opt outside experts on to his team if required;
4 is assured of the continuing interest and backing of senior management, despite the fact that he is presiding over a cost centre rather than a profit centre;
5 is required to work to a realistic but firm programme, timetable and budget.

Starting with the collection of ideas generated by the brainstorming session or any of the other sources described above, the product development manager (as he will usually be called) and his team can expect to go through something like the programme set out below.

1 Screening

If the idea-collecting stages, especially the brainstorming sessions, were conducted in the right uncritical atmosphere, no idea, however harebrained at first glance would have been rejected yet. But primary screening will probably result in the rejection, for perfectly valid and objective reasons, of 80–90 per cent of the ideas processed. Many will duplicate either some existing product or each other. Some will contravene the law. Some will contravene established company policy. Some will be outside the scope of the company's skills or resources. And so on. But don't be too tough at this stage.

2 Business analysis

The next step in the programme will be to subject the surviving ideas to a hypothetical business analysis. What is the size and what are the growth prospects of the market segment into which the new product would be introduced? What are the existing products in the market, and how does the proposed new or improved product compare with them? How formidable is the competition? How would the company bring the product to market? What are the risks? What would be the likely sales volume on the most favourable, least favourable and most likely assumptions? What would be the gross profit contribution? What would be the likely marketing costs? How long would it take for the new or improved product to come into profit? What level of profit?

There would of course be a large element of enlightened guesswork in these calculations, and at this stage the prospective new product should be given the benefit of any reasonable doubt. But if, on the most favourable assumptions, there is no reasonable prospect of the product ever earning an adequate profit it should be abandoned. This is likely to be the fate of at least half the surviving ideas. Too often however an idea is allowed to survive against the evidence for its rejection – for all sorts of reasons, including the mischance that the idea came from a respected senior manager. Equally, the NIH (Not Invented Here) syndrome often causes the premature rejection of ideas. Beware of both motives. Be tough at this stage.

3 The development stage

The product ideas still surviving (possibly 5 per cent of the original number) can then be formally adopted as products under development, each of them endowed with a modest investment budget. Development, whether of a manufactured product or of a service, will normally proceed down two parallel but inter-connected paths. The first could be designated Formulation; in the case of a financial service the precise terms of the proposition to be put to the target customer group, together with the benefit offered. The second could be designated Presentation; meaning the way in which the proposition and benefit are explained to prospective customers, and the supporting literature, contract forms, promotional material and so on. In this stage the details of the 'for real' pricing policy, which is an integral part of any product, will also need to be worked out.

If the project is at all complicated, outside agencies or consultants may well be involved; it will probably be worthwhile in such cases for the project manager to prepare a simple network analysis in order to keep the project in line with target dates. Be realistic.

4 Primary testing

It is more than likely that several of the final short-list of product ideas will drop out in the development stage, either because the market opportunity disappears or because unforeseen practical snags emerge. But there should be at least some which emerge in fully fledged prototype form. These should then be subjected to small-scale testing along market research lines, probably involving exposure to a representative sample or panel of consumers and at the same time exposure to some open-minded salesmen and distributors (or in the case of a clearing bank system, branch managers). It would be unrealistic to overlook the latter, because they can often make constructive suggestions and because a thumbs-down by salesmen and distributors will ensure that a new product flops, however favourably disposed the ultimate consumer may be. Be receptive.

5 Test marketing

For those products which come through the primary testing stage, plus any modification this stage may necessitate, the question then arises: do we introduce it into a test market or do we go immediately into a broadscale launch?

The prudent manager will usually opt for a test market, on the grounds that however thorough and careful your development work and preliminary testing may have been you can never really tell whether a product will sell until you have sold it. Repeatedly. On the other hand, mounting and evaluating a major market test can take up to a year, a year during which you may miss the tide of market opportunity and your competitors will certainly be watching your performance, analysing your product and making their own dispositions. If the product or product improvement is not very revolutionary, nor the investment at risk very high, it may make sense to skip the test marketing stage. Indeed in financial markets it may cost as much to carry out a thorough test market operation as a general launch.

But when in doubt play safe and organise a market test. Competitors seldom react as fast as might be feared; and a properly mounted and evaluated market test does have the advantages that (i) it provides insurance relatively cheaply against a total and expensive failure; (ii) it provides some measure of eventual sales volume and hence of the level of marketing and sales effort which will be justifiable; (iii) the trial run enables you to evaluate and strengthen your marketing and promotional plan; and (iv) all departments of your organisation will get to hear of it, including some who ought perhaps to have known before and who have a contribution to make.

To be of practical value, the test market must be as nearly as possible a microcosm of the final broadscale marketing operation. This means that the starting point should be to write the broadscale plan and then to scale it down to the test area; that the test area should be as representative as possible of the total market, in terms of advertising media and sales outlet availability; and that nothing should be done in the test area which cannot be reproduced on the larger scale (the temptation has to be avoided of getting emotionally involved in the test and making special efforts to ensure its success which cannot subsequently be reproduced). But, again, it is better to err on the side of too much support for the new service or product than to be too sparing. Because then, if it fails, you will be fairly sure that more support would not have made it succeed. For example, if you spend more on advertising than is really affordable nationally and it still fails, you can safely discard it. But if you had spent less would it be correct to discard it?

And finally, with or without a test market, we come to the launch of the new product on to the market. How long has all this taken and how far has a systematic approach eliminated the risk of failure? It is impossible to be specific about timing. It may be a matter only of a few months, or less in the case of a minor product improvement or of a product designed and introduced to meet the special needs of a local office or region. (There is no reason in so multifarious an industry as financial services, with so wide a scatter of branches and so many subsidiary organisations, why every new service should be offered in every location.) At the other extreme it may take a matter of years to plan and implement a major entry into an important new product sector.

The risk of failure can never be entirely eliminated. But a methodical approach along the lines described can improve the odds from, let us say, 20:1 against to 2:1 against success, measured in terms of ultimate profitability. Still, be lucky!

Pruning the product range

We have talked so far mostly about improving existing products and adding new products to the product range. But commonsense, supported by the practical experience of salesmen and managers burdened with an ever-swelling portfolio of products which they are expected to master and market, makes it obvious that too great a clutter of products will clog up the whole system. So provision has to be made for pruning out those which have passed their prime and obstruct the growth of the young and vigorous.

At this point the marketing concept of the 'product life-cycle' should be introduced. This concept, in effect, likens the life-cycle of a product to Shakespeare's seven ages of man, except that only five ages are identified. As illustrated in Fig. 5, the first of them is the period of introduction, when sales volume is low and revenue from the product is insufficient to meet the cost of producing, marketing and administering it. Sometime in its second age, of growth, it should, if all goes well, cross the breakeven line and begin to earn a profit. In the third age, of maturity, profits should be substantial and growth should be continuing. Then comes the fourth age of saturation, when competition multiplies, with increasing pressure on price levels and profit margins. Finally comes the fifth age, of decline, when both the sales volume and profit contribution fall drastically and euthanasia or artificial respiration is required to avoid drifting into loss.

That at least is the concept. But there are many variations in the way it works in practice. The life-cycle may be very long, as in the case of a product like Birds Custard which has passed its hundredth birthday; or very short, as in the case of children's toys, which may not survive a single season. And marketing men have come increasingly to realise that the ages of saturation and decline can often be indefinitely postponed by a judicious policy of product improvement. It is very often cheaper, easier and less hazardous, as we have already said, to improve and modernise an existing product than to kill it off and launch a new product in its place.

However, the principle still applies that sooner or later decline is inevitable and the product should be put painlessly to sleep. Some companies provide for this eventuality by having an annual review system, whereby all the products in the range are evaluated and classified in separate groups. One such classification system provides for green-light

Fig. 5. The product life-cycle.

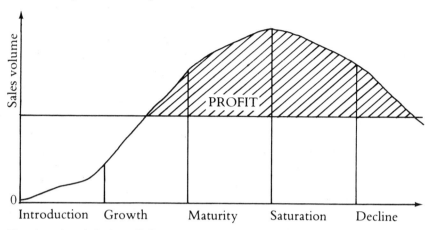

For the sake of clarity, all five phases are shown as being of equal duration: in practice they will be of very different lengths.

products with a bright future that merit top priority marketing effort; yellow-light products which are still earning a useful profit but should be watched and probably milked of their profits while they last; and red-light products which have no future but perhaps need to be kept alive for political reasons.

Major diversifications

When the need arises to move into a major new product area, management can elect to follow the road of product development from within (the route followed in the case of the Barclaycard and Access credit cards, born from an original US idea); or it can follow the road of acquisition, adopted by the British clearing banks when they moved into the hire purchase finance industry, and by Midland Bank when it moved into the travel industry through the acquisition of Thomas Cook, and Lloyds Bank in buying estate agents. The two roads are not of course mutually exclusive. Since the availability of a suitable case for acquisition is a chancy affair, it is no bad idea to develop a product range independently of the acquisition and merge the two if and when the acquisition comes off – a sort of internal test marketing.

Marketing may or may not be invited to participate in the identification of suitable businesses for acquisition in target industrial sectors. Sometimes the need for speed or secrecy will over-ride the advisability of investigating not simply a company's profit record and physical assets and the calibre of its management before signing a cheque, but also of examining the state of its customer relations and of the product range on which its future depends. But if marketing is invited to participate in the process of evaluation it may well come up with a rather different picture from the financial analysts. A company, for example, with most of its major products in the early stages of their life-cycle will probably have a brighter future than its recent profit record would indicate; contrariwise, a company with most of its products in the stage of maturity or saturation could well be on the verge of a serious downturn in profitability, despite its currently good figures.

Whether a company elects to follow the internal product development road or the acquisition road is largely a matter of temperament and timing. Some companies are bursting with innovative ideas, others have bulging moneybags. The internal development route will probably involve a smaller investment initially, but an increasing one over the years, with a fairly long wait for a substantial return. Acquisition, if all goes well, should assure the acquisitive company of an immediate return on a much larger investment; but the problems, to judge from the success rate of mergers and acquisitions over the post-war years, will then begin to mount up. Either road is a difficult and rocky one, but inescapable if a company is to go on growing, or, indeed, in the long run to survive, for its own traditional services will surely decline, unless updated.

Summary

In this chapter we have stressed the importance of a comprehensive, balanced product range, offering the target customer groups most if not all the financial services they need, so long as it is legal, feasible and profitable for the company to provide them.

We have classified product development activities into the two main categories of product improvement or range extension and the development from scratch of totally new and original products, saying cautiously that the former, though less glamorous, can often provide a better, safer return for a given investment of time, money and effort.

We have said that in both cases the starting point for a product development programme is an idea; or rather a great number of ideas, since many ideas are needed for every one that will work. We have listed a number of different sources for such ideas, and mentioned brainstorming as a useful method for multiplying and improving them.

We have said that a multi-disciplinary product development team, dedicated to the task of turning seminal ideas into profitable products, a methodical development programme and assurance of senior management backing are vital ingredients for success in the product development field. And we have sketched such a programme, progressing from the screening of the original product ideas through a stage of business analysis to a development programme involving formulation on one side and presentation on the other, with due attention to pricing policy. We have then mentioned the need for testing, initially by market research methods and then, if the project is sufficiently important or hazardous, by test marketing before the final launch.

We have also said that in order to avoid clogging up the company's production, marketing and administrative system, provision should be made for reviewing the stage in its life-cycle reached by each of the company's products and disposing of those which have reached a stage of decline from which they cannot be economically revived by product improvement methods.

Finally, we have compared the alternative methods of major diversification; through internal product development or through acquisition of an existing company with an established product range in the target market sector.

CHAPTER TWELVE

Selling and distribution

Selling services versus selling products

When British banks and other financial institutions emerged from the second world war it was a new and less comfortable world that confronted them. Before the war the market for financial services was small and select on the personal side; and on the corporate side, though competition existed, it was relatively gentlemanly.

After the war the personal side turned from a minority market into a mass market, which could not have been handled without the development of the computer; and the corporate side was exposed to increasingly vigorous competition from overseas banks and other institutions moving into the UK.

Hence the message that has flowed with growing insistence through the management ranks of banks and others: 'Whoever and wherever you are, if you come into contact with the customer at any level, either face-to-face or by telephone or by letter, you are a salesman (nowadays salesperson).'

The message came as no surprise to those who recognised that the banking, insurance and other financial service industries would never have grown and prospered as they have if they had not actively sold their services over the years and centuries; and if a goodly proportion of managers had not been of an expansionist rather than a conservative disposition. But there were also a number of individuals who proclaimed, or muttered, that they had not joined these industries in order to emulate the grocery salesmen; they had aimed for a position of dignity, a measure of power to dispense favours to the rest of the community.

For both groups, and for those with mixed feelings between the two, it was a case of accepting the inevitable. The blurring of boundaries between the specialist financial service institutions, with each beginning to offer more and more of the others' services, together with the arrival of fresh competition from within and from abroad, made it inevitable that more emphasis should be placed on the selling, and in turn therefore the marketing, function. This was particularly so because many of the new arrivals were less inhibited than the entrenched establishment about their selling methods (the Americans for instance seem positively to enjoy selling) and began to make inroads into the more vulnerable sectors of the establishment's business.

Happily for all concerned it rapidly emerged that selling services is a very different affair from selling packaged grocery products; the temperamental characteristics of the banker or actuary, which would probably make him an indifferent soap salesman, can be a positive advantage in his own environment. A salesmanship pundit once said that the qualities required of a good salesman are a judicious blend of empathy and ego-drive. The empathy is required so that he can understand and sympathise with the customer's motivations (including possibly his motive for not wanting to buy the salesman's product on the terms offered); the ego-drive is required so that the salesmen will get his own way in the end and strike a bargain as nearly as possible on his own terms. Clearly the desirable proportions in this blend will vary according to the selling situation and the product.

In financial services, where the product in broad terms is assistance for the customer, whether corporate or personal, to find the resources to further his personal or commercial objectives, or to deploy the resources he has to the best advantage, the requirement for empathy predominates. The customer's needs and motivations are likely to be more complex, and his or her ability to assess alternative courses of action without professional assistance is likely to be more limited, than those of the grocer or housewife making the unmomentous choice between two brands of washing powder. So the financial salesman must know his customer as well as his product.

Moreover, the sale of a financial service is not based on a fleeting contact between ships that pass in the night and may never meet again. It is either the beginning of, or an episode in, the development of what should be a long-term relationship. In this context winning a transitory advantage by slick or bullying tactics is unlikely to pay off in the long run. For a large element in what the financial service company's representative is selling is himself or herself; and through personality and behaviour they either enhance or diminish the company's corporate reputation. Neither of these last factors implies that the individual should be soft; the element of ego-drive is still required. But a fair bargain, struck in the light of a full understanding of the customer's position, is preferable to a ruthless battle of wits.

In the rest of this chapter we shall be looking at aspects of banking as they relate to, or are similar to, retailing and other service occupations. This may give the reader the impression that the chapter is only of general, non-specific relevance. Not so: our intention is to encourage the reader in the habit of learning from what is common to his industry and others, to make connections across common ground, and to apply to his trade some techniques and practices that have evolved elsewhere.

The selling sandwich

In most of the guide books to effective selling, primary emphasis is put on the actual selling interview, and various mnemonics (most of which we find eminently forgettable) are advanced to ensure a successful outcome. We prefer to think that in financial services the actual selling interview, important as it is, is the filling in the sandwich of which pre-sales analysis and post-sales service are the bread and butter; and that the bread and butter is what does most to maximise the success rate resulting both from the immediate sales interview and from subsequent interviews to sell additional services in a developing relationship.

The pre-sales activity is certainly not an unfamiliar concept to the great majority of bank managers, corporate finance managers or insurance representatives. There can be very few who fail to brief themselves in advance of any important interview, whatever its purpose, with such information as is readily available on the customer's or prospective customer's financial situation, likely requirements and previous dealings with the company. When the purpose of the interview is wholly or partly to sell one or more of the company's services, this preliminary briefing should in theory be widened to cover not only past history but reliable information or research-based hypotheses on the individual's or organisation's personality, policies, motivation and objectives. But theory has of course to yield in practice to the practicalities of information availability and affordable cost. If the information system which we sketched in the previous chapter were fully operational, and could be relied on to deliver all the information in a bank's possession instantaneously when and where it is needed, the pre-sales activity would be greatly facilitated. As it is, the individual on the brink of a selling interview, possibly at short notice, has to limit his preparatory work; and even if the notice is not short, he must consider whether the cost of assembling the ideal information file ahead of an interview is justified by the potential benefit to the company which may arise from the interview.

But one thing costs very little: constructive thinking in advance about the sales opportunities which may arise from an interview, or programme of interviews, not planned primarily for selling purposes. It is a frequent complaint of branch managers and others that too much of the time they have available for face-to-face interviews is devoted to castigating the bad rather than encouraging the good and, of course, prospective customers. The constructive thinking we suggest should be devoted to preparedness through:

1 recognising, on the basis of such information as is available, that any selling activity should be directed more selectively to customers or prospective customers representing the best business development opportunity for the company (i.e. the admirable principle that all customers are equal in the sight of the company should be modified to the extent that big customers are rather more equal, and entitled to rather more selling time than small customers);

2 refreshing the memory, if not on all the details at least on the key selling points of the services most likely to be relevant to the interviewee's needs. In principle, no interview, except with thoroughly undesirable customers, should be entered on without some idea of the services or additional services which might benefit both company and customer. The ideas may of course be totally wide of the mark, but their discussion can generate new ideas.

The implications of this preparedness principle, which would apply not simply to managers and designated business development officers but to all staff in contact with customers or potential customers, (that is, everyone) can be summarised as follows.

1 The customers and prospective customers within the ambit of the individual manager or staff member should be classified, as far as availability information will permit, into different desirability/probability categories in relation to the major services which the company is anxious to sell (a given individual or company will obviously rank higher in relation to some services than to others).

2 When the desirability/probability rating is high and the prospective return on a successful sale is attractive, more information should be

collected about the individuals or categories concerned as a preliminary
to positive selling efforts.

3 The information should be pooled among all those likely to have
contact with the target customers, either accidentally or on purpose.

4 These company personnel should also be armed with the main selling
points for the service or services at issue, recognising that the emphasis
to be placed on each of the main points may well differ from one
prospective customer to another. (See Table 2.)

Concerning the after-sales slice of the sandwich, the main point to
be made is that in selling a service, you are selling as a rule not a tangible
product which can be inspected and tested, but a promise of future
performance. The extent to which that promise is fulfilled will affect not
only future sales to the same customer but the attraction of new customers
through word-of-mouth recommendation. So part of the sales programme
has to be preparatory work to ensure that all the arrangements for
delivering the promised service are sound; this means, of course, that
those members of the organisation whose role is nominally only administrative are in a very real sense salesmen for the company. The cashier
who smiles when she cashes your cheque, the telephonist who keeps
coming back to you when the extension you want is busy, instead of
leaving you hanging in the air, are both contributing significantly to the
total sales effort.

The before-sales preparation and the company's reputation for
after-sales service can, as we have said, make the *face-to-face selling
interview* very much easier; and the softening up process represented by
media advertising and other forms of marketing communication make it
easier still – in some cases (for instance the postal marketing of credit
cards) totally eliminating it. But in most cases it is the face-to-face
interview at the heart of the sandwich, between the company's representative and the customer or his representative, which makes or mars the
sale. And the question arises how far the sometimes rather mechanical
selling methods suggested by the sales experts for consumer or industrial
product salesman can be usefully followed by the part-time or full-time
salesmen of financial services.

The answer will vary from one individual to another. There is of
course always something to be learned from studying the way other
people have handled a similar though essentially rather different job. And

Table 2. Key steps to gaining and keeping customers

Pre-sale	Selling	After-sales service
Identify key prospect groups/individuals	Explain the benefits to *them* of your own brand of product/ services; often face-to-face but sometimes not	Keep to any promises made
Describe them		Check from time to time that the developing needs of the customers are still being met as fully as possible, offering new services as required
Analyse their needs	Ask for business	
Work out the best fit of *their* needs and *your* services		
Promote yourself/ your services to them		

the rules propounded in most of the sales manuals ('identify the customer benefit', 'describe the product from the customer's point of view', 'anticipate and meet the customer's objections', 'close the interview by clinching the sale') are sensible enough. It would be a mistake to denigrate the contribution which the professional sales trainer can make to sharpening the techniques of those unaccustomed to selling.

On the other hand there is a great variety of different selling situations in the typical financial services organisation, from the specialist selling of a specific service package, possibly with a highly technical content, to the more frequent situation of the generalist manager whose customer interviews are usually only partly of a selling nature and whose task may as often be that of identifying opportunities to pass on to his technical colleagues as of actually completing a sale. The approach cannot be as planned or systematic in the latter case as in the former. Moreover, it has always to be remembered that an important part of selling a service is inspiring confidence in yourself as a key element in that service. From that viewpoint the painful mastery of selling methods and techniques which go against the grain of your own personality may be an obstacle to inspiring confidence; people who are obviously putting on an uncongenial act do not inspire trust. If, for personality or temperamental reasons, a person cannot accept selling as part of his natural self then he ought not to be employed as a salesman. But someone who can, and who is keen to learn, will soon develop his own style – and that, so long as it is based on a proper understanding of the role, is to be welcomed.

The sales management function

At present the role of sales manager, business development manager or marketing manager with an executive selling responsibility is not very frequently found in the financial services industry. This may well change in the future as the selling task becomes more difficult and more specialised. But for the present, management of the sales activity is more likely to be part of the responsibility of a general manager, competing for a share of his attention with a heavy load of administrative, personnel and other functions. This makes it all the more important that the sales management responsibility should be well understood and organised *systematically*.

Sales managers, whether of financial services or of other commodities, must sometimes hanker after the bad old days when life was simple if inglorious. In those not so long ago days the sales manager's task boiled down to appointing a salesman or sales agent for each sales territory, giving him a brief indoctrination course in the virtues of your product range (it was as well not to tell him too much, particularly about your cost structure), equipping him with a bagful of sample biscuits, spanners, insurance policies or whatever, plus a take-it-or-leave-it price list, and waiting for the orders to roll in. If the level of orders was unsatisfactory or if you began to get complaints from customers about the moron or bully boy who was calling on them in your name – or, alternatively, complaints that they never saw your representative – you would have fired the fellow and tried again.

Nowadays, in almost every market E.M. Forster's admonition 'only connect' has been followed only too faithfully. Almost everything in the commercial and industrial world connects with everything else. The sales achieved on any given sales territory or catchment area depend only partly on the efforts of the salesmen or branch manager responsible for that territory. In the first place many of the customers using the product or service in the area will not have the authority to decide which of a number of competitive products or services they will use. That decision will have been made, more and more often as the power and reach of multiple organisations extends, at head office, usually after hard bargaining about terms and about the service to be provided at branch level. The area manager or salesman for the servicing company will in fact contribute to the sale and to the retention of the business by the level of service and follow-through he provides; but he will not always get the credit for it.

In the second place, an important but usually unquantifiable contribution is made to the level of sales by the central, as well as the local, advertising and sales promotional activities of the servicing company. Sometimes this will do no more than open the door for the salesman, and in most cases he will be needed to clinch the sale; but the effort required from him will be increased or diminished according to the weight and effectiveness of advertising support. Sometimes it may make sense to cut down on direct selling effort and expense in order to spend more on sales promotion; sometimes the reverse may be the case. Always there will be an interplay between the two.

Thirdly, it is probable that a proportion of the sales on the territory will be made over the telephone or by post without any direct involvement by the salesmen. A number of organisations, for instance the classified advertisement departments of newspapers, have calculated the relative costs of a telephone call and a physical visit to a prospective customer. They have concluded that when the *purchasing decision* is not a very important one, telephone calls, though less effective individually, are most cost-effective overall. The same can be true of certain types of financial service.

A final factor, complicating the sales manager's task, is the fact that pricing and terms structures have to be more flexible in the buyer's market of today and tomorrow. If not the individual salesmen, at least the area sales manager must have discretion to negotiate on terms; and successful performance has to be measured not simply in sales but in profit contribution.

So sales managers have to think not simply of meeting or beating sales targets through their own efforts and those of the salesmen who report to them, but of the cost-effective deployment of all the selling resources at their disposal, supplemented by the support services on which they can call. They have to think also in terms of allocating a proportion of these selling resources to supporting or following through sales made in other parts of the organisation, and must find a way to account satisfactorily for these diversionary activities.

The task of the modern sales manager – or of the area manager or the general manager with selling responsibilities – could be summarised in job specification jargon along the following lines:

1 to identify the potential demand for his company's products or services in the area for which he is responsible;
2 to determine as specifically as possible which of the available customers or customer categories have authority to make their own financial or other purchasing decisions, and which need to be approached through head offices outside the territory;
3 to make the most cost-effective use of the selling resources at his disposal in;
   (a) increasing the level of profitable business with existing customers;
   (b) making selective selling approaches by the most appropriate means at the most appropriate level to prospective new customers likely to be profitable to the organisation;
   (c) following through and servicing the local branches and subsidiaries of customers with head offices outside his territory;
4 to train, direct and motivate personnel under his control who can
   (a) negotiate the sale of existing or new company products and services to new or existing customers;
   (b) identify and report sales opportunities with new or existing customers;
   (c) contribute indirectly to the acquisition and retention of business by the level of service provided;
5 to co-ordinate the selling operations under his control with central sales promotional policies and activities, including the effective use of central sales, service and other specialists;
6 to agree with management quantified sales and profit targets and to monitor progress towards their achievement;
7 to agree with salesmen and others under his control who contribute to the total sales effort individual objectives and targets, and to monitor their achievement.

Like most job specifications this looks fine on paper, but is not so easy in practice. It is only likely to be achieved if the sales manager:

1 works to a version of the marketing plan already described, whether it is written for him or by him;
2 establishes a level of communication with his staff which enables them

to understand the part they play as individuals in the total selling effort and equips them to play their part effectively (hence the need for line management involvement in training instead of its total segregation in a separate training department);

3 has organised a flow of usable management information reports and statistics which enable him to monitor progress against targets (including any developments which may affect the achievement of targets), both overall and at the level of the individual salesmen and sales support personnel. The latter of course ties in with the various versions of Management by Objectives adopted by a number of large organisations.

For the conscientious sales manager, who may have personal responsibility for large customers and administrative responsibility in addition, there is the ever-present problem of how many tasks can be fitted into a working week. There can be no glib answer to this problem. We can only suggest that the best personal solution may be found somewhere in the triangle represented by personal priorities, delegation and 'systematisation'.

In speaking of *personal priorities* we have in mind that the individual manager should regard himself, together with his salary, expenses and overheads, as a company resource on which he should earn the best return. This means allocating his own time – as much time as he has available after the mandatory tasks have been completed – so as to show the best long-term return to his company. (We say long-term to emphasise the fact that the time spent on staff training, which may show no immediate return, can be more valuable in the long run than time spent on the personal negotiation of a short-term deal.)

By *delegation* we have in mind the observed fact that the most effective personal salesmen are frequently indifferent sales managers; the growth in their value to the company stops abruptly when they reach the limit of their personal selling contacts.

By *systematisation* we have in mind the fact that the computer can be either a good servant or a complete curse, depending on the precision with which its users specify their requirements. The sales manager's task of controlling his patch will be made easier if he insists on getting clear summaries of relevant information. It will be made even harder if he is subjected to a flood of print-outs which he has no time to absorb, analyse and act on.

The sales-effective shop

An additional complication to the highly complicated financial services selling theme is that, unlike most producers, financial services organisations tend to own shops or chains of shops. We do not intend to be derogatory to the marbled halls of the bankers or the glass and steel palaces of the large insurance companies in describing their premises as shops. We want simply to underline the fact that from the marketing viewpoint they are a resource, comparable to any supermarket, on which a sales and profit return should be earned.

This of course does not mean that they should look like supermarkets. The rock on which a financial services business is built is confidence; and too obvious an effort to attract customers, particularly by what look like huckstering methods, may in the long run cheapen the image of the organisation and detract from that essential confidence. But always bearing in mind the corporate image factor, it must be a constant preoccupation of marketing and sales either to attract the maximum number of profitable customers into the shop and/or to service the maximum amount of profitable business out of it. In this, due allowance must be made for the changing climate in which financial organisations find themselves; what was considered appropriate in the 1920s is unlikely to be thought so nowadays. It is not unreasonable therefore to have 'shops' which have moved some way towards a 'supermarket' appearance, except of course where the branch office has a 'Harrodian' rather than a 'Tescovite' customer base.

But how to do it? Most banks and other financial service institutions are established in expensive purpose-built premises which cannot easily be disposed of. So even if an institution wholly subscribes to the principle of cost-effectiveness in its branch development, this has in practice to be diluted by a large element of make do and mend, not least because of the growing tendency of local planning authorities to feel that what they regard as offices have no place in High Street premises. The relatively rapid change achieved by the multiple grocers all over Europe (from chains made up of numerous small shops with a large element of personal service to much less numerous chains of self-service supermarkets and hyper-markets handling a far greater turnover despite their smaller numbers) is unlikely to be duplicated in the financial services market. Changes are taking place, but they are likely to be relatively slow and undramatic. The main factors that have to be considered by management in developing cost-effective shops are listed below.

1 Relating the character, facilities and style of the shop to the type of business and the type of customer for whom it is intended.
The branch bank or money shop which is intended to service personal customers will differ increasingly from those branches designed to service principally corporate customers. And, given the conspicuous absence of a classless society, personal customer branches may themselves be designed differentially to appeal to specific economic or social, or other, segments of the public. The racial, as opposed to racialist, branch is needed to provide for cultural and linguistic differences; the women's lib branch is probably not needed but may yet manifest itself.

2 Location
This is a factor which is getting more attention from the marketing-oriented managements of financial institutions than it did in the past. Not so long ago the dynamic new general manager of a large insurance company proclaimed that within the next twelve months his company would have a representative office in every major town in the land. His loyal lieutenants embarked on a crash programme of new branch openings, to be followed, shortly after his somewhat premature departure from the company, by a less conspicuous but still urgent programme of branch closures, covering the very substantial proportion of new branches which quite clearly had no prospect of ever yielding a return on the investment they represented.

More prudent managements recognise that it is a difficult and expensive matter to find suitable locations for new branches; and that it is wise to preface any final decision on possible locations with a rigorous analysis, aided by market research, of the profit potential in the catchment area of the location concerned.

3 Layout
There are a number of constraints of which experts in shop layout must be aware if they are going to be helpful to organisations marketing financial services. There is the obvious constraint of security, when substantial sums of money are being handled; there is the need to sustain an image of reliability and solidity, which may detract from the welcoming

impression which a shop should give; and there is the basic question of the extent to which the organisation actually wants to attract 'store traffic'. It may be policy to do as much business as possible at arm's length and to regard the branch primarily as a servicing unit for those customers who need or prefer an element of personal service.

Nevertheless, there is and will continue to be scope for making the individual branch a more congenial environment for personal shoppers, and an efficient outlet through which to market new or peripheral services. It seems likely that, as financial service organisations become more responsive to market segmentation, there will be a trend away from the standard branch layout to a variety of layouts, adapted to the customer segments (personal or corporate, up-market or mass market) which each branch is intended to serve.

4 In-store merchandising

Whatever the level of 'store traffic', it is clearly a legitimate marketing objective to sell, or make the first step towards selling, as many relevant services as possible to the individuals passing through the branch. Banks and other financial service organisations in the UK have made a lot of progress in the direction of the 'silent salesmen' as represented by an effective display of leaflets and brochures. But with the development of audio-visual and other electronic devices there will be scope for much more effective sales promotional devices than brochures, enabling interested customers to get fuller details of particular services in words and pictures – always remembering the need not to turn branches into bazaars.

5 Staffing

A more important factor than layout, in creating the right environment for a particular customer segment, is staffing. This is a matter not simply of determining what size and character of staff is needed to provide the marketing thrust and service back-up that is required, but how much expenditure on staff is affordable. With well-trained and competent people an increasingly scarce and costly resource, the consideration of cost-effectiveness looms even larger.

6 Automation

The impact on the financial services industry of the computer, aided and abetted by electronic communications, has already revolutionised branch banking. There is more to come. It is no longer fanciful to foresee a day, not very far ahead, when virtually all routine transactions for which customers now come into branches of banks and other financial service institutions will be handled on a self-service basis through computer terminals, cash dispensers and so on; and human resources will be concentrated on the more useful aspects of dealing with individual customer problems, ensuring that customers are aware of and buy the services they need.

Summary

In this chapter we have said that people involved in selling financial services need a larger element of empathy and a smaller element of ego-drive in their make-up than the salesmen of consumer or industrial products.

We have described the 'selling sandwich' and said that well-organised pre-selling activity and post-selling follow-up are as important as the face-to-face selling interview in the middle of the sandwich, and that they make the interview a great deal easier and more effective.

We have suggested that individuals involved in selling interviews should study the procedures and formulas advanced by experts in this activity, and then throw them away and develop their own selling techniques. We have also stressed the importance of identifying sales opportunities in the course of interviews initiated for other purposes.

We have listed the seven major elements in the sales management function; and we have discussed the extent to which the branch of a bank or other financial institution can be regarded as a shop for selling the institution's various services.

CHAPTER THIRTEEN

Marketing communications

The basic definition of 'communicate' is 'to succeed in conveying one's meaning to others'. That is difficult enough in all conscience; people's capacity to misunderstand each other knows no limit. But the marketing man asks more of communication. In his language, successful communication involves not only conveying an understandable message to the audience he is interested in, but getting them to do something about it. Marketing communication involves persuasion, resulting either in some desired action such as buying a particular product or service, or in a change of attitude or behaviour which is likely to lead eventually to the desired action.

The success or failure of the marketing man's communications effort will depend essentially on four inter-related factors:

1 the power of the original message;
2 the clarity and force with which it is expressed;
3 the media through which it is communicated;
4 the level of expenditure.

He can sometimes do very little about the original message, though it will substantially affect the ease of his task. If the message is that the local branch of Bink's Bank is giving away £5 notes it should not be too difficult to get the word around and precipitate action. If the message is that Bink's Bank is best it will be a good deal more difficult to persuade people to change their attitudes, particularly if Bink's Bank is not noticeably superior to its competitors. Occasionally it may be possible to introduce a genuine price advantage, though in financial markets such an advantage will probably be short-lived. But usually the selling message will have to emphasise benefits other than price.

Expressing a message in words or pictures with clarity, precision and persuasiveness, so as to have the maximum impact on the target audience, is one of the essential skills of the specialist marketing man.

But the understanding of his fellow beings which is needed is not necessarily confined to the business school graduate or professional advertising man (nor always to be found in these paragons). The effective general manager should also be a good communicator, and he will get better work out of the specialists if he briefs them with clarity and precision.

Nor are the media of communication necessarily confined to those which come automatically to mind in a marketing or advertising context. Television, newspapers, magazines, radio, posters and so on attract most of the attention in marketing treatises and most of the advertising money; and they are an undoubtedly efficient means of mass communication. But (as described later) there are other means of getting your story across to your target audience, particulalarly when it is a numerically small but very specific one. Using a rifle to hit your target requires more skill than using a sawn off shotgun; but there are many situations in which it is more effective.

In every marketing situation requiring the use of communication (what marketing situation does not require it?) cost-effectiveness should be the watchword. It is not simply a question of getting a message across, nor even of getting a message across in a way which stimulates action; it is necessary to relate the cost of the communication to the benefit accruing to the organisation as a result.

In short, the questions to be asked before any communications activity is undertaken, questions that are sometimes easier to ask than to answer, are the following:

1 Who do we want to reach?
2 What action or change of attitude do we want to bring about?
3 How should the message be framed so as to acheive the maximum impact?
4 What medium, or combination of media, is most cost-effective for conveying the right messsage to the right people?
5 How much is it worth for us to get the message across?
6 Can we do it for the money?

To put it this way is perhaps to over-simplify what the expert communicators, in common with most experts, have contrived to develop into a highly complicated procedure, liberally sprinkled with its own esoteric jargon. And so far we have talked only of the likely awareness of the communication among the target audiences. Success may depend in part on their ability to afford the product being offered, or on their ability to make good use of it, or on their ethical acceptance of an idea. Perhaps we should look at it all, and the above questions, in more detail.

Identifying the target audience

Two relatively useful marketing in-phrases are 'decision-makers' and 'opinion-formers'. (In banking, obvious examples of these potentates are finance directors, solicitors and accountants.) If you want to persuade people to buy your product or service, or at least to let them know it is available in case they want to come and get it, you need to know the type of individual, family group, small or large organisation which should be interested in buying it (if you follow the best marketing procedures you will have designed it with them in mind); and you need to take a view, whether based on research or experience or commonsense, or a combination of all three, about those who are likely to make or contribute to the purchasing decisions. Then you can address yourself to people as human beings and not simply shout your message from the housetops, hoping that somebody will hear.

Equally, if you suspect that your 'corporate image' is not all it might be and that people are not as anxious to do business with you or work for you as you would wish, you need to decide who are the key people you want to influence, either because their own opinions are important or because they can influence the opinions and actions of others. Once again, if you address yourself to them as human beings, you are more likely to get results than if you were addressing the whole faceless mass of ' the general public'. *It pays to particularise.*

Establishing customer motivation

Especially perhaps in so competitive a field as financial services, which so many people simply take for granted, it is an odds-on bet that your customer will be less interested in buying your product or service than you are in selling it to him. He has many other things on his mind, and many other people prepared to sell him something not very different from what you have to offer. Hence the interest in motivation research as a preliminary to major advertising campaigns. Often the results of such research, based on 'in depth' interviews, group discussions and similar attempts to adapt the methods of psychology to commercial ends, are not particularly helpful; seeking to plumb the depths of hidden reasons for this decision or that often results in the revelation that far from being deep-rooted the decision was largely accidental.

But sometimes unexpected reasons do pop up. And usually the exercise is worthwhile, if only because it forces the inevitably self-interested producer to pause and look at his product from the customer viewpoint, asking the crucial question, 'What's in it for *them?*' *It pays to empathise.*

Designing the message

Manufactures of branded products have in principle the choice between two different approaches to their marketing communications. They can on the one hand, like the H.J. Heinz Company, place major emphasis on the company's name and fit every product they put on the market into the elastic framework of the Heinz 57 varieties; or they can choose, like Procter & Gamble, to emphasise the brand name and leave it to the small print to reveal that Daz and Tide and Fairy Liquid are all made by the same company. In the same way a chain of retail shops can theoretically choose between promoting the shops as such or promoting the exceptional products or exceptional bargains that can be bought in them. (For some products that are bought only once, establishing a brand name is difficult: consider wedding rings or coffins; though to the trade both *are* branded.)

A financial services organisation, doubling the role of producer and 'shopkeeper', can be said to face the same theoretical choice. It can seek in its marketing communications to build the impression that the customer who wants the best range of financial services should come to one of its 'shops'; or it can promote the main services individually, seeking to communicate in each case with the customer segment which the service in question is designed to satisfy. Of the British clearing banks, for example, Barclays seem to favour the 'umbrella' approach of using the parent name to identify some of its main consumer products (Barclaycard, Barclayloan, Barclaybank); while Nat West tends to promote its individual services or subsidiaries independently.

It is not of course a black and white choice. It is possible to adopt both approaches in separate sales promotional and advertising campaigns, though it is advisable in such cases to make sure that the individual campaigns are compatible in tone and presentation, reinforcing each other rather than clashing. And it is equally possible to combine them in the same campaign; the large preponderance of retail advertising in practice seeks to attract the target segments of the public to the retail outlets by describing a selection of the goods they offer for sale, chosen to enhance the reputation for quality, cheapness or universality that the particular retailer seeks to establish.

Whichever approach or combination of approaches is chosen, the process of designing an effective marketing message starts with a very precise understanding, agreed between the originator and the professional communicator, of the specific news or claim to be conveyed and the general impression about the company and its services which the message should reinforce. Far too many advertisements, brochures and simple selling letters start out with a good idea and then become bloated and shapeless through the well-intentioned addition of superfluous items: 'While we're at it why don't we tell them this and maybe this and perhaps that as well, it won't cost much.' In fact it may well cost you the whole message! *It pays to specialise.*

Getting attention

If the communicator has won his first battle by keeping the message clear and simple, he has then to apply himself to the problem of catching the target recipient's attention. The communicator who is not face-to-face with his audience in the awe-inspiring environment of the headmaster's study or the bank manager's parlour must fight to gain attention in the midst of a babel of other belligerents. (If you doubt this stop and think, when you fold up your newspaper or turn off your television, just how many of the advertisements that passed before your eyes you can actually recall in any detail; or chat to a direct mail expert about the huge sense of triumph he experiences when as many as 10 per cent of the recipients respond to his mail-shot.)

Getting attention is not simply a question of shouting louder than the next man, printing your advertisement upside down, introducing a naked body or some other startling device. What all these may gain in attention they can lose in effectiveness through failing to convince the audience that the advertiser should be taken seriously. Effective attention is more often a matter of tuning in to the recipients' wavelength. People, to put it baldly, pay attention to what interests them. Over forty years ago George Gallup, the doyen of market researchers, undertook a series of studies into the advertisements which caught people's attention, and made the then startling pronouncement that women were more likely to look at illustrations of women and men at illustrations of men; not a question of homosexuality before it became fashionable, but simply of self-identification. (Incidentally, their second choices, it is said, were babies for women and dogs for men.)

On the same principle, if you happen to be suffering from toothache your eye is much more likely to be caught by a feature mentioning this malady than if your teeth are not bothering you; and the chances of your noticing an advertisement for your own company or a competitor are much greater than they would be if these companies meant nothing to you. So the professional communicator seeks first of all to flag his target customers, featuring in words or pictures something which he knows or believes to be of lively interest to them.

But interest, once awakened, will not be sustained for long if there is not some immediate indication of a *benefit* for the recipients of the communication. The toothache sufferer will lose interest and patience very rapidly with an advertisement which simply tells him that toothache is a misery; he knows that already. But his interest will be sustained if the advertisement goes on to say not that the advertiser's product can cure the condition (apart from the penalities of being found out, the Code of Advertising Practice forbids exaggerated claims of that nature) but that it will relieve the pain and tide him over until he can get expert help from his dentist. Similarly, an overdraft will not cure a company's fundamental financial weakness, but it can tide it over a bad patch and give it a breathing space in which to take expert advice.

A key benefit is all very well, but why should those on the receiving end of your communication believe you, particularly when there are so many others making much the same claim? This is where the professional communicator starts searching for one of his essential instruments, the *'reason why'*. Is the reason because the old firm has been in business for a long time? Not all that convincing; it could just mean that they have grown lazy and old-fashioned. Or is it because the service is cheap? A convincing reason in some contexts, but suspect in situations where reliability is essential and 'cheap' may be taken as meaning 'cheap and nasty'. Or, 'We have made a special study of this area and know more about it than others.' This can be persuasive, if you can give chapter and verse. Or, 'We have satisfied other customers just like you, so why not you?' Again pretty convincing, so long as the target customer does not number among his friends some of your other customers who were far from satisfied. Or, 'We have some special advantage which others lack', such as the special tax concessions which off-shore banks can pass on to some of their depositors. Excellent, if you are fortunate enough to enjoy such a special advantage.

The choice of the reason why is crucial, and it cannot be made in isolation from the facts. It is self-defeating for example to advance as a reason for doing business with your company that it is 'friendly and approachable', if your switchboard operator answers rudely and your receptionist never smiles.

The 'product difference' is another tool much sought after by the communicators. How does your company's Home Improvements Loan differ from your competitors' schemes, or if it is not actually very different, how can it legitimately be made to seem different? It is fairly easy to create a superficial visual difference, particularly if the scheme is presented as a package, complete with brand name, brochures and integrated sales promotion. But to be different only in superficial respects does not get you very far when there is a serious decision to be made by the customer. The problem is to find a product difference (or an image difference for the whole organisation, if the promotional approach is along corporate rather than product lines) which is both genuine and important enough to the reader for it to matter to him.

One school of advertising thought combines the concepts of customer benefit, reason why and product difference into one portmanteau phrase 'the unique selling proposition' (sometimes abbreviated as 'USP'). The essence of this theory, which developed out of the marketing of branded and packaged products, is that the communicator should find a central claim, which describes an important benefit to the user or purchaser of the product that he can find only in this one product. If this ideal combination of circumstances is not available, the recommended recourse is to be the first to fasten on to a claim which others could also well advance, and by constant reiteration identify it with yourself or your product. An example of this theory in action was the dogfood PAL, with was advertised with the slogan 'Prolongs Active Life'. This was not a unique claim. Much the same proposition could have been advanced for other brands of dog food, on the grounds that a dog which is not fed is unlikely to live very long, actively or otherwise. But it became identified with PAL, and not only because the initial letters coincided. 'Players

Please', 'Guinness is Good for you' are other examples from an earlier era.

A clear and simple message, an attention-getting device, a customer benefit, a reason why, a product difference – with these you begin to have the makings of an effective advertisement. Whenever feasible, one additional element should be added. This is a clear indication of the action the recipient of the message should take if you have persuaded him that you have something to offer. At one time it was thought undignified for financial services institutions to 'ask for the order'. The result was the practice of so-called 'tombstone advertising', which is still not wholly obsolete. This slightly morbid phrase describes accurately enough advertisements which record the name, address and capital resources of the institution in question, but add nothing else – not even RIP.

It may be that in these more competitive days fashions have swung too far in the direction of importuning the customer to come and buy; but that is a matter of tone and degree. Those on the receiving end of advertisements or other forms of sales promotion are in no doubt that whoever paid for the campaign is anxious to sell a product, a service or an idea. They are unlikely to be surprised or offended if the communication tells them what they should do if they're inclined to buy; whether to fill out a coupon, get in touch with a local manager or agent, or simply send for more information on the subject. Even an institutional campaign, designed for cumulative long-term effect, will not necessarily suffer from an invitation to take some short-term action.

So much for an individual advertisement or series of advertisements. If it is to develop into an effective campaign, two key watchwords need to be observed. The first is *simplicity* and the second is *repetition*. Simplicity has already been mentioned in relation to the message to be conveyed. It applies equally to the way in which the message is expressed. For most people, whether as individuals or as the managers of businesses – not to mention the politicians who supposedly steer our economy – finance is a horribly difficult and complicated subject. The financial services expert, who has spent a lifetime mastering its complexities, can very easily forget that what is now simple to him may be incomprehensible to his customers; and that the technical language he uses, rightly, in communicating with his peers will need to be translated into simpler terms when he seeks to communicate with the uninitiated. So it is wise to keep the *language* of communication as well as the message simple without being condescending.

For this reason it is as well, when embarking on an advertising or communications campaign, to prepare an agreed 'copy policy' setting out the essential message and the impression which has to be conveyed, in pretty specific terms. This provides a creative discipline which can be invoked, if an accretion of small improvements by individuals anxious to put in their two-pennyworth threatens to obscure the original message and intention of the campaign.

As for repetition, the communicator has to accept that however boring it may be for him to say the same thing over and over again, repetition plays an essential part in getting all but the most dramatic messages into the heads of an audience at least half of whom are only half listening. To avoid losing the attention of those who *are* listening in the first place, it may be advisable to express the message in different ways or through different media. But the gravest mistake in any otherwise effective advertising or sales promotional campaign, a mistake committed over and over again by advertisers worried about becoming bores, is not going on too long, but stopping or changing too soon. It is sometimes said that the advertising agency gets bored with an advertisement before it appears – the advertiser when it appears, the public never – because it is changed before they have even had a chance to read it? *It pays to standardise.*

Picking the right media

The marketing communicator with a defined message to convey and a target customer segment to aim at still has to make the choice of the most appropriate or cost-effective vehicle to carry the message. Depending on the size of his budget and the size and nature of his target, he will make his choice from a considerable range of media, each with its special characteristics.

If he has a large budget and is interested in reaching the bulk of the population he may well think first of television, in those countries where a commercial television is well established. It is a medium which combines the attention-getting attributes of sound, pictures, colour and movement; and it has repeatedly proved its capacity to stimulate a quick response. But it has its disadvantages in that it cannot easily sustain a long or complicated message which needs serious consideration; one or two basic ideas and a powerful atmosphere is the most that the normal commercial can convey. And it tends to be unselective in the audience it reaches; if your target customer segment is a narrow one you will have to pay for a lot of viewers you do not want in order to reach those you do want to communicate with.

Newspapers, particularly their financial pages, are obviously more selective. Each has its own more-or-less loyal readership, large or small; and each has different editorial characteristics, which can be expected to have some influence on the attitude of readers to the advertisements the pages carry. But they too have their limitations. The press is a difficult medium in which to create a dramatic effect, or to stand out as a financial services advertiser among the welter of competitors' advertising offering similar services in the financial sections of the most frequently used papers.

Magazines, particularly the specialist financial or trade and technical journals, have a still more narrowly defined readership. But advertising in them, though superficially inexpensive, can in fact be costly in proportion to the number of readers. Between these and newspapers it is a choice between expensive rifle shots and cheaper buck shot. You pay your money and you take your aim.

For the advertiser with a geographically restricted catchment area, posters, local radio, cinemas or the local press may be the most economical public media. But because of their nature, most posters can only carry a single headlined message; local radio is about as unselective as television in its audience; cinema-going is a habit which is more or less abandoned after the first flush of youth; and the amount of persuasive weight carried by most local papers is somewhat suspect.

Then there are the less obvious media, like direct mail, a particularly economical way for financial service institutions who must in any case communicate regularly with their customers, to inform customers of a new service or one that is particularly relevant to their individual requirements. (A well-organised financial services institution, with a well-programmed computer, should know enough about its customers not to mail suggestions for will appointments to teenagers, suggestions for dealing with the intricacies of inheritance tax to struggling newlyweds or offers of piggy banks to captains of industry.) As a means of reaching new customers, direct mail can be relatively costly unless the communication is sufficiently pursuasive and the mailing list sufficiently reliable to produce a 'good' response rate – i.e. one that is cost-effective.

Other media, often lumped together under the heading of 'below-the-line' are the leaflets, pamphlets, explanatory guides and manuals which can be used to support the selling activity on a particular service; point of sale display material, either two-dimensional or three-dimensional (in this electronic age mobile or audio-visual devices are beginning to take over from the humble showcard); the variety of visual or mechanical sales aids which can be used to help the salesmen make a more effective presentation; representation at shows and exhibitions; the sponsorship of cultural or sporting events which with luck and supporting publicity should shed some reflected glory on the sponsor; the organisation of training courses for customers' employees, with mixed educational and promotional motives; and a variety of other devices related wholly or partly to the furtherance of the company's business. How much of such activities can be put under the heading of advertising or promotion and how much should be regarded as a matter of public relations is an arguable question, as indeed is the relationship of the public relations function itself to marketing. (For banks, insurance companies and other financial services institutions, PR in its broader sense of creating and maintaining a high level of understanding and co-operation with all levels of the community from government downwards, is clearly of the first importance. But in the narrower sense of securing favourable mention in the media of the organisation, its management and its products, it can also be a valuable weapon in the armoury of marketing communications.)

How some of the various media listed above might prove useful is illustrated in Table 3 and Table 4 (overleaf). But it should be emphasised that the choice of media is not just a rule-of-thumb operation, nor can it safely be left entirely to the advertising agency's computer, which will tell you with a spurious air of precision that if you use this media schedule the average member of your target audience will have 7.83 opportunities to see your advertisement; whereas if you use that schedule, they will have only 6.29 opportunities to see it. The accuracy of the audience research on which the computer analysis is based is not always beyond dispute; and, more importantly, the factor of creative impact – how many of those opportunities are taken and lead to the desired action – gets left out of the sums. Reading and noting studies show that, commonly, only one in every five of those who have the opportunity do actually take it.

Selecting the best medium, or more often combination of media, to achieve a defined communications objective is as much an art as a mathematical science. But, whatever the balance, it is important to pick the particular media which at least reach the target audience. *It pays to plan.*

Table 3. Communications grid – 1

MESSAGES	AUDIENCES			
	Company staff	Prospective customers	Government	Share-holders
Good to work for	✔			
Makes good profits				✔
Good products or services		✔		
Socially responsible			✔	

While there will be many messages the company wants to transmit, and many audiences it will want to reach, not every message is equally relevant to each audience.

Measuring cost-effectiveness

We have already emphasised the importance in principle of making sure that the results of a marketing communications exercise justify the cost. But it would be wrong to disguise the fact that converting principle into practice presents certain difficulties. There are some forms of advertising, most particularly so-called 'direct response advertising', where precise measurement is quite easy. If you run an advertisement inviting people to write in for particulars of a new unit trust you can use keyed coupons to measure what percentage of the coupons were returned; and you can go on from there to measure the proportion of those returning coupons who ended up buying and paying for the product. Even in that case, of course, the effectiveness of the *offer* rather than the effectiveness of the *advertising* may be the main factor determining reponse rate. The same principle applies to direct mail advertising. But keyed coupons (i.e. coupons which include an identification of the medium used, its date, etc.) do enable you to compare media, even if none turns out to be effective enough.

Table 4. Communications grid – 2. The 'Prospective customers/good products or services' cell enlarged

Messages	Prospective customers			
	Accountants			Others
	in practice	in smaller businesses	in large companies	
We give fast service	Direct mail; advertisements*	Advertisements* PR	Direct mail; telephone calls	etc.
We have standard prices	Not relevant	Advertisements*	Not relevant	etc.
We are friendly and helpful	Diaries	PR	Lunches	etc.

This example is designed simply to suggest that the 'how' of getting a message to a relevant audience can take many forms. The 'hows', or channels of communication, are almost limitless in number.

* Of course different advertisements, different at least in their copy, may well be needed to communicate each message.

But it is very much harder to get any reliable measurement of cost-effectiveness when advertising or other marketing communications activities are only part of a long-term drive to change people's attitudes and behaviour. In such cases it is very difficult both to measure what may be quite a slow rate of change and to disentangle the element which is attributable to the communications effort from all the other contributory factors. The communicator who wants to assess cost-effectiveness has to fall back on intermediate measurements such as the proportion of people who can recall the advertising message; or the relative standing of his organisation among a target group, where 'standing' is based on several factors such as 'friendliness', 'success', 'social acceptability'; or on the tenor of commments made about his company in the media; or on a number of other surrogate measurements which specialists in communications research will advocate from time to time.

None of these approaches is wholly satisfactory but they are all better than simply hoping for the best.

What it comes down to is that in all but a limited set of circumstances definitive appraisal of cost-effectiveness is impossible. Not only because it is difficult to separate the effect of various strands of the total communications package, but also because some effects take a long time to show through, so the benefits come long after the investment (and every reader of this book will know the difficulties of assessing investments). One must look carefully at all the evidence and try to peer into the future. So too with communications. *It pays to scrutinise.*

Setting budgets

Finally there is the question of what funds to put into an advertising/promotion/PR/communications programme. Ideally you would set the goals to be reached, work out the cost of reaching them and the total would be your budget. Of course, life is not at all like that, not least because in a competitive world the goalposts keep moving. 'To be as well known as competitor X' may sound all right as an objective; but it is impossible to respond to and plan for if competitor X is himself moving, or planning to move, in directions unknown to you.

In practice, communications budgets are normally set in relation to last year's expenditure (updated for the nowadays inevitable inflation) modified by considerations of 'affordability'. If the computer has to be replaced, advertising may have to be cut, along with other costs, to pay for the replacement. Such a decision may well be absolutely correct. Indeed, even a highly marketing-oriented senior management has to balance a number of demands for resources, and cannot accord an unquestioned priority to the communications function. But given a budget, it is fortunately not all that difficult to sort out how much to allocate to the various elements in the marketing communications programme. What is important is to ensure that all the elements pull in the same direction. *It pays to co-ordinate.*

Who said that?

One of the more irritating outcomes of communications research is for researchers to find a good level of 'recall' for the advertising message but also to find that it is attributed to the wrong company. This happens quite frequently to new entrants to a market dominated by some long-established name; a quite substantial proportion of casual readers attribute the new entrant's advertising, and the new benefits he is offering, to the old-established competitor the newcomer is aiming to dislodge. So whatever other deficiencies your advertisement, brochure or sales letter may have, do make sure that there can be no doubt about the name of your company. Name registration associated with an action-provoking or attitude-changing message is the ideal; but name registration in a vaguely favourable context is better than nothing. After all, its *your* money. *It pays to be identified.*

Summary

In this chapter we have emphasised the need for the communicator to get quite clear in his mind (and the minds of those working with him) what categories of individuals he wants to reach, what action or change of attitude he wants to bring about, and whether the desired effect, if achieved, will be worth the cost.

We discussed the essential principles of designing the message: keep it simple, attract attention, state a customer benefit, give a reason why, indicate a 'product difference', and whenever possible ask for the order.

We said also that in extending a single advertisement or mailing shot into a campaign it is of primary importance to keep the underlying message clear and to keep on repeating it, though not necessarily in identical words. To ensure continuity of theme it is a good idea to record the basic campaign message in a formal, written 'copy policy'.

We suggested that, because every message will not be equally relevant to every target audience, the use of a 'communications grid' can help to systematise the whole communications programme.

We outlined very briefly the salient characteristics of the main media through which the communicator can choose to convey his message(s). We mentioned the availability of computer-based schedule analysis services, observing that while it is obviously prudent to use all the aids to cost-effective media selection that are available, the computer should not be relied on unreservedly to measure the cost-effectiveness of an advertising campaign. Arriving at the optimum mix of media and message involves more than arithmetical analysis. The campaign, we have said, should be evaluated as nearly as possible in terms of *total* effect and *total* benefit.

We added a final word on the importance of name registration, without which any communications expenditure is wasted.

CHAPTER FOURTEEN

Internal communications

Of all the topics covered in this book, internal communications is the most likely to evoke the response 'So what? That's commonsense, we do that already', or 'my people do what they're told!' It is probably true that only well-run organisations will already devote considerable thought and effort in this area. But what we mean is that a consistent, structured, well-planned, and above all recipient-oriented communication pro-gramme is very, very important. Indeed, we have not attempted to disguise the fact that, although new marketing initiatives are essential if a company wants to grow, or indeed in the long run to survive, the majority of such initiatives fail to achieve fully the objectives their originators had in mind. Whether the failure rate is two out of three or nine out of ten, or some other figure, depends on the stage in their life-cycle at which the initiatives are evaluated and the severity of the criteria used in the evaluation.

In fact formal evaluation is not as frequent as it should be; managers, like doctors, prefer to bury their mistakes. But in many, if not the majority of cases a totally honest evaluation would show that a failure of *internal* communications has been a large contributory factor in the failure of the whole project. The product or service itself may be well designed to meet a customer need, well presented and competitively priced; the external communications may be soundly planned and efficiently executed. But if the various members of the organisation responsible for selling and sales promotion, or the many other necessary support services, do not understand or believe in the product, it will not be as successful as it should be. Nor will an initial success be sustained and built on if there is not continuing provision for reporting progress and sustaining interest among all those involved.

A personal experience in checking the progress of a savings scheme launched by an Irish banking group is typical. The writer approached the cashier in one of the bank's branches enquiring whether he could open a savings account with them (a pretty small account it would have been, given the state of his finances). She was a sweet girl and honest to a fault. 'Oh, I wouldn't lodge it here if I were you,' she said, 'you get a much better rate of interest at the savings bank down the road.' She was of course right. But there were arguments other than the rate offered which were in favour of the bank's scheme and they had clearly not been effectively communicated to her.

One of the first things a manager at any level should think about, when initiating a scheme either to increase sales of an existing service or to introduce a new service, is the question *who* within the organisation will be in a position to influence its sales for better or for worse; and *how* best to get them wholeheartedly on his side. This is likely to involve communication upwards to superiors (few people are in a position to say as Harry Truman did that 'the buck stops here'); sideways to equals whose co-operation must be secured by persuasion; and downwards to subordinates who must also be convinced by explanation and persuasion.

Communicating upwards

In the plainest terms, if you do not secure the understanding and continuing support of your boss and perhaps of those above him for your project, you will have deprived yourself of an invaluable asset, particularly if the going should get rough. But your boss has a lot more to worry about than you and your goings on. Failure to think through the implications of those two salient facts has damaged the careers of many otherwise bright young men and women.

Yet the implications are so obvious if you put yourself into your boss's shoes, and after all, empathy is a natural requirement of all good marketing people. He needs all the help you can give him in making the right decision fast; and he needs assurance that it really is the right decision, so that if he is challenged about it he can feel confident that he knows and can explain what is going on.

Hence the need for communications, whether written, oral or visual, to be clear, brief and to the point. Winston Churchill's famous request during the second world war. 'Pray tell me on one half sheet of paper', may not always be feasible in a complex situation. But it is an ideal to be aimed at. At least remember that every manager in some degree is fighting a continuous war; and that endless rambling essays, designed to show how thorough and how clever you have been, are likely to backfire.

Bosses have their idiosyncratic methods, which would repay studying. But if you put yourself in the place of your typical general manager or marketing manager (a place that you no doubt aspire to occupy in due course), exposed to the marketing proposals and projects of a lot of bright young men and women, you will probably look for a brief but convincing answers to some such list of questions as the following.

1 What is the problem to be solved or objective to be achieved?
2 What do you propose to do?
3 How?
4 Who in the organisation will be expected to do what?
5 How much will it cost?
6 What is the benefit if it succeeds?
7 What are the penalties if it fails?
8 How will you check progress, and keep me informed?
9 What do you want *me* to do now?

The extent to which you as the boss would want to study the evidence or dig into the details of the project would vary, depending on the importance of the project. If the project were a relatively unimportant one, and you had confidence in the bright young male or female, you would probably take it as read. More often, you would either want to ask a few probing questions just to make sure that the bright young male or female *had* collected all the evidence and *had* thought the project through; or you might want the supporting evidence and details to be attached to the proposal in a series of appendices and supplementary documents which you could either read or just skim through. What you would not want is to be forced to plough through pages and pages of blether in order to extract the significant points. What you would look for is a direct simple *solution* to the problem, not an endless account of the problem itself; you have enough of your own. (We go into this topic in more detail in Appendix III.)

Communicating downwards

The days when a boss could say to his subordinate 'Go thou', and he goeth, are long passed in our egalitarian western society. Nowadays if a manager says 'Go thou' too roughly, his subordinate goeth all right, probably to his shop steward to lodge a complaint. How far this is an overdue recognition of the fact that all men (and women) are equal, and how far a brake on efficient management, is immaterial; it is a fact which must be allowed for in the way management communications are transmitted down the line. There must be just as much awareness of the need for downstream persuasion and explanation as there is in upwards communication. If not more.

In the marketing context, management communications are likely in most cases to revolve around new devices for marketing existing services, special sales drives and promotions, or the introduction of new or 'repackaged' services. For this the first essential is *'product knowledge'* i.e. the individuals who are being asked to sell, identify opportunities for selling, or simply recommending new products will not get very far unless they understand the benefits of the product or service well enough to be able to explain them clearly to others. In a financial services organisation, whose stock in trade is to have a product available to meet every identifiable customer need in the financial area, this is more easily said than done. It may salve the communicator's conscience to put a full technical description of the new service on paper, and add it as service number 937 in a fat manual. But fat manuals mostly do not get read. So it may seem sensible for a company to segment its selling organisation and to ask individuals to master only a narrow range of services. That can sometimes help, but it is dangerous unless the generalists in the organisation, and those who provide back-up services, are not only fully aware of more than merely the broad outlines of the services concerned, but also available when they are required.

The best practical solution to an almost insoluble problem is to be as clear and simple as possible in the basic description; to supplement written descriptions when possible with personal briefings, or some form of audio-visual communications as described later in this chapter. Internal spadework of this kind, supplemented by clear guidance on where the individual who gets out of his depth can refer enquiries, will at least reduce the risk that a blank stare will greet any customer who is spurred to action by the advertising or other promotion for a new service and tries to buy it.

A second principle in downwards communication is to *secure and sustain the interest* of all those who should understand and act on the communication. This essentially means that the communication should be presented in human terms, related so far as possible to the personal experience of the recipients, and therefore be understandable, and specify the benefits it will generate both for customers and for the organisation. It also means that a single communication will probably not be adequate.

A programme of reminders reporting progress, success stories and mod-ifications in the product or marketing plan (if any) can be as important for effective internal communications as for external advertising campaigns.

A third principle is to *be as specific as possible about individual tasks and objectives.* If a manager says vaguely that 'We are confident that we can count on your local co-operation in doing your best to publicise and sell this outstanding new service' he will not have much to count at the end of the day. If he says to individuals that 'I am looking for ten enquiries and three firm orders from you each month and will expect a monthly report of your progress against target' he can hope for results.

The fourth principle to consider is that of *motivation*. Why should the individuals down the line do what you ask with any real enthusiasm? At one time salesmen of manufactured products were very directly motivated, since they were remunerated largely or wholly by commission on sales; if they didn't sell they didn't eat. That is no longer the case in most manufacturing companies, since it has been recognised that selling is a complex operation which does not depend solely on the eloquence of the salesmen. Selling on commission would never have been appropriate in a responsible financial services organisation and it is seldom found today (though it is occasionally practised in exceptional or even disreput-able circumstances). In general it is very rightly felt that the salesman of financial services should not be encouraged to disregard the welfare of the prospective customer by making it a life-or-death matter for him to conclude the sale.

Of course, being paid will always be important, and reward for effort an acknowledged spur. But if money is not to be the only motivator, what should be added, and in what proportions? Pursuing this question too far would get us into deep water, beyond the scope of marketing, since it relates to an organisation's whole policy of personnel development and remuneration. But money can be a considerable help if the organi-sation operates some version of Management by Objectives, whereby individuals are set performance goals and have regular meetings with their superiors at which the degree of success achieved in pursuing the goals is discussed, with subsequent repercussions on merit payments or promotion prospects. In the financial services organisation few of the large number of jobs which have some marketing content are concerned purely with selling; so the ranking of selling in the hierarchy of goals specified for the individual may not be particularly high. But provided it is there, and taken seriously, its inclusion in the crucial performance discussions can be an effective motivating factor. On a less formal basis localised competitions can be organised; and if all else fails, a simple 'thank you', a phrase too often forgotten in the large organisation, can work wonders.

Whatever form of motivation is introduced, downward communication is seldom really effective in the marketing context if it is a one-way traffic. However well thought out and well researched a marketing project may be, it is impossible to anticipate all the detailed problems which will arise at the final interface between company and customer; or to foresee the progressive changes which may occur in the ever-changing market place.

So feedback from the front line is of vital importance to the marketing executive or manager who wants to improve his plan of action. Feedback developing into a dialogue, has furthermore, a role in increasing motivation. There will be a better, more imaginative, contribution by those directly concerned with selling if they can feel that their problems are understood and responded to.

Lateral communications

In many marketing organisations, as we said in an earlier chapter, those concerned directly and full-time with marketing are likely to be in a staff rather than a line job. For them effective communication with other managers at roughly the same level is vitally important. A marketing project or package that is no more than a selling proposition will not succeed. It has to be an integrated part of the organisation's operational system. For this purpose the support of line management is certainly essential; but so also is the support of the various service departments. An administrative muddle or a failure in computer programming can kill a project just as effectively as failure to impress the customer.

So the project manager has to think very clearly about the departments or individuals in these areas who need to be not only infomed but also persuaded, if not to support the project enthusiastically, at least not to undermine it.

In this aspect of communications, securing and sustaining interests can be even harder than in the upwards/downwards context, since the contribution of effort or readjustment that is required from those involved may offer no obvious reward for them. It is just another chore.

Even so it is very well worthwhile spending time to explain precisely what contribution is needed from the department or individual concerned, the reason why it is needed, and ways in which the practical problems, real or imagined, can be overcome. Networks (see Appendix II) can be very helpful here.

Finally, never forget that the marketing man needs a sense of proportion as well as persuasiveness in his internal communications. Using the squeaky wheel principle (of getting colleagues to yield up the oil of co-operation rather than endure the noise), he should insist on getting the help he needs; but the wheel should not squeak so loudly that it upsets the whole applecart.

The means of internal communication

Organisations in the financial services field are addicted, for obvious reasons, to written communication. Get it in writing and the responsibility for any slip-up can be clearly identified. But (as writers we hate saying it), writing alone is seldom the best way of conveying information or securing action. Teachers and other communicators have long been aware that a combination of the written and spoken word, (even the old-fashioned lecturer with his blackboard, indulging in 'chalk and talk') is more effective than either in isolation. If pictures can be added to the written and the spoken word, and if on top of that the pictures move, there is a pretty good chance that even an originally uninvolved audience will get hooked. Hence the increasing interest of the educational system in closed-circuit television and audio-visual cassettes as a reinforcement of the teachers' own efforts to communicate.

There is no need, in a financial services context, to argue the case for electronic communication. With computer terminals and visual display units, the most confirmed addicts of traditional methods have modern technology thrust upon them. But this does not always mean that good use is made of the available range of technological aids in communicating marketing information or stimulating marketing action. There is quite conclusive experimental evidence, for example, that the salient points of, say, a new insurance policy will be more quickly grasped by the company's salesmen if the general manager and underwriter communicate them personally (or as good as personally) via audio-visual cassettes or closed-circuit television. It can be expensive, at least in terms of the initial capital investment; and a supplementary written description will be needed to deal with the small print. But even if the managers concerned are not the greatest of actors, more of the essential points will penetrate and stick.

This is not intended as special pleading for communication by cassette, though undoubtedly this medium will grow until it is superseded by some more modern or inter-active method, such as audio-visual discs. It is, rather, a plea that those concerned with internal marketing communications should think just as hard about the most cost-effective medium, or combination of media, for the job in hand as they would in planning an external advertising campaign. It is unlikely that the communicators will ever devise anything to beat the face-to-face interview, supplemented by visual aids when appropriate. But the range of available alternatives or supplements is growing all the time.

Towards an information and communications system

It would be easy to say that an organisation cannot have too much marketing information or communicate it too widely. But of course it is only too easy to have overkill in this area as in any other. The productivity of the computer in particular is a constant temptation to inform everybody about everything, and thus ensure that nothing will be assimilated and acted on. So as well as thinking what to communicate to whom and how, it is just as important also to think about what *not* to communicate in order to leave people with some time for thought and action.

This means devising and constantly improving a system whereby an input of information is organised, filtered, stored and then fed out to those who can trigger, initiate or modify action in the light of the information. The number of subject areas covered by the information will increase and the detail diminish as the individual becomes more senior and less specialised. But there should always be provision for more detail to be provided on request.

Establishing such a system can take months or years of work, if it is planned thoroughly enough to include analysis of individual needs, the design of regular forms (for example, salesmen's report forms; consistency of format and regularity of reporting add enormously to the usability of information), and indoctrination in converting information into action.

And major changes in organisational structure can leave it all to be done again.

But it is still worth doing.

Summary

In this chapter we have said that effective internal communications are vital, meaning not gossip, not routine exchanges, but purposeful, persuasive, action-oriented communications; and that a breakdown in them is one of the most frequent reasons for the failure of otherwise valid marketing projects.

We have also discussed and described the three directions of communication – upwards, downwards and lateral – emphasising the importance of deciding who needs to be persuaded to do what; and how much information needs to be communicated in what form both to achieve the required short-term action, and to maintain continued interest and support over the long haul.

We have said that although the written word, clearly, sensitively and succinctly written, will retain its importance in internal communications, there are other available media, particularly the proliferating audio-visual devices, which will help in developing an effective internal 'communications mix'.

CHAPTER FIFTEEN

Some problems of pricing

Of course the price one pays for any product or service is relevant and may even be important. But it is very seldom 'all important'. Indeed cheapness is sometimes seen as a disadvantage by the purchaser. Nevertheless pricing is near the heart of marketing strategy if for no other reason than its direct link to profitability. A scientific approach can be helpful – and we give an example later – but pricing always was, and remains, part of the *art* of marketing.

The generalities are easy. First, price is a very powerful marketing tool. In a now highly competitive but once cartelised market like financial services – where it is difficult to create and sustain either a true 'product plus' or a conspicuous advantage over competitors in the level of service delivered – it is tempting, though dangerous, to regard price as the only effective competititve weapon and to precipitate a price war which in the end benefits nobody.

Second, as every marketing textbook will tell you, price should be based on customer demand as expressed through a market mechanism rather than on the cost of producing the goods or services in question. This is true, but only a half-truth, even in theory. Production costs must come into it since companies which sell their range of products for less than it costs to produce and market them, will not survive very long; and companies which charge a great deal more than the cost of efficient production and marketing are simply asking to have their business taken away from them by more realistic competitors. (Even apparent monopolies and theoretically watertight patents are seldom more than a delaying factor, since it is almost always possible to find another way to satisfy a genuine need.)

Third, pricing policy should be flexible, taking particular account of the factors of market segmentation and product life-cycle described earlier in this book. In some market or customer segments, quite clearly, price is a less crucial factor than in others (or, if you like, price elasticity of demand is lower). A marginal 20 per cent added to the price of a Rolls-Royce will probably not bother its fortunate purchasers too much; if anything it may enhance their feeling of superiority to the common herd who cannot afford such prestige symbols. But 20 per cent added to the price of a small family saloon, when competitors were holding their prices, could be catastrophic.

In banking we can see a very wide range of price sensitivities, one of the factors that makes banking so interesting. When it comes to buying money from or lending it to large companies which maintain accounts at more than one bank, price is a very senstive matter. That is one reason why base rates move in line, and why no single bank can stay out of line for long. At the other end of the scale, customer loyalty makes the price of services to individuals a very much less dominant factor in their choice of bank.

Similarly a new product or service, representing a real advance in customer benefit, can command a premium price early in its life-cycle (when costs are high and competitors have not yet caught up); but both price and costs will probably need to be reduced, if and when success attracts serious competition.

The point that a company needs some high profit margin products, not only to provide funds for investment in the future but to offset the products which, for one reason or another, have to be marketed at narrow margins, seems not to have been grasped by the various government bodies which have, from time to time, attempted to regulate prices. They appear to regard price from a moralistic rather than a practical viewpoint. But it is a particularly relevant point in many multi-product industries, including the British banking industry, which for many years has provided its basic personal current account service at or below cost.

The exposure of pricing policies to particularly searching government scrutiny is only one of the factors which makes the specifics of pricing *practice* in the financial services industry very much more difficult than the generalities of pricing theory. There is also the problem that the 'production cost' for an individual service is never an immovable point, fixed beyond all reasonable argument, on which the market price strategist can take his bearings. In an organisation with high overheads (in people, premises and so on) and relatively low variable costs, the way in which those overheads are allocated between the services has a major effect on the 'cost' of an individual service. It can be claimed that the accountancy profession has its 'laws' about the allocation of overheads. But as Lord Brougham said, 'If you would have your laws obeyed, see well that they are God's laws'; and accountants have adjusted their principles too often in recent years to inspire any confidence that they sit on the right hand of God. A new service can look very profitable, marginally profitable or distinctly unprofitable depending on the decision whether to allocate its share of overheads on the basis of variable costs, proportion of turnover or estimated load on executive time, space and so on. Indeed even with an identical set of rules by which the 'allocation' of 'overheads' is decided, say in proportion to funds lent, the actual charge on Product A can swing simply because of a change in the volume of sales of Product B; for example, home sales can benefit from extra exports. Is this proper? And should it influence the market price?

Moreover, the risk factor looms very much larger in the case of institutions which depend heavily on buying and selling credit, and whose main stock in trade is security, than it does in the case of manufacturing companies whose transactions are over and done with in a short space of time. The unacceptable risk of borrowing short and lending long is drummed into every young banker from the start of his career. The duration as well as the magnitude of risk has to be reflected in the price paid for borrowings or charged for loans. But how to calculate the 'right' price is a question which calls for experienced judgment as well as analysis of all the relevant facts. And of course it is a truism that it is risk-taking, in one form or another, that leads to profit.

But rather than carrying on about the difficulties, it would be more constructive of us to illustrate the ways in which the difficulties have been tackled in the context of the London clearing banks. (There are no absolutes in pricing policy; the problem *has* to be considered in context.)

First of all we should differentiate between those services for which prices are fixed centrally, singly, or in the form of a range of prices, and (as a rule) published; and those for which prices are negotiated individually with the customers concerned. For the main banking services, the position is normally as follows:

Fixed centrally
personal current accounts
deposit accounts
trustee and taxation
factoring
leasing
personal fixed term loans

Negotiated individually
business current accounts
overdrafts
merchant banking
international services
loans (fixed rate or base rate plus)

Pricing a basic service

In the centrally fixed sector, the 'price' charged for personal current accounts is a particularly complex question. It is an area where the competition enjoined by the Bank of England's 1971 document on 'Competition and Credit Control' can be particularly conspicuous, since almost everybody who had dealings, either personal or commercial, with a bank will have a personal current account. For just that reason it can be argued that the current account can legitimately be regarded as a low margin or even loss leader service (comparable to the introductory offers familiar in other markets), provided that the size of the margin either way is quantified and controlled.

But the argument that a keenly priced basic service will generate goodwill and attract new customers to the bank concerned collapses if a significant proportion of account holders feel that they are being discriminated against; and there are wide variations in account usage between the heavy users who take full advantage of most of the available current account services, listed below, and the light users who often are not even aware of the range of services they could call on.

Current account services
cheque cashing facilities
clearing other cheques
standing orders/direct debits
other debit items

credits
statements of account
a cheque guarantee card
a cash card
a credit card
safe custody facilities
a secure home for cash
financial advice
miscellaneous other services

So the marketing strategist is torn between the desire to have a simple price structure, which is easy to administer and to dramatise in advertising and sales promotion; and a reluctance to subsidise the heavy users at the expense of the light users.

In 1973, when competition for current accounts was hotting up, one of the smaller clearing banks resolved to stop playing follow-my-leader and strike out on an independent pricing policy, but to do so only after thorough investigation of the cost implications.

The first step was to ascertain the facts about the use made of current accounts by the bank's customers. Accordingly a sample of accounts was drawn from all of the bank's branches and quantitative data collected on the major variables affecting the cost of account handling:

number of automated credit entries
number of unautomated credit entries
number of automated debit entries
number of unautomated debit entries
average credit balance
minimum balance
debit turnover.

Whenever possible, the totals of and ratios among the key variables were validated against available computer-based 'census' information, to ensure that the sample did not differ significantly from the total customer population.

A price structure model was then made and programmed for use on a computer incorporating the data from the sample, in order to measure the sensitivity of revenue to changes in the charging basis. The outcome was the matrix illustrated in Table 5 (actual figures are omitted).

Table 5. Sensitivity of revenue to changes in the charging basis

	SENSITIVITY		
	High	Medium	Low
V A R I A B L E S	Charge per unautomated item	Charge per credit item	Charge per automated item
	Notional allowance on average credit balance	Level of average credit balance above which all charges are waived	Level of minimum balance above which all charges are waived
	Interest actually paid on any credit balance – minimum or average		Level of charges below which they are waived
			Notional allowance on minimum credit balance*

* Up to average credit balances of a few hundred pounds

Armed with factually based estimates of the likely effect on revenue of various charging formulae, the bank's management took the bold initiative of announcing the introduction of 'free banking'. More specifically, existing and new customers were told that if an account was maintained wholly in credit for a charging period (three months) no charge would be levied; otherwise a charge of 6p would be made for each automated item and 8p for each unautomated item, less a notional allowance equal to 5 per cent of the average credit balance, with charges of under 20p being waived.

In the event, the actual cost of the 'free banking' offer fell within the predicted limits and was more than justified by the benefit that accrued to the bank in terms of new customers and favourable publicity.

Pricing a subsidiary service

When the question of introducing a new or substantially redeveloped subsidiary service arises there will be little or no relevant historical data on costings. So the pricing strategist can feel freer to tackle the question, along orthodox marketing lines by first seeking to establish what the optimum marketing price should be and then working back to estimate affordable 'production' and marketing cost figures.

The first step from this starting point is to identify all existing competitive products (your own as well as those of competitors) which offer more or less the same customer benefits and to plot their prices. Unless it is a very unusual market, or one in which very few suppliers operate, there will probably be a range of prices, from the premium-priced services which claim some special or exclusive features down to those which base their sales appeal on a low price.

The second step is to determine approximately where in the hierarchy of prices the new product or service should be positioned, bearing in mind the special features or advantages which should justify its introduction. Consumer research can help to some extent with this. It should be possible to establish by talking to a representative sample of prospective customers – indeed, it already should have been established in the process of product development – how important the special features are, relative to the basic features which are common to most of the competing services. But it is not easy to quantify through this type of research just how much extra the customer would be prepared to pay for the special features. Hypothetical questions along the lines of 'Would you pay x pounds more or y pounds more?' encourage a hypothetical open-handedness which is apt to evaporate when people are invited to put their hands in their pockets in real earnest. So it is prudent, when possible, to set up a test marketing situation where actual packages are sold for actual money.

The third step, which will usually be concurrent with the second rather than following after it, will be to estimate the volume of sales which is achievable at the target price level, and calculate the related costings. There will be two categories of cost to consider: the fixed costs (or more or less fixed) of providing the service, and the variable costs of the raw material required (in the case of financial services this will basically be money), plus the planned expenditure on marketing it. As has been said earlier, the costs of administration and so on are partly factual, in terms of the additional workload on service departments which the new 'product' will generate, partly negotiable to the extent that a marginal costing approach may be agreed when there is under-utilised capacity in the organisation. The cost of money will vary both in direct ratio to sales of the new product and in response to the supply and demand situation for that type of money in the market place. The level of marketing expenditure is the only factor controllable by the marketing planner, and even this only within limits. There is no sense, for example, in settling on an unrealistically low level of sales and sales promotional expenditure simply to try and balance the books.

The fourth step is to juggle the inter-related variables of price, volume and marketing expenditure so as to maximise the net profit accruing to the company. The calculation needs to take into account both the time-scale over which the profit materialises (if there is a long wait, discounting principles will need to be applied) and the possible loss of revenue to other services in the bank's range adjacent to the new 'product'. Whether the calculations are done on a computerised model or on the back of an envelope will depend on the importance of the product and on the availability of data to support the assumptions which have to be made. There is not much point in mounting an elaborate statistical exercise when the amount at risk is not large and most of the relevant assumptions are no better than informed guesses.

In either case a fifth step is essential. If the sums work out, a price is agreed and the product is launched, into a test market or broadscale. The essential step then is to monitor the actual outcome against the assumptions and to take corrective action, whether by reducing the price or increasing the selling and sales promotional pressure, if results fall behind expectations. Since it is a rare experience for things to go according to plan, let alone better than expected, it is a reasonable rule of thumb when hesitating between two prices to pick the higher. It is always easier to reduce the price than to raise it; a high price leaves room for special discounts or deals with major customers; and in any case it is likely that the price will have to be reduced at a later stage in the product's life-cycle.

Pricing off the cuff

Any attempt at a 'scientific' approach to pricing recedes still further into the background in the situations, not all that infrequent in the marketing of financial services, where a responsible manager or businss development officer has to negotiate a fee or a charge more or less on the spot. There are usually guidelines or precedents in such cases, but there is still elbow room for the individual concerned to decide on the appropriate figure between the parameters laid down; or to blend two types of arrangement – for example an overdraft and a term loan – to produce a weighted average.

It would be easy to say simply that arriving at the right result in such cases is a question of 'experienced judgment' and leave it at that. But without decrying the value of experience or the importance of judgment we would argue that those who get it right most of the time are using instead of a computer, their *minds* (in themselves no mean computers, though with less reliable memories) to review the main questions which would be covered more elaborately by a computerised model.

1 What is the range of 'going rates' for this service?
2 What is the approximate cost to the company of providing it?
3 What are the cost sensitivities?
4 What, on previous experience, is the likely risk?
5 How important is this customer's (or this group of customers') business to the company?
6 How important is it to him/them to obtain this service from us?
7 How near the top of the 'going rate' range can I pitch the figure without prompting him/them to shop elsewhere?
8 How great is *his* 'experienced judgment'?

All that this adds up to, you may say, is an admonition to charge what the traffic will bear. Up to a point this is true. So long as banks and insurance companies continue to be commercial organisations they have an obligation to earn sufficient profit to cover their costs, including the costs of retaining their shareholders' funds, provide the safety margin which enables them to back risky ventures and smooth out rough passages, and provide resources for all the other things necessary to ensure the long-term stability of the company. Walking too narrow a tightrope between cost and price will not acheive this.

But there are three factors which would quickly quash any impulse to pitch the price too high. The first is competition; the second is the normal desire to stay in business for the indefinite future, and not to imperil that future for the sake of a quick buck; the third is a deep-seated concern to protect a reputation for probity and fair dealing, which is the most important asset of any financial services organisation.

Summary

In this chapter we have said that the orthodox marketing approach to pricing policy is to start from the end of customer demand (what the customer is prepared to pay for the benefit he receives) rather than from the more traditional end of calculating production costs and adding a 'reasonable' margin for selling costs and profit.

But in practice the question of cost *must* be considered, for the obvious reasons that prices too close to the cost of producing, administering and marketing a company's services will lead to bankruptcy; and prices too far above costs will invite competition to take the business away. We have also drawn attention to the difficulties which arise when a significant proportion of costs are indirect and have been – more or less arbitarily – allocated to a service.

We have described three representative pricing situations, among the many that confront any multi-product financial services organisation and have argued that, although the processes of arriving at the optimum solution may differ, the factors to be considered are much the same.

PART THREE

Marketing in action

In the six years since the first edition of this book was published, the marketing practices of UK banks have developed greatly in scope and sophistication.

It was difficult in 1980 to find case histories with a beginning a middle and an end that exemplified all the principles of coordinated marketing – preliminary research, product development, targeted selling, sales promotion and systematic monitoring of results.

Now, coordinated projects of this kind are standard practice in all major banks in relation both to the development of traditional banking business and to the banks' incursions into related financial services.

We have therefore assembled an entirely new collection of case studies (with one exception – which has been updated) to illustrate the way bank marketing departments go about their business in 1986 and the ways in which they are organised to achieve the best results.

The best results, that is, in current circumstances. The organisations listed below, for whose cooperation in providing case histories we are most grateful, left us in no doubt about their belief that in 1990 the state of the art would be different once again.

We are indebted to the managements of:

Barclays Bank plc
Charterhouse Japhet plc
The Joint Credit Card Company Ltd
Lloyds Bank plc
National Westminster Bank plc
The Royal Bank of Scotland Group
Standard Chartered Bank plc
Trustee Savings Bank Scotland
TSB Trust Company Ltd
Yorkshire Bank plc

CHAPTER SIXTEEN

Product marketing

Banking is sometimes described as just another form of retailing, with packaged services sold across the counter, in much the same way as grocery products used to be sold before the advent of self-service. The analogy can be misleading. The service and fiduciary aspects of banking make the customer relationship very different from the quick transactions of fast moving consumer goods businesses.

But many of the marketing techniques familiar in retail business have been adapted to bank marketing, particularly those of customer segmentation, product development and targeted promotion within a coordinated business development project.

In this chapter we describe four such projects, two of them savings 'products' aimed at attracting the savings of children, in the hope that they will grow up to become permanent customers of the bank concerned; one aimed at attracting adult deposits by offering high rates of interest; and one aimed at simplifying the process of obtaining business loans. All were attacking market sectors as competitive as washing powders or packaged holidays, with the same need for product differentiation.

SUPERSAVERS

The reason why all the large UK clearing banks are so generous in their offers to students and other young people is that, whether through loyalty or simple inertia, individuals usually remain for the rest of their lives with the bank (not necessarily the branch) where they first opened an account. Though the proportion is likely to decline with increasing competition (and something like 12% of students are enterprising enough to keep accounts – and no doubt overdrafts – with more than one bank) around 78% of current account holders have never transferred their accounts. So it makes sense to invest in attracting student customers, and to tolerate the unprofitability of handling their accounts in the expectation that they will complete a lifetime association on the right side of the ledger.

But if student customers make sense, doesn't it also make sense to catch them still younger – particularly if their accounts can be handled economically while they are still on the parental payroll? Barclays Bank was the first British bank to make a serious effort to attract the custom of the pre-student population as part of its segmented cradle to grave marketing strategy.

The vehicle developed for what was to become a long-term campaign was Barclays Supersavers Account launched in July 1982 and aimed at the 7–17 age group. Developing the product itself placed no great strain on the marketing department's ingenuity or the bank's systems infrastructure; the account was in fact an enhanced version of the standard 7-day deposit account. Where creativity was needed was in defining and communicating the benefits of the account both to the juvenile target audience and to their parents; and in sustaining accountholders' interest through the many changes of lifestyle between the ages of 7 and 17. It was also important to secure the active support and involvement of branch staffs, whose relationship with customers can tip the balance between a successful project and a flop.

The customer benefit was set out in a leaflet, written simply and clearly enough to be understandable to the 7 year old without appearing patronising to the 14 year old. The current version of the leaflet states clearly that 'it only takes £1 to open your account', that 'you'll always take out more than you put in' (because interest is worked out daily), that 'there are over 2,000 branches of Barclays where you can pay money into your account', that 'you can take out as little or as much of your savings in cash whenever you like', that you will 'know how much you've saved' from a six-monthly computer statement, and that 'in many of our branches you'll find a Receptionist or a team of Personal Bankers who'll be happy to help you with any problems or answer any of your questions'. This last feature was incidentally helpful in securing support for the project at branch level; counselling the kids made an agreeable change for Personal Bankers from dealing with their elders.

The customer leaflet also illustrated the account opening pack originally an austerity model costing the bank only 30p each, but upgraded a year later to meet competition into a blue cardboard folder with the accountholder's membership card in a slot on the outside; and a memo pad, ruler, felt tip pen, ball point pen, guide to running the account, statement holder and paying in book on the inside. The marketing men visualise accountholders carrying the folder proudly to school, demonstrating to their schoolmates that they are Persons of Quality and Substance – and customers of you-know-who.

Also illustrated in the leaflet are the product features designed to sustain accountholders' interest until they graduate into the student or young employed customer segment. These are membership of the Super-savers Club, offering competitions and special events, and the receipt three times a year by post of the Supersavers Club magazine, featuring these activities and appropriate money matters; the editorial problem of addressing such a wide age group is met by talking mainly to the older members of the group, but including a junior section. Competition prizes mentioned include 'a trip to Australia to meet Boy George and Culture Club, a chance to compete in a mini-Olympics in Sardinia, a week in Florida to see an American football game and a tour of London with a Club Sandwich tea in the Dorchester Hotel'; and there are tie-ups with outside bodies offering opportunities to participate in dinghy sailing and other sports activities.

Parental support for both the Supersavers Account and the follow-up Barclays Cheque Account is canvassed in another leaflet, designed as a statement stuffer, asking 'How much could your children get out of Barclays?' The tone and thrust of the answer is embodied in the first two paragraphs:

'It doesn't matter how old they are, you can't stop children spending their own money. It wouldn't be fair to try.'

But there are ways of teaching them to manage their money responsibly. Which is where we can help you.'

For branch staffs the main appeal is that the whole package shows sensitivity to the attitudes and interests of the young people it is aimed at, that its details are well thought out and organised and that it works. All customer contact staff are regularly sent illustrated promotional campaign leaflets in the standard format developed by the marketing department, detailing objectives, target market, selling points and product information for use in personal interviews together with details of the planned promotional package. Exchange of information between the central marketing department and the districts about results achieved and any problems encountered is constant.

Advertising in children's publications was combined with in-branch posters and literature and supported by personal selling. An offer on the back of Kelloggs Cornflake packs was particularly effective, resulting in the opening of 30,000 accounts. Altogether 200,000 Supersaver accounts were opened in this first year.

In 1983 competition in the children's market became fierce, with

Lloyds Bank introducing a more valuable opening pack supported by heavy advertising. A similar promotional programme was adhered to but there were indications of diminishing returns.

So the decision was taken to relaunch the product with the more valuable opening pack. Visual appeal of one promotion relied on off-cuts from the Warner Brothers Superman III film. The previous off-pack offer was transferred from cornflakes to soapflakes, producing this time around 130,000 new accounts. The relaunch in fact, as sometimes happens, was almost embarrassingly successful. A forecast of 20,000 new account openings a week over the peak promotional period was exceeded, in some weeks by 100%; there were production problems with the extra supply of account opening packs, and the administrative machinery began to creak. When the smoke cleared at the end of the year some 600,000 new accounts had been opened.

In year three the market was becoming saturated. NatWest had launched their heavily promoted Piggy Bank offer in December 1983 and the other banks were gazumping each other by offering progressively more lavish account opening packs and other inducements. A near repeat of the P & G off-pack offer produced the smaller though still satisfactory total of 80,000 new accounts.

Reviewing the position in 1985, Barclays marketing department was not unhappy with what had been achieved. They now had a million accounts in the target age group, with an average credit balance of over £30 each, representing about one-third of the banked children's market; NatWest probably had almost another third, with other banks sharing the balance. It was important to defend this share, but probably not worthwhile to spend heavily on increasing it. Maintaining child customer interest and satisfaction (as well as creating goodwill among their parents and teachers) was likely to be a more cost-effective use of available marketing funds; the primary objective after all was not to garner more deposits from children's savings (£30m is not a significant sum for a large bank) but to create good Barclay customers for the future, educated in the way to use a bank account.

So the emphasis shifted from media advertising to internal promotion, to building up the appeal and value to members of the Supersavers Club and above all to ensuring that the transition from child customer to young earner or student customer was accomplished without succumbing to the blandishments of competitors.

A small team in the central marketing department carried the responsibility for market sector development, including sales promotion and advertising, liaison with the districts and branches, encouragement of in-school activity, publication of the magazine and organisation of joint promotions and competitions with companies interested in the children's market that were compatible with the Barclays image. Everything seems to be under control with a substantial customer base and regular recruitment of young people to Supersavers – unless this is interrupted by a competitor or changes in children's tastes and habits.

SAYING 'YES' TO CHILDREN

The Trustee Savings Banks had their roots among what would today be described as the 'small savers segment'. Indeed their origin in the early nineteenth century lay precisely in this market sector and was a wholly new concept, introduced by a minister in the Church of Scotland. Within half a century there were over 600 TSBs across Britain dedicated to encouraging saving. In those early days that was virtually all they did – Personal Loans were many years into the future. Indeed not until the mid-1970s were government restrictions lifted to allow the TSBs to blosssom into the efficient and flourishing financial services group they have become.

With such a background, and re-inforced by the technology to handle the volumes economically, it is no surprise that childrens' savings should be a market segment of special attraction to TSB Scotland. It was one of several marketing initiatives which followed the bank's formation in 1983 from the merger of four Scottish TSBs.

Children are the customers, not only of today, but of tomorrow and for many years to come, and they are important members of families and extended families whose brothers and sisters, parents, grandparents, friends and acquaintances may also be, or may become, customers.

Recognising the pivotal role which children can thus play in customer relationships in general, and long-term customer loyalties in particular, the bank focused its attention on its child customers. Looking at banking from *their* point of view, highlighted the need for a customised package which would attract young children and keep their interest alive.

The Marketing Department, working in close consultation with Baillie Marshall, their advertising agency, studied a variety of options which led to the participation of Joe Austen as a consultant on the project. Joe Austen is the creator and author/illustrator of a highly successful series of children's books known as the Magic House series, and also acts as the presenter/storyteller of a BBC Television series featuring the Magic House characters, in addition to making other children's programmes for the BBC and working in other publishing and marketing activities which involve young people.

The Magic House and the characters who live in it, such as Uncle Teapot, Kitty Kettle, PC Pot and so on, were already very popular with children through books and television, and the Magic Bank scheme was designed to capitalise on that popularity.

A moulded plastic Magic Bank shaped like the Magic House was designed with a slot in the chimney to accept money, holes in the windows through which the child can peep at its growing savings, and an opening in the base (which can only be opened by a TSB teller) through which the money can be removed for deposit in the child's account.

Great care was taken to ensure that this savings bank was highly attractive and colourful in appearance, and completely safe for a young child to use. The branding of 'TSB – the Magic Bank' was also featured very prominently in the design, and its effect reinforced by prominent incorporation in the wide range of promotional and other supplementary material. This included a kit which accompanied the bank – namely an attractive box, containing a savings frieze for stickers which are issued each time a child makes a deposit, a Magic Bank passbook, an explanatory leaflet, and a free Magic House book, which re-inforced the identification of the Magic Bank with the Magic House, to marketing advantage.

This highly attractive package, of conspicuous retail value was given to the child *free* when a Magic Bank account was opened for a minimum sum of £2.00, and the market demand which resulted was overwhelming, with some 30,000 accounts being opened in the first six months, at a start-up cost of around £6 for each account.

Gratifying as this response has been, it is being regarded by TSB Scotland, not as an end in itself, but as the first step in a long-way strategy. Central to this strategy is the concept that when a child opens a Magic Bank account, he becomes a member of the Magic Bank Club, which is designed to keep alive his interest and enthusiasm for the Magic Bank. Club membership entitles the child to various benefits, including a free quarterly comic called, 'The Teapot Times'. 'The Teapot Times' not only contains full-colour picture stories featuring the Magic House characters, but also competitions for Magic Bank Club members with numerous attractive prizes, pages of Magic Bank Club news, photographs, birthdays, and artwork, but also a Playgroup page which features aspects of Playgroup activities.

The special relationship which exists between TSB Scotland and the SPPA (Scottish Pre-Schools Playgroup Association), is reflected in such things as a specially designed Playgroup account, TSB sponsorship of Playgroup events, promotions and competitions, and financial advice and other services. The TSB's existing strength in primary schools is also being extended through the Magic Bank scheme by a variety of means, including promotional visits to schools by the Magic Bank's own Magician, sponsored events and other initiatives.

The strategy of advancing the Magic Bank scheme through such non-banking channels as the Playgroup network, the Schools network and the market outlets of various commercial companies, is essentially a soft-sell and goodwill exercise rather than one of aggressive financial marketing, and the intrinsic attractiveness of the Magic House material and the cheerful friendliness of its presentation, gives an acceptability to this marketing technique which a more open and aggressive policy might be in danger of losing.

Its launch in November 1984 was preceded by a period of preparation, production and most importantly by staff briefings and training sessions. Every TSB branch was issued with a series of posters, window stickers and display material, and a "Paint your Mum" competition was launched, bringing in many thousands of entries.

This was followed by a two-week tour of branches which proved highly effective and served to launch the Magic Bank scheme with great success in the pre-Christmas period.

A number of conclusions may be drawn from the success of this integrated approach, among them the conviction that considering customers as individuals, whatever their age, rather than merely looking at their bank balances, actually can result in higher profits to the bank as well as improved customer relations.

Another conclusion must be that involving specialist expertise in areas other than banking can make very good banking sense indeed.

DESIGNING A HIGH INTEREST ACCOUNT

If you reduce banking to its barest essentials, there are three key ingredients in a profitable business – the cost of attracting funds (the banker's raw material), the rate at which you lend them out to borrowers, and the administrative cost of running the show. Whilst marketing always considers administrative overheads it can take action to improve profitability by attracting deposits in a cost effective manner and by promoting the more profitable forms of lending.

In the early days of 1984, the funding side of the equation did not look very bright to the clearing banks. Competition, particularly from the building societies, was steadily eroding the banks' share of consumer savings held in current accounts and 7-day deposit accounts and forcing them to rely more and more on the expensive wholesale money market for their funds; the government's requirement, about to be implemented, that banks should deduct tax from depositors' interest at the same composite rate as the building societies instead of paying interest tax free (benefitting non-tax payers) was likely to highlight interest rate differentials and accelerate the drift of funds to the building societies. The banks' unanimous reaction was to introduce a variety of high interest deposit accounts or interest-bearing current accounts, each with some special twist, keeping their fingers crossed lest the effect would not simply be to encourage their customers to transfer deposits from low interest to high interest accounts, without any significant increase in total funds.

Barclays Bank marketing department did not dissent from the general view that it was necessary to introduce a high interest account, which would at the same time enable them to compete with the building societies and the other banks for deposits from the growing number of customers who are sensitive to interest rate differences; and to attract funds at lower cost, after allowing for administration and promotion, than the cost of wholesale funds. But given the competitive necessity for such a product, they sought to design it in a way which would contribute to some of their other basic marketing objectives.

One such objective was to increase customer convenience. It was obvious to anyone watching competitive promotions and researching customer attitudes that the proliferation of special accounts with special conditions was both confusing and irritating for the public. What is the interest rate on this one? What balance do you have to keep? What notice of withdrawal? Do you get a cheque book? What restrictions on its use? And so on.

Barclays, following the time-honoured KISS principle (keep it simple, stupid) decided that the shortest road to convenience is simplicity, both in the product's features and in the conditions attaching to it. So the terms were kept simple – minimum of £1,000 deposited, variable rate of interest which always exceeded the 7-day rate, no cheque book, no charges, withdrawal on demand without penalty, immediate transfer to current account by telephoned instruction – and embodied in a simply written brochure.

A second objective was to give special protection to the most affluent 10% or so of personal customers who tended, as in other banks, to be more valuable individually to the bank than the less prosperous, because of keeping larger balances, positive or negative. They were provided for by offering a still higher rate of interest for deposits over £10,000, the higher interest applying to the whole amount.

A third objective, appropriate to the new competitive climate, was to attract deposits from the customers of other banks or building societies. It was made clear that private customers who did not already bank with Barclays would be more than welcome – as indeed they would be. Their deposits would unquestionably be new money for the bank, not just transfers from 7-day deposit accounts.

The principle of simplicity was carried through to the name of the new account. From a number of names submitted to consumer testing, a simply descriptive name, The Higher Rate Deposit Account, was selected in preference to more 'creative' alternatives.

A heavy promotional campaign announcing the new account was launched in the middle of March 1985. It hammered the two main themes of high interest and withdrawal on demand supported by the slogan 'the more you put into it, the more you get out of it'. The hammering was driven home, literally, by a consistent visual theme of three fairground try-your-strength hammers, each more potent than the last, linking the media package of television and press advertising, in-branch posters and statement stuffers.

The importance of securing support for the project at branch level was recognised by distributing to Personal Bankers, Saturday Bankers, Cashiers, Receptionists and all other customer contact staff a promotional campaign leaflet (one of a series) stating – once again in simple terms – the objective of the campaign, the target market and the main selling points to be made in face to face interviews; and illustrating the available sales support material – in-branch posters, leaflets, statement and account opening pack – with the suggested use of each item.

By September, six months after the launch, some 220,000 accounts had been opened, and total deposits had reached £2.0 billion. Even better, a substantial amount of new money had been attracted from the building societies and elsewhere, with the result that the effect on the bank's net cost of funds was broadly neutral. In addition branch staffs were happy with the product as one that could be offered with confidence to their customers – a confidence that was demonstrated by a number of bank employees shifting their own funds out of building societies into the new account.

Barclays' marketing department reckoned that they had a success on their hands. The next step would be consolidation, product enhancement – for instance, by making the account available to trustees as well as personal depositors – and keeping a watchful eye on competitors, in case they embarked on any new tack which needed to be covered.

BUSINESS LOANS

In the late 1970s all the clearing banks more or less simultaneously, became acutely aware of a fact that they had known in a general way for some time; the need to segment their business. There was a recognition of the need to strengthen their market positions by developing services specifically tailored to meet the needs of particular groups of customers.

The small and medium-sized corporate market was one such focus of attention, offering growth opportunity, spread and stable earnings. This contrasted with the intense competition in the 'blue chip' large corporate sector with margins squeezed particularly by the foreign banks; and in the personal market, with growing pressure from the building societies for retail deposits.

In this situation the clearing banks' marketing departments were faced with the problem of how best to implement their managements' strategic objective of improving the banks' service to small and medium-sized businesses. The same problem for all, but as usual in a competitive situation, rather different solutions.

Review of market situation

Lloyds Bank undertook a thorough review of their own and competitors' relationships with small and medium-sized business customers in the early 1980s, concentrating initially on the lending position – not the whole story of a relationship, but an important part. From a simple market share viewpoint the situation was not unsatisfactory; the bank's market share of lending to this segment was on the increase. However, competitors had opportunities to market, more overtly, their well-publicised business lending schemes. NatWest was promoting Development Loans, designed for the purchase of a business or professional practice, or of plant and machinery or for additional working capital. Barclays was offering Business Expansion Loans to allow expansion via the purchase either of capital assets or another business. Midland had equivalent facilities. Lloyds themselves had launched two schemes in previous years, Asset Loans and Enterprise Loans. However, neither of these schemes had made the expected impact on the customers for whom they were designed or on the branch managers who were selling them.

In total, product lending accounted for no more than a fraction of the bank's lending to smaller businesses, most of which remained in the form of overdrafts or branch arrangements drawn up locally.

What was wrong with the existing schemes? Questionnaire-based research plus group discussions with customers and potential customers suggested two major defects in both schemes which were confirmed in detailed discussions with branch managers.

First, there were faults in the design of the two products, specifically rate structure inflexibility, particularly the lack of a fixed rate for longer term loans, and in one case the absence of a variable interest option, linked to base rate. Secondly, the procedures for seeking and screening loans were complex so that both customers and managers were impelled to find a simpler arrangement, particularly for the small loans that constituted the majority of applications. The result was a proliferation of local branch arrangements to the detriment of the national product scheme.

Objectives of the new product

When the marketing group responsible for the project had completed their market analysis, designed and researched the new product and drafted a marketing plan, they were able to put the commercial objectives of the scheme to the General Managers for approval in the following terms: 'The recommended loan scheme would enhance loan volumes and earnings growth. Earnings would be generated largely through increased fee earnings (the introduction of an arrangement fee), from the switching of maturing non-scheme branch loans, through improved margins resulting from conversion of maturing overdrafts to loans and the active use of a "managed" fixed rate option. Targets for Year 1 activity would be set as a means of monitoring progress.'

Product features

The twin keynotes of the new product, directly resulting from the consumer research and discussions with branch managers, were simplicity and flexibility in a product designed to match the best that competitors were offering, with an added element of uniqueness. *Simplicity* began with the replacement of two schemes by a simple composite product; the presentation was straightforward, as were the application form and branch handling procedures.

One simple application form replaced several complex ones, negotiating procedures were simplified and formalised – customers, as seldom before, were given their own copies of simply-stated, binding agreements – and care was taken to ensure there were no obstacles in the administrative system which might deter branch managers from supporting the scheme.

Flexibility was embodied in the extension of the maximum loan term to 20 years with provision for early repayment; the widening of loan limits covered by the scheme from a minimum of £2,000 to a maximum of £500,000; and the option to choose between a fixed interest rate and a flexible rate linked to base rate. The element of *uniqueness* lay in a five year review clause in all agreements, allowing for both fixed and flexible rates to be reviewed (or for a switch from one to the other) every five years. This benefits the customer, who can seldom forecast his financial situation more than five years ahead.

Marketing and promotional plan

By contrast to some earlier marketing ventures by both Lloyds Bank and its competitors, the main emphasis in the run-up to the launch was on getting the operational details right and securing the support of the branch network in addition to consumer promotion.

The launch plan included a large-scale burst of advertising in the national dailies coinciding with the launch. This was supported by brochures and point-of-sale posters in the branches and there was a successful drive to obtain press publicity. However, there was no attempt to brand the new product with some glamorous and easily forgettable name. This was felt to run counter to the principle of simplicity, requiring continuous large-budget advertising to support and to be more appropriate to the personal customer market than to the negotiations attending a business loan. The new business loan scheme was promoted simply as 'Business Loan'.

In addition, members of the marketing department briefed regional offices, explaining the logic of the proposal, the key negotiating points and the simplified administrative procedures. The message was relayed via branch marketing groups throughout the country.

The outcome

Targets for 1984 and 1985 which had been set ambitiously by comparison with previous performance were exceeded by a substantial factor; by the end of 1985 the total portfolio had reached almost £500m, which was well beyond earlier expectations. Ten percent of Lloyds' medium sized and small business customers had taken advantage of the scheme and many new customers were acquired.

The future

Lloyds Bank regards the Business Loan as an important success and a permanent constituent of a wide product range, although it will need to be modified over time in the light of changing circumstances and competitive initiatives.

It can be claimed, however, that the scheme has not only been successful in its own right but has highlighted four important principles of new product marketing; a competitive product, clear and simple communication, a sound administrative infrastructure – and the first people to sell to are your own sales force.

CHAPTER SEVENTEEN

Marketing the plastic card

As every practising banker knows, passing cash to and fro across the counter is highly inefficient – both expensive for the bank and time-consuming for the customer. Plastic cards, linked to electronics, are much more efficient than cash, linked to people. The trouble is that customers are addicted to cash and slow to change established habits.

A long-term marketing task is to persuade the man and woman in the street that the use of plastic cards to obtain cash or to substitute for it has benefits for them as well as for the banks. In this chapter we describe the marketing steps taken by two banks to persuade their customers to transfer an increasing proportion of their withdrawal transactions from cashiers to ATMs (automated teller machines) and we bring up to date the marketing history of Access, one of the two leading cards in the UK.

AN ATM DEVELOPMENT PROJECT

By 1978 Yorkshire Bank had installed five first generation through-the-wall ATMs in their 200-odd branches. Customers found them inflexible and unreliable. Management found the level of usage wholly insufficient to compensate for the cost of installation and maintenance, quite apart from the complaints about non-functioning machines. There was no clearly defined responsibility for planning and managing the whole ATM situation as a commercial operation. It was still essentially a technology-led activity, with Management Services reviewing the equipment offered by the various hardware manufacturers without much concern for the customer's viewpoint.

However, there was an economic argument for increased investment in ATMs, provided that greater reliability and flexibility could be achieved and that both the bank's customers and its staff could be persuaded that there were many advantages in handling routine trans-actions mechanically at any hour of the day or night, instead of over the counter during banking hours. Yorkshire Bank's personal customer business was growing rapidly, resulting in considerable pressure on staff and premises. At a given level of usage the installation and maintenance costs of an ATM would compare favourably with the cost of recruiting and training an additional cashier, let alone opening an overflow branch.

Also it could be argued, since competitors were steadily increasing their establishment of ATMs, that installation of a Yorkshire Bank network would assist in the acquisition or retention of customer accounts – once again provided that customers were persuaded that it was a useful facility. So in June 1978 management set up a multi-disciplinary working party, with representatives from Finance, Data Processing, Inspection and Marketing and with the Planning Manager in the chair. The working party's terms of reference were to 'report to General Management on a cost effective strategy for the introduction of automated teller machines in Yorkshire Bank.'

The working party submitted its report three months later recom-mending that an initial batch of 13 installations should be allocated to branches in major population centres; since the population in Yorkshire Bank's catchment area is heavily concentrated in cities and conurbations, this meant that over 50% of the bank's customers would be within 5 miles of an ATM. It was also recommended that after a brief period off-line, the ATMs should come on-line to the main-frame computer; that the machines should offer deposit and balance enquiry as well as cash withdrawal facilities; that, given an acceptable rate of usage, the system should eventually be extended to accommodate up to 80% of Personal Current Account holders; and that the use of lobby and remote site, as well as through-the-wall machines should be investigated.

A recommendation to go ahead was probably not too difficult to arrive at in view of the fact that other banks had already embarked on a programme of installing ATMs. (Not being the pathfinder, but learning from the mistakes of others while technology and consumer acceptance both advance is not the worst of marketing policies, provided you don't fall too far behind). But the strength of the working party's report lay in the thoroughness of the organisational planning, in the tight financial disciplines, and in the recognition that in the end success would depend on convincing the consumer.

The main features of the plan were a financial appraisal, a promotional plan, and the various operational requirements for card distribution and control, card preparation and administration, and staff training. Specific targets for card uptake and utilisation were written in, with appropriate deadlines and provision for research data; and the working party sought management permission to assume executive responsibility for the project, with the marketing department's representative acting as product manager.

The financial appraisal set out to compare the cost of installing and operating the eventual network, assumed to be either 32 or 50 ATMs, over the projected 10 year life span of the equipment, with the benefit defined in terms of staff savings and the acquisition or retention of customers. The conclusions presented a formidable challenge to the working party; breakeven point would be between 1,000 and 1,500 transactions per week, compared with the average of under 40 a week recorded by the admittedly unsatisfactory first generation machines.

The promotional plan began with a review of the competitive situation. By 1978 some 15% of the 'Big Four's' current account customers were known to possess, though not necessarily to use, cash dispenser cards – an increase of 50% on 1976. Cardholders were predominantly among the young (15-34) and the upmarket (ABC1) – a common phenomenon in the acceptance pattern of any new product. It was encouraging that acceptance was growing, making customer education easier; not so encouraging that growth was faster in the ABC1 group, since Yorkshire Bank's market share in this group was relatively low.

Points to be learnt from a study of competitors' products and from research into the attitudes of their customers were the relative popularity of optional product features such as withdrawal limits, deposit facilities and hours of availability; the advantages and disadvantages of Lloyds Bank's emphasis on ATMs within the banking hall, as against the more frequent through-the-wall siting; and the consumer benefits and resistances which had to be covered in the promotion.

Benefits appreciated by customers who had acquired and used cash dispenser cards were, according to the research, mainly different aspects of convenience but also the advantage of impersonality; it was less embarrassing to be told by a machine that your balance was only £2.84 and that was all you could withdraw than to get the same bad news from a cashier. The main obstacles for those who had not acquired – or acquired and failed to use – a card were the ATMs' reputation for unreliability; and their fear that once in front of the machine, card and

PIN number in hand, they might fail to master the intricacies of making the withdrawal and have their card humiliatingly impounded. Fear, needless to say, was less frequent among the young, who had grown up in the computer age, suggesting that time was on the ATMs' side.

From an analysis of the research and other data, the working party concluded that the target audience for promotion of the new service should be those of the bank's existing or new current account customers who, in the branch manager's opinion, could be trusted with a card – probably about 50% of the total, as with a cheque card; that they should be invited to acquire one after a full explanation of their benefits and the simplicity of using them instead of having them issued automatically like the early Access cards; and that everything possible should be done internally to avoid malfunctioning.

The main methods of communication would be on-site demonstrations by branch staff and simple, explanatory brochures for study at home; local press advertising would be used only to announce the installation of a new ATM. The main benefits to be communicated should be privacy, convenience and constant availability of cash (clearly much more popular than the other facilities the machines could offer). The tone of the promotion should demonstrate an understanding of customers' fears and emphasise the ordinariness of the service in an electronic age; and the machine should be named to help personalise the relationship. (The name was in fact extensively researched through discussion groups; names like the first generation machines' 'Yorkash' were disliked as too gimmicky and 'American', and the less colourful but more descriptive 'Minibank' preferred.)

Provision against malfunctioning was made by meticulous planning of machine installation and operating procedures; by pre-testing of the early machines on site (the bank's staff were employed as guinea-pigs); and by great emphasis on staff training and motivation. Members of the working party visited each of the branches in which a new machine was to be installed with a slide presentation, to explain what was planned and what was required in the way of local co-operation; the importance attached by regional managers to the success of the project was left in no doubt; and interest was sustained by regular feedback of results, as they were achieved.

Despite all the research and pre-planning things did not go smoothly, with Murphy's law taking over in the early days of the project. When the system was introduced it was not on-line, branch staff had to withdraw and transcribe the machine's journal on to vouchers for posting in the same way as counter transactions. The facility for depositing cash was only used by about 10% of customers with cards and took longer than withdrawals (annoying other customers who were waiting to withdraw cash), sometimes jammed the machine, and was expensive for the branch to service. The deposit facility was eventually withdrawn.

Inevitably too, the local villains found ways of overcoming the anti-fraud precautions and obtaining cash to which they were not entitled, though this was made more difficult when the system came on-line early in 1981. It was a continuing struggle to control the level of avoidable breakdowns, due to such factors as lack of cash (some particularly busy machines had to be reloaded by branch staff during the weekend), journal rolls running out or customers inserting bent cards.

Nevertheless, thanks to constant monitoring by the working party and co-operation by branch staff it was clear by the beginning of 1981 that the project was a success. With only the initial 13 machines installed 10.7% of the bank's 544,000 current accounts holders had cards and the average number of weekly withdrawals was well above the breakeven target of 1,500. Customers using cash withdrawal cards, though still a small minority, were evidently pleased with the facility and branches, which had begun by regarding them as a burden, now recognised that they reduced workloads instead of adding to them (with transactions on line to the central computer) and were eager to have more installed. Management agreed to instal them progressively outside those branches where a satisfactory level of usage could be predicted.

By July 1981 the establishment had been increased to 26 machines, to 62 by July 1982, to 79 by July 1983, to 119 by July 1984 and to 145 by July 1985. At the last count 54.3% of personal current account customers, now increased to 886,000, held cards and average weekly withdrawals had risen to 250,000.

In 1985 approximately 46% of cash withdrawals by Yorkshire Bank customers were made by ATM rather than over the counter, equivalent to a saving of 150 cashiers – or more positively making it possible to re-deploy 150 prospective cashiers to more constructive occupations such as small loan officer.

Equally important the availability of 'round the clock banking', as the brochure describes it, was a competitive asset in the battle both against the national banks, none of which had reached the same level of card usage, and the building societies.

But there remained plenty for the Product Manager to do, apart from monitoring progress. There was still room for growth in the proportion of current account holders with cards, and even more in frequency of use. The latest check into the latter indicated that only one-third of cardholders had used them within the last month, one-third had used them on some occasion in the past and one-third had never used them. There were peaking problems in some high use areas, which made excessive enthusiasm about encouraging usage inadvisable; but reminder messages were included selectively in the statements of dormant holders.

There were also regular monthly meetings with the machine supplier to discuss possible improvements in the hardware, as well as ways of increasing reliability; at the same time every machine was monitored and corrective action taken internally to deal with trouble spots. One source of trouble, for example, was the larger average size of withdrawals, spurred by inflation, exhausting the machines' stock of notes; this was handled by increasing note denominations first to £10 and then to a combination of £10 and £20 at heavy use sites. The Bank of England's parsimony in issuing new notes was no help here; note sorting arrangements had to be made in Head Office to ensure that the machines would not be loaded and clogged with crumpled notes.

But the most important question was where next to move down the road to automated banking, as customer acceptance grew and more versatile machines became available. One experiment in Wakefield where three ATMs were located in a vacant shop alongside an existing branch looked interesting; and NCR had developed a new CAST terminal, capable of issuing insurance and making personal loans on a credit-scored basis. Was the unmanned – and unwomanned – branch just around the corner?

CASHLINE – AN UPDATE

The Royal Bank of Scotland launched its cash dispenser network in 1977, the first in Scotland, and by October of that year had installed eight of them and issued 4,500 cards. It was, and is, an on-line system.

In mid-1982 the Royal Bank's 239 machines were linked to the 84 of its sister bank, Williams & Glyn's, giving a national network to be shared among some 700,000 cardholders.

Plans are now well advanced for this network to be joined with those of Barclays Bank and Lloyds Bank in England and Wales and the

Bank of Scotland (in which Barclays Bank previously held a large stake) probably early in 1986. Such a move will produce a network of some 3,500 machines (and many millions of cardholders) while the other two major clearers, Midland and NatWest, already operate a second joint network – in their case off-line. Building societies and the TSB are also of course, active promoters of their own cash dispenser services.

It is estimated that over £10,000 million is now withdrawn through the cash dispensers of the major clearing banks each year. Even allowing for inflation – which has roughly doubled prices in the last ten years – this is an impressive change in the public's habits since ATMs were introduced. It is appropriate therefore to update an earlier study by the Royal Bank which won the marketing award in the 'Ideas at Work' competition in 1980.

The earlier study stated, 'The bank's prime objective in introducing the Cashline facilities was to transfer as many customers' cash withdrawal transactions as possible from conventional methods to a Cashline machine; efforts were linked to the growth in number of machines becoming operational. The success of the service would enable the bank to save costs by:

(a) reducing counter and other staff costs associated with cash withdrawals, balance enquiries and associated tasks. Staff costs account for approximately 70% of the bank's total costs excluding interest payments;
(b) reducing the need to expand some branches' premises, as a result of;
(c) reducing the existing level of congestion in branches.

Secondary objectives included the desire to show that the bank remained the leader in Scottish banking, in particular that it was seen to be up-to-date, go-ahead and innovative.'

Cashline therefore gave the bank the opportunity to provide an improved service to customers and at the same time cut down costs. It was considered, however, that the most important development lay in improving the service to the customer. Cashline has enabled customers to carry out routine banking transactions at the times most convenient to them and normally at a charge lower than for a conventional type of withdrawal. Increased customer satisfaction can strengthen the relationship between customer and bank and can lead to a greater awareness and usage of other bank services.

Now, some ten years on from the initial planning stages, we can ask whether or not the original objectives have been met. Clearly they have been, even though the cost savings have shown up as a slower rate of growth in costs rather than as a reduction. For example, branches became less congested than before and thus the need to extend them or to open extra branches nearby has receded. In addition, staff at all branches – but especially those with Cashline machines – could obviously be deployed to a greater extent on other duties, giving the opportunity for more varied and more interesting jobs.

Of course merely installing the ATMs was not enough to ensure their usage. Apart from training the branch staff on maintenance procedures it was necessary to train them on selling the new service to customers. And the customers themselves had to be reached by other means too, mainly advertising. The final group was non-customers to whom the idea of an extra service not obtainable elsewhere (at least at the launch period) had to be explained.

In time the new technology led to new services to customers, but more of this aspect later. The first need was to draw up a total plan and the marketing needs were prominently featured in it. So a considerable marketing effort was launched to persuade appropriate customers to apply for a card, although of course this effort had to be kept in step with the installation of the Cashline machines.

The first target group of customers were current and deposit account holders and these were addressed by way of letters to them enclosing an explanatory leaflet and inviting them to apply for a Cashline card. This 'solicited' approach – as distinct from a mass mailing of cards – was decided upon, even though it might have meant a slower take-off, because it was felt to be better in terms of customer relations.

Within two years of the launch the number of cards issued had risen from 4,500 to well over 100,000 while the number of ATMs installed rose from 8 to 43. Having issued many thousands of cards upon request it was obviously important to encourage usage. Letters were sent to cardholders who had not used their card after an interval, and of course branch displays reminded customers of the existence of the machines.

But the greatest spur to use was undoubtedly the efforts of branch staff, explaining, demonstrating and generally enthusing about their branch's ATM. Was it a successful campaign? Yes it was. In various studies the Cashline network in Scotland has been shown to be the most heavily used in Europe. In June 1985 for example, one machine in

Falkirk dispensed over £550,000 and handled 24,000 transactions. The whole Royal Bank network in England, Scotland and Wales in the first half of 1985 dispensed some £600 million through nearly 18 million withdrawals – and also handled nearly 12 million enquiries about the balances on customers accounts.

And new services for customers? Apart from offering customers instant information on the balance on their accounts displayed in the Terminal 'window', it is also possible to obtain a printed record of the six most recent transactions on the account, including any through a cash dispenser that day. The amount which is still available for withdrawal that day is also given. In addition, provision has been made for customers to order – by a single key depression – a new cheque book or a full statement, which is then sent to the customer's home address from their branch. In a further development introduced in October 1983 Royal Bank of Scotland Access cards can also be used in Cashline machines. Any cash withdrawn is debited to the cardholder's Access account in just the same way as if the cash had been drawn at a branch of an 'Access Bank'.

A wholly new account was developed a couple of years after the first machines had been installed. It is called the Cashline Deposit Account, in which credit balances earn interest and up to £100 a day can be withdrawn through the ATM network. In addition, the mini-statement service is available (full statements are only provided at pre-set intervals, not on demand) and, of course, the balance on the account can be displayed. There is no facility for an overdraft. Finally, wages can be directly credited to the account and standing orders or direct debits operated from it.

The marketing effort aimed at gaining customer acceptance of this virtually paper-less account was directed mainly at Pass-Book Account holders. A very considerable number converted, and in effect leapt from Pass-Books to Plastic Cards in a single step, missing out cheque books. Many of course also have an Access card, so perhaps they are the customers nearest to the future.

THE ACCESS STORY

Pre-launch marketing activities

We have emphasised in the various parts of this book that the success of any marketing operation is largely dependent on the preparatory work that is done before the new product or service is launched, in market research, the definition of marketing strategy, detailed pre-planning and preparation of the required back-up services. The launch of the Access card was no exception to this rule.

Market research and analysis
The first plastic cards in the UK were T & E (Travel and Entertainment) cards. The first well-known name, Diners, was launched in 1963, followed by American Express which entered the UK market in 1966. Neither offered credit, though some customers took it.

The first UK credit card with an extended credit facility was Barclaycard, which was launched by Barclays Bank in June 1966 with an initial base of 1 million card-holders and 30,000 retail outlets. (Barclays Bank, in fact, naturalised in the UK the blue, white and gold card scheme of Bank Americard, now called VISA worldwide.)

Throughout the 1960s the other clearing banks were studying the market and observing Barclaycard's mounting progress.

By about 1970, the five key factors listed below were emerging from the market studies.
1 Barclaycard had begun to penetrate the current accounts of the other banks; just under 20 per cent (250,000) of the card-holders did not bank with Barclays.
2 Research showed a clear profit potential for a scheme with as many card-holders as Barclaycard.
3 Market research indicated strong resistance among retailers to each bank introducing its own credit card scheme.
4 There would be significant economies of scale if the banks were to enter the market on some kind of a joint basis.
5 Finally, the other banks took the view that there was room in the UK market for only *two viable* general-purpose cards.

As a result a somewhat unusual event occurred. Lloyds, Midland and National Westminster Banks, who are in competition with each other, formed a joint working party to examine the possibilities of launching a common credit card. In 1971 a joint press release was issued by these banks, stating that they would launch such a card in September or October 1972; and that a common service company would be formed, which is now known as The Joint Credit Card Company. Before the launch Williams & Glyn's Bank also joined the Access set-up.

The basic marketing tasks

With this commitment there were four basic marketing tasks to be accomplished during the pre-launch period:

1 to recruit 3 million card-holders;
2 to recruit 60,000 retail outlets;
3 to create the advertising and promotional platform and programme for the launch;
4 to select a name for the new credit card (Access was chosen after duly diligent research).

Just as important as the four marketing tasks was the task of establishing the necessary computer operation facilities. This went on in parallel with the marketing activities.

Advertising and promotion

All the appropriate media for delivering persuasive messages to potential or existing customers, such as press advertising, leaflets and direct mail were considered, as also were the point-of-sale support materials, such as display material in shops.

What had to be recognised was that the new card-holders in most cases would have had no previous experience of using a credit card; so their knowledge and acceptance of the benefits to be gained from intelligent use of the card would be low. The prime task of the advertising and promotion would be to encourage use both of the card itself and of the extended credit facility which it represented.

Analysis of the consumer research, supplemented by creative imagination, suggested that the intangible concepts of instant finance and flexible repayment could be made more tangible when expressed in terms of the things that people want and of when they want them.

Things have a value over and above their intrinsic worth – the value which is conferred on them by being available at a particular time; they can be more valuable at certain times than at others – what was called 'the time utility of money'. A refrigerator, for example, tends to be more valuable in summer than in winter, and a family holiday is more valuable when the children are on holiday from school than two months later. And winter clothes must be bought in good time, even if, say, a car repair bill arises suddenly.

The new credit card, it was concluded, could provide access to things when they are needed, when they are most valuable. From this, and involving the name of the new credit card, came the launch slogan 'Access takes the waiting out of wanting.'

Execution of the marketing plan

While the basic thinking was being done on the advertising and promotional approach and on the name of the new card, preparatory work was being done in the two recruitment areas: card-holders and retailers.

Card-holder recruitment
This was carried out in four stages.

1 The Access department sent each branch of the collaborating banks selection criteria for new card-holders with a suggested target figure.
2 Each branch supplied a list of potential card-holders, with proposed credit limits assigned to each name.
3 The bank's Access department analysed these lists and made the final decision on which current account customers should be offered an Access card.
4 After the basic advertising theme had been agreed, an introductory mailing kit was created and assembled, to include the new credit card. The objectives of this mailing were:
   (a) to provide the necessary explanatory details of the new service to the card-holder;
   (b) to encourage use of the new facility through the 'Access takes the waiting out of wanting' theme.

Retail recruitment
This essential task was entrusted to a brand new salesforce set up by the Joint Credit Card Company Ltd. Because Access was going to be a financial service offered by the banks to their customers, it was decided to recruit the salesforce from bank staff. An establishment of 145 salesmen and sales managers was agreed on.

By January 1972, nine months before the launch date to which the original three banks had publicly committed themselves, the salesforce was ready to go.

Outcome of the launch phase

One month before the stated launch date the target of 60,000 retail outlets had been exceeded; 70,000 had been signed up. The final figure could have been still higher, but the retail recruitment programme was stopped at this point, for fear that the computer operations centre would not be able to cope with the volume of business generated by a larger retail base.

The target of 3 million card-holders was also exceeded by half a million. Moreover, the initial use of the card, thanks to the way in which the concept had been sold, was considerably higher than had been expected.

Access – the follow-up

So far so good. But just as important as a successful launch in any marketing operation (if not more so), are the various follow-up stages, including adjustment to changes in

the economic environment;

government restrictions on credit cards;

increased understanding and experience of the credit card industry.

Five phases, in retrospect, were important.

1 The launch period 1972–73

The banks, as it turned out, were lucky in the period chosen to launch the Access card. It coincided with the height of the Barber boom, when consumer financial confidence, expenditure and demand were at a record level. The white-collar section of the public at which Access was aimed (60 per cent of card-holders are ABC1s, who represent around one third of the general population) was in a receptive mood to be told of the availability of instant finance for large purchases, linked to the flexible repayment facility. And it was appropriate that the advertisements should be deliberately designed to appear luxurious, featuring high-value merchandise.

2 The post-launch period 1974–76

Towards the end of 1973 the Barber boom collapsed. In November the government announced an emergency budget which had the basic objective of reducing the money supply. The most directly significant elements of this budget for the credit card industry were the imposition of two restrictions to become effective on 1 January 1974. These were:

15 per cent minimum repayment on the amount owing on each statement (up from the initial 5 per cent), with a minimum repayment of £15 (up from £5);

£30 maximum cash advance; down from the open flexibility of the launch agreement.

This change of climate and legislation meant that the very successful launch campaign had to be abandoned. The only property of the credit card that could be promoted in the new circumstances was its convenience as a method of payment. Only very minor emphasis could be given to the flexible repayment feature.

The level of advertising expenditure was substantially reduced. It was not expected that the campaigns would have the same impact as the launch campaign. But in retrospect it appears that the advertising was less effective than it might have been, even allowing for the reduced expenditure, because of the lack of singlemindedness: three different campaigns in as many years are more likely to confuse than to penetrate the public consciousness.

3 The readjustment period 1977–78.

Towards the end of 1976 the attitude of the government and the Bank of England towards *responsible* promotion of the major purchase facility offered by the credit card showed signs of softening. In the changed circumstances a new campaign was devised to illustrate the fact that an extended credit facility, if used responsibly, could bring tangible economic benefits.

The advertisements illustrated the cost of high-value merchandise and showed that, including the interest charge on repayments spread over six, nine or twelve months, there could be significant savings for cardholders using the credit facility to make a cash purchase. The campaign was supported by yet another slogan 'Access makes the most of your money.'

By the end of 1977 inflation was declining and wage increases were resulting in the first real gain in consumer buying-power since the Barber boom. Restrictions on money supply were relaxed and, in the April 1978 budget, credit card restrictions were lifted. Once again there was a new economic situation, requiring a new promotional approach. As there was new market research information indicating that through ignorance or timidity, many card-holders were not getting the full benefit of the facilities the card represented, the campaign consisted of advertisements with dramatic illustrations such as a birdcage with an Access card on the perch, captioned 'If you let it out will it fly away with you?' The campaign's basic aim, to reduce card-holders' fear of using the card, was underwritten by the slogan 'Use Access to make the most of your money.'

Developments on the sale side

While the marketing and promotional side was trying to adjust to changing economic circumstances, the Access salesforce was able to follow a rather more consistent course. For the salesmen the year following the launch, 1973, was something of an anticlimax. The intensive recruitment effort of the previous year was replaced by a predominantly servicing role, and the lion's share of salesmen's time in 1973 was spent in calling back on retail outlets signed up in the previous year as a servicing, consolidation and public relations exercise. Call sheets were completed which sought retailer reaction to questions about the efficiency of the Access service, whether retailers were happy with the level of business transacted, and so on. Display material was replaced where necessary and any problems in the operation of the system relating to sales voucher stocks, the imprinting machines and so on, were dealt with.

In 1974 a start was made with broadening the retail base for Access into less obvious sectors. A special services section of the salesforce was set up to expand credit card activity in the rapidly growing mail order market; to research, approach and recruit the major insurance under-writers; and to develop Access business in the holiday and travel trades.

Since 1974 other 'non-standard' service industries have been recruited, such as rating authorities, water boards, home fuel distributors, the professional services, opticians, dentists, and others; and the salesforce has been required to absorb an increasing range of retailer/service product knowledge, as well as developing tailormade sales approaches for the very varied categories of 'buyer'.

The beginning of a new approach, 1979–1980

1979 saw a change in the political and economic climate in the UK.

Changes to the levels of direct and indirect taxation resulted in consumers being uncertain in their reactions. Increases in the levels of VAT saw the Access frequency of use falling and the Access marketing team began to adopt a more positive and reassuring theme to Access advertising.

Role of Access advertising
Following a change in advertising agency in 1979 the cartoon characters of 'Access' and 'Money' were used to promote the Access facility. The advertising slogan 'Access – your Flexible Friend' was introduced with the initial campaign concentrating on increasing usage of the Access card. 'Money Talks' was the commercial which introduced Flexible Friend. 'Out and About' and 'Shopping List' were commercials which emphasised the potentially wide usage and convenience of Access. 'Cheque Book' appeared in late 1979 focusing on a key usage benefit – that of no £50 ceiling as with cheques. However, the large VAT increases in 1979 actually saw frequency of use fall.

In 1980 the Access advertising effort excluded TV as it was felt that the economic and political climate was not conducive. As a result, recruitment suffered although an advertising presence was maintained with press ads which concentrated on:

1 explaining the general benefit of Access AND
2 promoting usage.

The development of Flexible Friend, 1981–1984

Despite lower inflation rates the UK economy was experiencing major recession. Major business collapses and high unemployment predominated. Limited recovery was led by a consumer boom which in many cases led to increases in import levels. This consumer boom assisted growth in Access business. By end 1984 Access was the largest single credit card company in the UK with a turnover of nearly £4 billion and cardholders exceeding 7.5 million.

Role of Access advertising
In 1981 Flexible Friend returned to TV with two new commercials 'Hotel' and 'Ticket Office'. These commercials represented a significant shift in strategy. For the first time Access advertising concentrated on a

key benefit for potential cardholders – that of coping with the unexpectedly large bill. This successful formula was used again in the 'Garage Repairs' commercial in 1982.

In 1983 the campaign developed further, using the theme of dealing with a minor financial crisis. Both 'Old Bill' and 'The Visit' treatments communicated very directly how a credit card could be used. The theme adopted in these commercials was made possible by a softening of attitudes generally on credit and credit cards. It became possible for Access to be more direct in what was said through advertising.

Similar changes in execution took place in press and poster advertising with the 1984 press campaign developing a question and answer type approach to facts about Access. However, in the period TV remained the dominant medium.

The Salesforce

By 1979 the salesforce had settled down to a role which involved not simply servicing the collaborating retailers but stimulating them to more positive efforts on behalf of Access. Staff training sessions were organised for retailers and specific trade promotions undertaken, featuring both cardholder and retailer incentives. Town centres events were organised, including window display competitions, and personalised promotions arranged with individual retailer chains. Since 1979, despite the overall contraction of the general UK retailer base the development of the Access retailer base has continued, with the salesforce continuing to expand into areas of committed expenditure.

Many more large turnover retailers emerged and commanded more salesforce time and training, especially considering increases in the levels of credit card fraud. Salesforce time therefore needed to be much more planned, and retailer publications were developed to allow a large section of the retailer base to be kept fully informed, without visits from Access staff. This enabled time not only to be concentrated on major retailers but also on the introduction of technological advancements at the point of sale.

Forecasting Access turnover

The Joint Credit Card Company's Corporate Information Department has been successful in the difficult task of forecasting turnover. The basic historical premise in isolating turnover is that:

$$T/O_x = DT_x \times ATV_x$$

Where:

T/O_x = Turnover for month x (sales plus cash advances less returns)
DT_x = Number of debit transactions in month x (sales plus cash advances less returns)
ATV_x = Average transaction value in month x

The validity of such a model for forecasting relies on the accuracy in predicting the number of Cardholder Transactions and their average value.

As the business matures and cardholder behaviour becomes more homogeneous, JCCC has been progressively more successful in predicting the number of debit transactions and the number of occasions of use, i.e.

$$DT_x = DA_x \times F_x$$

Where:

DA = Number of 'Debit Active' accounts in month, i.e. persons who used their Access card in month x
F_x = Frequency of use in month x by by 'Debit Actives'

These components have not historically been significantly affected by external factors in the UK economy, although, over a period, they tend to be more in line with the generic trend towards increased credit-taking.

In relation to Average Transaction value, a lagged historical relationship between the money value and Retail Price inflation has been identified. The relationship is lagged because Access cardholders tend to 'anticipate' movements in the Retail Price Index in their spending patterns. As an additional factor, the trend of 'real' i.e. deflated transaction values has been isolated. Therefore, for the purposes of the forecasting model,

$$ATV_x = RATV_x + Hx + 1$$

Where:

$RATV_x$ = 'Real' or Deflated Average Transaction Value in month x
$Hx+1$ = Henley Centre for Forecasting's estimate of Retail Price inflation in month $x+1$

Forecasts derived from this method have proved to be generally accurate insofar as the Henley inflation forecasts are reliable. This model can only respond to changes in inflation and is likely to deviate when unforeseen major fluctuations in other external factors (such as Personal Disposable Income) occur.

Forecasting Model (Extended):

$$(DA_xE \times F_xE) \times (RATV_xE + H_x + 1) = T/O \text{ Estimate}$$

Where:

DA_xE	=	Estimate of the number of 'Debit Actives' in period x
F_xE	=	Estimate of Frequency of Use by Debit Actives in period x
$RATV_xE$ =		Estimate of 'Real' ATV in period x
$Hx+1$	=	Henley Estimate of Retail Price inflation in the subsequent period $x+1$

In 1985 the model was used by Joint Credit Card Company Limited both for forecasting Access turnover and for sales targeting purposes. By deflating Average Transaction Value, it has been possible to calculate retrospectively the effect of various events (e.g. Consumer Credit Act) and thus to place Access more accurately in its market environment.

CHAPTER EIGHTEEN

Related Financial Services

A senior manager in any of the large UK clearing banks if asked the time-honoured question 'What business are you in?' would be as likely to answer 'financial services' as 'banking'. Where the breakdown of barriers between formerly self-contained industries will end nobody can say for sure – certainly not the politicians whose competitive and deregulatory legislation speeded the whole process on its way.

In this chapter we describe some beginnings – the beginning of a business in the home transfer market by a leading clearing bank, the direct entry of a bank trust company into the car insurance market, and the more aggressive marketing posture adopted by the merchant banking subsidiary of a clearing bank group.

THE CHARGE OF THE BLACK HORSE

Considerable alarm and despondency was caused when Lloyds Bank announced in May 1982 that they had taken the first step towards building a wholly owned national chain of estate agencies by the acquisition of a small East Anglian estate agency chain. The many practitioners engaged in one or other aspect of the house transfer business, sniffing a threat to their livelihood, protested that the bankers' appetite for diversification was getting out of hand. While those commentators who are underwhelmed with admiration for British bankers' commercial management expertise forecast that Lloyds would have difficulty in reconciling the idiosyncratic culture and low cost structure of small local estate agents with the management systems and attitudes of a large banking group.

In fact the bank's decision was a classic example of the logical approach to marketing innovation: first identify the opportunity through conceptual thinking, supported by market research and analysis of profit potential, next develop and implement an operating plan, finally monitor progress and further develop the operating plan.

The opportunity

With hindsight the opportunity for a large British bank to enter the house transfer business seems obvious; and it is surprising that so far Lloyds is the only one of the four biggest UK clearing banks to have seized it with enthusiasm. Buying or selling a home is probably the largest and most complicated financial transaction undertaken by most people during their lifetimes (albeit one that, in the case of mobile individuals like bank employees, may be repeated several times).

In a 'property-owning democracy' like Britain, financing and nego-tiating the sale of one house and purchase of another is a growth industry. Already, in 1985, 62% of families owned their homes, a figure which should pass 70% in the early 1990s; and house sales – at prices rising faster than inflation – have risen from 685,000 in 1971 to 790,000 in 1981 and an estimated 850,000 in 1985.

Yet, until they actively attacked the mortgage market in 1981, the clearing banks gave their competitiors, the building societies, a very clear run to lend on mortgage to house purchasers, many of whom were bank customers; and offered these customers very little help in finding their way through the jungle of collateral negotiations that could include:

— selling through one agent;
— buying through another agent;
— getting a survey and valuation elsewhere;
— getting money from a building society or bank;
— arranging insurance through a broker;
— consummating the legal transaction(s) through lawyers;
— getting a bank loan or store credit for new furnishings.

For Lloyds Bank the concept of pre-empting even stronger building society competition resulting from de-regulation, and at the same time filling what appeared to be a consumer need was particularly attractive because if fitted the bank's long range strategy of increasing the cost-effectiveness of their delivery system through rationalisation and seg-mentation; and using the rationalised delivery system as a framework for product development. Estate agents' offices, being both specialised and inexpensive to run, could make a useful contribution as delivery points in such a system.

Additional research served to confirm and quantify the belief that there was an opportunity to market a one-step house transfer product range through a wholly owned chain of estate agent offices. The estate agency business was highly fragmented. In 1981 there were 6,600 firms and 11,500 branches with no single firm claiming more than a 1% market share. Profitability, on investigation, proved to be good; characteristically, return on investment was over 30%, despite an image of mediocre service and very moderate standards of efficiency. Commission charge averaged around 2% – as much as was justified perhaps by the service provided, but very much less than that charged in North America and some European countries, where commissions of up to 6% were paid for a much more extensive service. It looked as though there might be scope in the long run for achieving the marketing ideal of a higher price for a better product. Consumer attitude research confirmed at least the second part of this proposition (which many of the bankers involved could confirm from first hand experience). There was widespread dissatisfaction with the service provided by estate agents, expressed by one exasperated home owner in the comment that 'moving house is the greatest hassle in God's earth'.

Finally, talks with the relevant professional bodies, the RICS (Royal Institute of Chartered Surveyors) and the ISVA (Incorporated Society of Valuers and Auctioneers), confirmed that, while certain sensitivities needed to be watched, there was no insuperable obstacle to a bank entering the estate agency field.

The action plan

The purchase of the East Anglian Estate Agency in 1982 was thus the first step in a thought through plan to build, mainly by acquisition, a national network of house transfer delivery points which would retain their local identity, but be linked by common services and standards and a common symbol. The notoriously difficult problem of retaining the support and enthusiasm of the existing owners after acquisition was to be tackled by converting owners into boards of management with a considerable degree of local autonomy.

By 1985, after several other acquisitions, a chain of 160 offices was linked together by the Black Horse symbol – the already well-established trademark of the Lloyds Bank group – by their common ownership and by an increasingly effective internal communications system. This still represented less than 2% of the market; but already the Black Horse

Agencies were the largest single group in the business, well on the way to a national chain. With other acquisitions in prospect, the target of a 5% market share was clearly realisable.

Product development

Within the concept of one-stop shopping, product development proceeded in step with the build-up of the delivery system. The essential point, the marketing people felt, was to keep the customer's interest to the fore-front – developing a relationship approach, with one adviser understanding all the needs of the individual customer and avoiding the temptation to develop too rigid and mechanistic an approach.

Freedom of choice would be important; so there should be no insistence on using the bank's insurance facilities, or even its borrowing facilities, if a better deal was available from a building society or other sources. In a sell/buy situation easy access on a computer matching basis to other properties being handled by the chain would be useful, but only to a limited extent until the chain was larger. Conveyancing, as part of the one-shop service, would have to await the passing of deregulatory legislation and even then be voluntary.

Meanwhile there were other creative aspects of the service that could be progressed. One was a chain breaker facility, related to the situation peculiar to English law, where no house sale or purchase is irrevocable until contracts have been exchanged; so one house that sticks can hold up half a dozen related transactions. Lloyds Bank, will undertake, for a reward appropriate to the risk, to break the chain by purchasing the obstructive house. Another product, which a substantial bank-owned estate agency could offer but a small independent could not, was a corporate employee relocation service for companies transferring their operations to a new site. Yet another product range extension for the personal customer, offered on an experimental basis, was a pre-packaged contents scheme whereby customers could get both a bank loan and a design scheme for the carpets, curtains and other furnishings needed for their new homes. And, as well as the personal sector, the estate agents' existing connections opened up new opportunities for the bank to develop their services in the commercial and agricultural property markets, bringing in both fee and interest earnings.

Developing the environment

An important part of High Street retailing (a description which applies to certain aspects of banking as well as estate agency) is creating the environment in which the service or product range is sold. The Lloyds Bank marketing people recognised at the outset that the extended product range and the Black Horse symbol would not be sufficient by themselves to change the image of a newly acquired estate agency office from a sometimes old-fashioned purveyor of houses for sale, to a well informed and informative supplier of a complete range of property transfer and investment services. So a long-term programme was initiated to give the offices a more welcoming, up-to-date look. Financial Service Desks were installed in the larger offices, selling house purchase loans, surveys, valuations, and insurance for mortgage protection, property and contents. Some offices were used as outlets for the promotion of personal loans and credit cards, identifying them more closely with the parent bank; in some, ATMs were installed, identifying them even more closely with the bank. Electronics, that familiar token of modernity were added to the environmental mix with some caution, partly to keep overheads down but mainly to maintain the emphasis on people and personal service. However, terminals were installed on all Financial Service Desks, providing competitive insurance and mortgage quotes, thus enabling those manning the desks to be genuine advisers, not simply salesmen of the group's products.

Finally, self-service banking experiments were set up in selected estate agency branches, where the site was suitable and space was available. At the same time Black Horse Agency sales brochures were introduced into suitable Lloyds Bank branches and eleven in-store banking outlets.

Promotion

By the nature of their business, estate agents are bound to promote their own names locally, while promoting the sale of their clients' properties. It was a relatively straight-forward step to infiltrate the news that the local agency was now part of the national Black Horse Agency chain by adding the symbol to advertisements, fascia boards, and 'for sale' signs. As soon as there were enough branches to justify the cost, television advertising was added to support the corporate identity.

Less straightforward was the problem of promoting the new breadth and level of services offered by the chain. The rate of change was bound to differ between acquisitions and between individual offices, as was the rate at which new services and service enhancements could be introduced. And, as every experienced advertiser knows, making promises and failing to deliver can be exceedingly counter-productive. The policy adopted was to use central advertising skills to improve the presentation of brochures and other promotional literature such as house magazines for the larger members of the chain; and at the same time to develop Black Horse brochures describing major products such as relocation services to be offered selectively and delivered either centrally or by regional offices with the necessary resources.

Monitoring; further development; trouble-shooting

The third phase of monitoring progress on this major long-term project, while continuing its development, is now well under way. The scope for development is virtually unlimited. When the target 5% market share is achieved in delivery terms, the need to widen and strengthen the product range will continue – just as fast as people can be trained to understand and deliver with competitive efficiency both the entire interactive range and its component parts.

Undoubtedly some of the component products and members of the estate agency chain will be more successful than others. Hence the need for an efficient management information system and central monitoring. Undoubtedly also there will be problems arising from internal failures or from changes in the environment or from the external competition that any successful project must anticipate. But at the end of the first three years the bank is entitled to say with some satisfaction 'so far, so good'.

CAR INSURANCE FOR TSB CUSTOMERS

The Trustee Savings Bank Group is one of the most dramatic examples of change in the changing financial services market. Still a loose confederation of regional savings and loan associations in the early 1960s, more akin to the American 'thrifts' than to the UK's High Street banks, by

1985 it had a central policy-making management (still more respectful of regional differences than the big clearers) and was poised for fully commercial privatisation.

In making the transition it could count on a number of marketing assets – notably a national branch structure and a more friendly relationship with its six million customers than the more commercially-orientated clearers; it also had a number of marketing liabilities – notably a distinctly downmarket clientele, essentially C2D, and a shortage of wholesale banking business and expertise. The Group's overall strategy was to move away from the thrift image – thrift having become an obsolescent concept in the new sociological environment of spend now, pay later – and to move closer to the diversified commercial banking groups, while retaining the same friendly relationship with customers. By a happy coincidence this policy involved the often-stated and only intermittently practised marketing principle of looking first for the customer benefit in any new product or marketing initiative; and only then considering whether it would be profitable to the Group. It also involved ensuring that the benefit offered by the product or service was actually delivered by all parts of the organisation contributing to it.

The TSB Trust Company was launched in 1968 as part of the TSB Group. Brian Brown, its Managing Director, is a rare phenomenon among British Chief Executives in having a marketing background; and even rarer among bank divisional managers in staying in the same job for the better part of twenty years. Over that period the Trust Company's employee strength grew from an initial 24 in 1972 to over 1,000 in 1985, including a sales force of 400; the latter is employed primarily on liaising with the TSB branches and following up introductions from them to customers who are likely to benefit from one or other of the Trust Company's products.

Life insurance, either unit-linked or as protection for mortgage loans, was an early product. By 1984, TSB Trust Company could claim to be the country's leading unit-linked life insurance company, having overtaken Hambro Life. It had also established separate unit trust and general insurance marketing divisions, the latter handling personal customer business; and TSB insurance brokers, as a separate entity, predominantly handling commercial business. But it was not until that year that active steps to enter the motor insurance market – a low priority hitherto because of the erratic performance of other motor insurers – were seriously considered.

The main questions which the Trust Company's marketing department sat down to look at in the spring of 1984 were:

(a) could motor insurance be regarded as a logical extension to the range of services offered to TSB's personal customers?
(b) did it have an affinity with existing bank products or would it conflict with them?
(c) could the TSB branches be persuaded that this would be a product they could confidently recommend to customers?
(d) what would be the 'product difference' from all the other motor policies offered by competitors?
(e) how could adequate profitability be ensured?

The tentative answers which the marketing department arrived at were:

(a) after death, marriage and house purchase (all of which the Trust Company's existing insurance products catered for) the purchase of a car is one of the major events in family life; so assisting in its mechanics should be an acceptable customer service.
(b) there was obvious synergy with the personal loans offered by the bank for car purchase; and TSB's ownership of the Swan National car rental company could offer interesting opportunities.
(c) initial talks with branch management produced some negative reactions. Didn't the marketing boys realise that branches are understaffed with constant administrative and training problems and need another new product to worry about like a hole in the head? And what would it do for customer relations, when the accidents started and the Claims Department was awkward? Something clearly would have to be done about this.
(d) A 'product difference' which had worked with other Trust Company insurance policies was *simplicity*. A policy that was simple to take out, easy to understand, and avoided arguments about claims settlement, had attractions both for the prospective policyholder and to the sales force – attractions that could compensate for not being the cheapest product on the market. Getting away from the no-claims bonus (when do you keep it, when do you lose it?) could be a major simplification.

(e) But dispensing with the no-claims bonus – or, looked at another way, not loading the premiums of the accident-prone – would clearly have an adverse effect on profitability. What to do about it?

Designing the product

Brainstorming within TSB and with prospective insurance carriers did not produce any revolutionary new product concepts – perhaps not surprising in as competitive a field as this. But it did produce an attractive package including:

— monthly premium payment by direct debit at no additional cost on the annual rate
— nationwide network of recommended repairers
— 'new for old' replacement parts
— 'new' replacement car
— cover for personal property
— immediate broken windscreen replacement service
— free Green Card
— legal assistance cover for excess compensation claims
— discounted car rental through Swan National
— optional breakdown/recovery protection.

The no claims bonus question was neatly sidestepped by offering all policyholders a 'safe driver discount', accepting as policyholders only those customers who had already qualified for a no claims bonus with another insurer, providing in premium calculations for a normal incidence of accidents – but planning to ask the unacceptably accident prone to find alternative cover. In effect, the problem of avoiding excessive underwriting losses without a complicated no claims price structure was taken care of by policyholder selection.

All of these features were embodied in a simply-written 'no nonsense' policy and checked through group discussions. Responses were generally favourable. The positively stated 'safedriver premium' was warmly welcomed by customers who prided themselves on their safety record and resented having to pay high premiums for the misfortunes of others, as was the facility for paying by monthly instalments without additional cost. TSB was regarded favourably as a potential seller of motor insurance, by many for the same reason as brokers are often preferred to postal cover from a large insurance company – the possibility of discussing a problem face to face.

The delivery system

How to handle selling, policy issue and renewal and claims settlement so as to obtain the support of the TSB branches without putting an excessive administrative load on them was as important a question as the contents of the policy. The first step was to appoint a carrier with the necessary skills and organisational facilities, as well as a congenial attitude to customer service. A systematic selection process was undertaken, using a scoring matrix for such features as depth of resources, empathy, price, flexibility and claims settlement reputation, and agreement was finally reached with Royal Insurance (UK) Ltd. The Royal undertook to set up a direct response handling unit in Manchester to process direct mail quotation requests and to add a TSB section to its new business/claims department in Southampton with a direct line to the Trust Company's computer in Andover and a Freefone number for claimants.

Meanwhile an in-company project team was working on internal systems and procedures against a rapidly advancing deadline (when the project was initiated in April 1984, the Trust Company's marketing department had set the ambitious target of a launch in February 1985). It was decided that the branches of the regional TSB companies needed to be fully briefed on the car insurance product, and the thinking behind its introduction, so that they could co-operate in the identification of suitable customers and in providing sales support; but the administrative work, including the issue of cover notes and policies, would be centralised in the Trust Company. Information packs and sales promotional material – written in as simple terms as the policy itself – were distributed to the branches. Because time pressures did not allow them to be researched in advance, they were accompanied by questionnaires inviting suggestions on how future editions could be improved; this produced valuable feedback from the branches, and stimulated interest.

Sales promotion and advertising

The selection of an advertising agency was handled in the same systematic way as the selection of a carrier; in the end a direct marketing agency (now called Ogilvy & Mather Direct) was preferred to a large general advertising agency because it was felt that their practical experience in direct marketing was most likely to sell policies. The media advertising theme, used in both press and TV, stressed 'bumper to bumper cover' for safe drivers, and introduced a mildly knocking element by announcing 'a comprehensive policy, designed for car drivers, not insurance companies'. The same theme was followed through in branch display and direct mail material.

Targeting and monitoring results

Of TSB's six million customers, some four million are car owners; and about half of these were believed to conform to the target customer specifications (age 25–75, three years accident-free driving). In addition to the two million or so potential among their own customers, an incremental return of unknown size could be expected from non-TSB customers responding to the couponed press advertising (on advertised unit-linked insurance products over 60% of enquiries had come from non-customers).

On the other hand, while insured motorists may be interested enough to enquire about a new policy, they are much less likely to switch to a new insurer before the renewal date for their exisitng policy. So the TSB marketing people reckoned that they would know very soon how interesting the product proposition was by measuring the enquiry rate; but they would not know how successful they had been in actually selling policies until renewal dates had arrived and the computer's reminder to enquirers that D-day was here, had succeeded or failed in eliciting action.

The response to the initial burst of five press advertisements was encouraging, even embarrassing; the forecast level of enquiries was exceeded by 200%, necessitating a doubling of capacity in the Royal's Manchester direct response unit and postponement of further advertising. Now the nail-biting period has arrived of watching the conversion rate slowly build up, while initiating other promotional activities to generate more enquiries. The product seems to be near enough right, the promotion seems to be working, the profit formula is watertight (Royal carries the underwriting risk and TSB handles the promotional aspects, for which it receives a fixed percentage added to the premium). From now on, as always, the customer will decide.

A MERCHANT BANKER'S APPROACH TO MARKETING.

The conventional marketing man's wholly erroneous notion of merchant bankers is that there's no place in their convivial, opportunistic lives for systematic marketing. Whether it was ever true that business was won simply by knowing the right people and belonging to the right clubs is questionable. It is certainly not the case to-day. Merchant banks can be more flexible about *means* than the inevitably more ponderous clearing banks – which is one reason why the major clearers find it essential to incorporate a merchant bank in group organisations. But in defining *ends* they are every bit as dedicated to the basic marketing principles of market segmentation, concentration of effort, market research, planned communications and adherence to long-term strategy.

Selecting a market niche

Charterhouse Japhet, now the merchant banking arm of the Royal Bank of Scotland Group, decided in 1975 that establishing a solid base and reputation against its larger competitors in an increasingly internationalised merchant banking market would require concentration on carefully selected market niches, rather than trying to be all things to all people. They went down the logical road, travelled by many others, of analysing the market for the major merchant banking services of fund-raising, organising mergers, acquisitions, flotations, strategic business development advice to clients, and so on, in search of industrial segments with high growth potential, likely to be capital-hungry and likely to need skilled financial advice. Still not alone, they identified Information Technology as such a segment.

They then went a bit further down the road and selected the closely linked sub-segments of communication by satellite and cable as offering special opportunities. Both were hugely under-developed areas in which big money was looking for investment opportunities; both were areas in which hard information and informed judgment was difficult to come by; both had strong connections with television, in which Charterhouse Japhet was already deeply involved; and both in the long run were bound to flow into each other.

The first problem was to find the best point of entry. In the satellite sector the bank, having by now nominated one of their senior partners as Mr. I.T., decided that buying into a specialist satellite consultancy would be the quickest way of acquiring and keeping up to date the necessary market information. They were under no illusion that this would be a profitable investment in itself – an attitude that will not astonish consultants who tend to confirm the adage that the cobbler's children have no shoes; but they calculated, rightly as it turned out, that an investment of $250,000 or so in the right consultancy would pay off in the knowledge, contacts and early warning system of new developments that it provided.

Through a company broker, Charterhouse Japhet found a consultancy in California, which met their specifications and was not averse to a minority investment by a 'limey' bank. Starting from this market knowledge base, the bank's executives progressed methodically along the familiar path of getting to know, and making themselves known to, everybody who was anybody in the international satellite field. This involved attending the right conferences, circulating market information to clients and non-clients alike, holding little lunch parties, where A was introduced to B and C to their mutual benefit, and taking all the other P.R. measures needed to bring about the desired situation – namely that when an entrepreneurial organisation wanted to discuss a financial problem with a merchant bank that understood their business, Charterhouse Japhet would be one of the first names to come to mind.

By 1985 the small (four-man) I.T. group in the bank had acquired enough confidence in their own market expertise to invest the bank's money in satellite hardware. In that year they were actively involved in the retrieval of the satellite that went missing from Discoverer and in selling the recovered hardware.

The cable market, tackled in parallel with the satellite sector, was at a much more developed stage. Already there were successful businesses, particularly in the US and continental Europe, piping TV information or entertainment services and programmes to local communities, and preparing for the day when the landlines could be utilised for home shopping, home banking and other inter-active services.

The bank decided that in this case, buying practical experience was more appropriate than buying knowledge and gave a company broker a very tight brief to find them a US cable operator in which they could buy a 20% to 30% interest for around $20 million. The specifications included such requirements as the operation of two separate franchises, one in an under-developed, the other in a developed but under-peopled area; an entrepreneurial and congenial partner in charge; a weak financial director, who could be replaced by a British nominee; and accessibility to a port of entry.

Almost unbelievably, the broker came up with a business near Seattle that met the specifications. Months of negotition followed, culminating in failure on the edge of success when a rival investor stepped in with a higher bid. So how to pursue the main strategy when the favoured tactic had collapsed?

What Charterhouse Japhet – by now as well informed about cable as about satellites – elected to do was to adopt another marketing strategy. They constructed and publicised a computer suite, programmed to evaluate sales and profit potential for organisations applying for cable franchises in the UK or in continental Europe (where prospects are considerably brighter).

They also offered a free headhunting service to companies entering or expanding in the cable field – an exchange of immediate revenue for possible future favours which only long-term thinkers would countenance.

By 1985 they had been appointed as merchant bankers to three such organisations and were once again on course for the inevitable day when cable and satellite would coalesce.

What part did the bank's Marketing Department play in all this? It has to be admitted that there is no bank Marketing Department. The bank's senior managers take the view that it is more important for them to be well-informed, methodical and imaginative in their business development activities than to employ specialists to do it for them. They could be right.

CHAPTER NINETEEN

Marketing organisation

In the end, successful marketing depends on the calibre of the people who plan and do it, the way they are organised and (when marketing, as in most banks, is a staff function) the way they relate to all levels of line management.

None of these factors are constants. The right people and the right organisation in one bank may not be appropriate to another; and what is appropriate for the same bank in 1985 may be inappropriate five or ten years later.

In this chapter we describe the different states of marketing organisation reached in 1985 by two large banks, one with its main emphasis on domestic business, the other with the larger part of its activities distributed among a variety of overseas markets; we also describe the functions and organisation of a central intelligence department, servicing the needs of decentralised group marketing departments.

ORGANISING FOR RESULTS

In the late 1960s and early 1970s the British banks were beginning to suspect that marketing, as practised in large consumer goods companies, might have something to offer them in an increasingly competitive market. But early attempts to introduce a marketing function, which took place more or less simultaneously in all the big banks, were tentative and seldom wholly successful. This was attributable partly to the prevailing culture – traditional bankers were seldom sympathetic to the notion of actively selling their services – partly to the fact that the banks were making good profits rather easily, which does not encourage any fundamental change of attitude or behaviour; partly to the emerging realisation that marketing techniques developed for fast moving consumer goods were not always appropriate to the financial services industry.

In all the big clearing banks the next decade was a period of finding the proper role and organisational niche for a marketing department;

and of slow but steady progress from a somewhat peripheral position, looking after the promotion of related banking services and so on, to making a more fundamental contribution to the planning and development of the bank's core business. While they were all moving in the same direction, seeking to improve the return on their investment in marketing people, the banks did not all adopt the same organisational structure as regards the perpetual issue of centralisation versus decentralisation and the responsibility for marketing functions like market research, advertising, P.R. and business development planning; nor was it certain that the organisation charts of 1985 would all look the same in 1990.

In 1985 Barclays Bank, generally acknowledged to be the most proactive of the 'Big Four' English clearing banks in its attitude to marketing, had positioned its central marketing department as shown in the Chart (opposite), reporting in a staff role to one of two General Managers responsible for UK operations. Its main functions, on paper, lay in the areas of market research, the development of new services and the organisation of promotions. Planning, advertising, P.R. and marketing training were handled by other departments; and local marketing activities were handled by regional marketing teams under the control of regional general managers.

But, as usual, the organisation charts told only half of the story about the real role of the department, its relationships with general management and with other staff departments and its growing influence on the course of events, particularly in the area of long-term customer relations. Unlike the functional heads of most other staff departments, the AGM Marketing had a permanent seat at the weekly General Managers' meetings. There was close liaison with the Planning, P.R. and Advertising Departments, including a regular input of market data and analyses. And through the District Support function there was a mutually supportive working relationship with the branch network; the regional marketing teams provided the centre with ideas and feedback from the branches, while the central marketing department supplied the field with research data, marketable products and sales promotional material.

Compared with its staff structure two years earlier the marketing department had changed in the direction of quality as against quantity. Staff numbers had been reduced by over 25%, thanks mainly to shedding routine clerical responsibilities related to automated payments. And direct responsibility for marketing training had been transferred to Personnel,

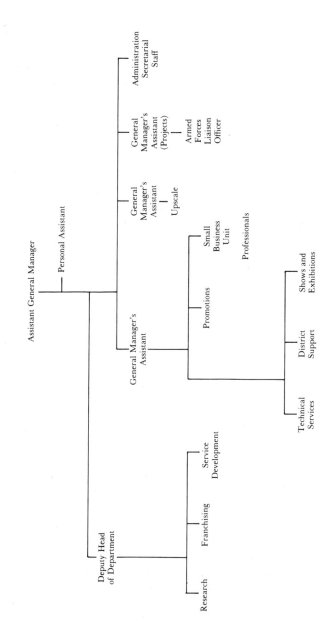

**Barclays Bank Marketing Department
Staff Structure as of July 1985**

though members of the department still participated in courses while the development of new services and promotions involved a substantial element of product knowledge indoctrination.

Members of the department were mostly career bankers with the exception of professional researchers recruited from outside the bank. This was in recognition of the vital importance of effective communication with all levels of line management. But those who took to marketing had the prospect of spending more than the conventional two or three years in the department, without detriment to their career prospects; and others returned there for a second stint after a spell in the field. A number of former career bankers, carefully picked from the line by the Department's senior management, had switched to a permanent marketing career with benefits to both themselves and the bank.

Not perhaps the textbook marketing organisation. But like marketing itself, marketing departments are most cost-effective when they are designed to meet real needs in real situations rather than achieve some theoretical ideal. On such practical grounds, Barclays Marketing Department is more than willing to stand up and be counted.

MODERNISING THE MARKETING APPROACH OF A TRADITIONAL INTERNATIONAL BANK

The Standard Chartered Bank Group could not claim in the 1970s to be literally 'old-established' as such, having been formed in 1969 out of a merger of the Standard Bank of South Africa and the Chartered Bank of India, Australia and China. But it and its component banks had established their commercial habits and traditions in the old imperialist days when you did not even need a better mouse-trap for the world to beat a path to your door, because the world (or those parts of the map that were coloured pink) had no choice in the matter. If you wanted to do business with a bank in Hong Kong, Shanghai or Nairobi, you beat a path to the dominant British bank. Marketing activity could readily be confined to the club, the golf-course and the race-course.

Even after the sun had set on the British Empire, Standard Chartered continued to operate from a privileged or protected position in many of the former colonial territories. It was often the first or at least among the earliest banks to be established. It had banking connections with the local business community and a depth of experience that newcomers could not match. And as other banks came in, there was a tendency to suppress the growth of any real competition through protective associations, agreed tariffs and other cartel arrangements.

But good times always come to an end. In 1979, when developing the bank's strategic objectives for a five year plan, management carried out an in-depth examination of the strengths and weaknesses of Group operations around the world. Marketing came high on the list of weaknesses identified by the examination. It was decided that organisational changes were needed; and that the initial thrust for more effective marketing must come from the top. A general management post was created in Head Office with the task, among others, of analysing the marketing weaknesses in greater detail and finding ways and means of correcting them.

The following were the most damaging of the specific marketing deficiencies found by the General Manager and his team in one or other of the bank's far-flung territories:

- calling on potential customers but ignoring existing (and usually more valuable) customers;
- failing to prepare for calls by reviewing the prospective customer's needs and identifying bank services which might persuade the customer to transfer business from his existing bankers;
- placing responsibility for marketing in the hands of relatively junior officers, without senior management support or involvement;
- segregating the marketing function in separate departments, which tended to become appendages, unable to get speedy or satisfying responses from operational areas;
- attempting to cover all segments of the market with the same people. (The need for an international bank to segment the market place, and develop particular and relevant expertise came through very strongly.);
- failing to co-ordinate marketing activities, particularly in areas where several members of the group – commercial bank, merchant bank, finance company – were operating independently;
- failing to record sales and sales promotional activity, resulting in duplicated effort and irritated customers after personnel changes;
- failing to complement marketing training courses for junior management with indoctrination of senior management;
- accepting regular social contact as sufficient fulfilment of marketing needs. 'They will ask me if they want anything', the standard response of senior management, was no longer adequate in a more competitive banking environment;

– focusing business development effort on asset business, while neglecting the liability side of the bank.

Diagnosing these deficiencies was, as always, far easier than putting them right; the culture of an organisation and the attitudes of people who have worked in it all their lives do not change overnight. Management decided that improving the bank's marketing performance had to be a progressive affair, taken step by step with responsibility for developing the various aspects of marketing assigned to the appropriate managers at every level.

Among the first steps was the expansion of the annual corporate plan to include a marketing plan. Or rather marketing plans. For it was very soon apparent that both the market environment and the bank's marketing performance varied greatly between territories, making it necessary to segment the over-all plan into separate territorial plans for each of the overseas territories. The need for segmentation of planning and organisation also became apparent in relation to the main customer sectors served by the bank. These were identified as:

– Central banks and other international banking institutions
– Correspondent banks
– Large multinational companies
– Large non-multinational companies
– Middle market companies
– High income personal customers
– General retail
– Technology driven areas – Cards, ATMs etc.

At the same time, information about the needs and attitudes of the various customer segments was being collected and analysed more methodically than in the past. This in its turn led to the identification of a number of gaps in the bank's product range, which had to be filled if it was to compete successfully in a highly competitive, rapidly developing environment. New product development became a high priority.

Closer relationships with multinationals were developed by the appointment of Account Relationship Managers, as part of a Global Account Management concept. Other companies were handled by Account Executives, operating within corporate banking divisions, which tended increasingly to assume responsibility for corporate relationships, leaving branch managers to concern themselves with the increasing demands of retail banking and the growing variety of counter services.

Other aspects of market and organisational segmentation included specialisation in supplying the financial service needs of certain industrial groups, such as energy; and the establishment of units to develop and deliver new services such as international cash management and special transactions such as countertrade.

In the early 1980s the move towards greater market orientation was stimulated by the acquisition of a substantial American bank. Standard Chartered found that the new subsidiary was at the opposite end of the marketing spectrum from its own inherited traditions and concluded that there was much to be learned from American methods. It was becoming increasingly evident that the generalist banker approach is an impediment in a world of growing specialisation, particularly in the world of technology. Finding the right balance between the generalist and the specialist was one of the biggest problems that they, in common with many other British banks, urgently needed to tackle.

The question of personal motivation was another urgent problem, highlighted by the American acquisition. British banking has been fortunate in living with good margins, thus allowing generous basic salary scales with automatic increases, provided only that you do not put your hand in the till. But now margins and thus earnings were under pressure, while overheads continued to rise inexorably. It became more attractive to develop some of the American style incentives, with reward more closely related to performance – and the non-performers no longer able to count on a lifetime of automatic increments.

By 1985 the centralised approach to marketing, essential in the early days of organisational and policy changes, was becoming less appropriate; and the need to adapt marketing strategies to fit the different situations in the different markets and market segments took precedence. The central marketing department was slimmed down, retaining responsibility for the Group's strategic marketing planning and the continued enhancement of Group marketing standards, but releasing operational marketing responsibility to the various territories.

It can reasonably be predicted that by 1990, when Standard Chartered has fulfilled its intention of joining the Committee of London Clearing Banks and winning a larger share of the UK market, the Group's marketing organisation will look different once again. One of the things that makes marketing so frustrating for the indolent, and so stimulating for the lively-minded, is that you never quite catch up with change. The moment you say 'this is it, we've got our organisation, strategy, product range and operational methods dead right', the marketplace changes; and unless you change with it, you really will be dead.

Standard Chartered's managers have seen enough changes in their various markets not to be surprised by the unexpected. Change and adjustment are continual in all parts of the organisation. But it looks as though the main directions, though certainly not the details of marketing organisation and methods are now established. The pioneer days of building marketing awareness are over, and the emphasis can now be on increasing effectiveness. The principle of delegating responsibility to the territories for carrying out marketing policy is likely to be enhanced, as marketing skills become more widespread. But at the same time the development of information and communications technology, together with the realisation that in the world of international finance everything interconnects, will force the central marketing department – strengthened in quality if slimmer in numbers – to be more proactive in the initiation of new policies. Above all the elasticity to cope with crises has been built into the organisation.

THE INFORMATION BUSINESS

In the early stages of becoming more market-oriented, the banks had little difficulty in accepting market research, economic reports and other forms of market intelligence as useful, if minor, contributions to running the business. They didn't cost much and you didn't have to take them too seriously if they suggested that all was not well, or that opportunities were being missed; profits were still good.

But in an increasingly competitive and volatile marketplace, both national and international, every bank is spending more on the collection and analysis of information; and the providers of information are correspondingly more concerned to ensure that the fruits of their expenditure make a cost-effective contribution to management decision-making at all levels.

The location of the market information function varies from bank to bank, often for historical reasons. In NatWest, the Market Intelligence Department is part of the central Business Development Division, whose other functions include corporate planning, public affairs, advertising and operational research. It is headed by the bank's Chief Economist (who says proudly that he is a one-handed economist, always ready to stick his neck out; none of your 'on the one hand this, on the other hand that') and is responsible for servicing the market information needs of 'customer' divisions and departments in the bank within an annually negotiated budget.

The main in-bank customers are senior management and corporate planners, responsible for the bank's business development strategy; the advertising and public affairs departments, devising and monitoring communications strategy; and the business divisions (Domestic, International and Related Banking Services) who carry the responsibility for implementing corporate strategy on the ground – and who have been heard to remark that it is they who earn the profits that Business Development and the other service divisions spend.

As in other banks there is continual debate about whether the market information function should be centralised or decentralised. The business divisions, each of which is a large business in its own right, have their own planning and marketing departments and are encouraged, but not compelled to resort to the central Market Intelligence Department for their market information needs; apart from procedural pressures, there is the practical inducement that central information is supplied 'free'. None-the-less the decentralisers argue that research related to tactical marketing projects loses some of its immediacy if it is carried out by or through a central department rather than by the marketing people directly responsible for the project. The counter-argument, which so far has carried the day, is that the results of research carried out for one division in the bank are often useful (with or without further analysis) to other bank divisions or subsidiaries; and that a concentration of research skills in one department produces a valuable degree of people synergy.

Responsibilities

In its central position in NatWest the Market Intelligence Department's main responsibility is to act as interpreter between the providers of market information – market research companies, the media, government departments and so on – and its 'customers', the users of market information within the Group. The prime measure of its success is the extent to which the information is applied constructively in making strategic and tactical business decisions, initiating business development or promotional projects, and monitoring their results. A secondary measure is the cost of acquiring and processing the necessary information.

Organisation

No organisation stays unchanged for very long. But at present the department is organised to discharge these responsibilities as illustrated in the Chart (opposite). The main units in what is still a relatively small (though expanding) department – in relation to the size and diversity of the Group – are the Economists, who have the key responsibility of forecasting the national and international climate in which the various members of the group will be operating; the Commercial Intelligence Section, which collates and reports on published information about the marketplace, competitors' activities and so on, both regularly and ad hoc; the Statistics and Market Research Section, which commissions and analyses field research; and the International Section, which specialises in servicing the market information needs of the international division (apart from such geographical sectors as the US, which is big enough to look after itself) and of those subsidiaries whose business is more national than international. Small though they are, the individual sections have tended in the past to become compartmentalised; it is a major concern of the present departmental head to break down any barriers, so that 'customers' can readily gain access to all the information that is relevant to their needs.

Problems

Even a staff department, operating as a cost centre rather than a profit centre, is well advised to think first and foremost about satisfying customer needs; it will not fare well in any organisational shake-up if it is generally regarded as uncomprehending and dilatory. For MID, as for many organisations the customer is a number one problem ('what a great airline this would be, if it weren't for the customers'). The problem arises in the first instance from the great variety of customers and potential customers in the group. Some, most particularly the domestic division, have made extensive use of the department's services; some have made little or no use of what was on offer. Some have been specific about the information they needed, some distinctly vague. Some have been sophisticated in the interpretation of research data, others unsophisticated and prepared to interpret information selectively to support whatever case they were making. The problem was compounded in the early days by the limited manpower of the department, which left no spare time for selling its

Structure of Market Intelligence Department, National Westminster Bank Plc

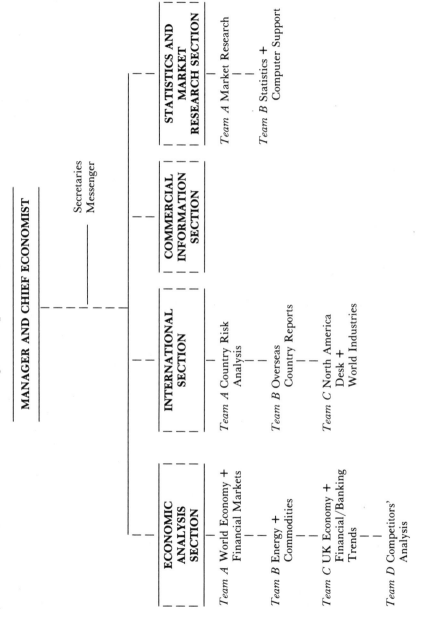

MANAGER AND CHIEF ECONOMIST

Secretaries
Messenger

ECONOMIC ANALYSIS SECTION

Team A World Economy + Financial Markets

Team B Energy + Commodities

Team C UK Economy + Financial/Banking Trends

Team D Competitors' Analysis

INTERNATIONAL SECTION

Team A Country Risk Analysis

Team B Overseas Country Reports

Team C North America Desk + World Industries

COMMERCIAL INFORMATION SECTION

STATISTICS AND MARKET RESEARCH SECTION

Team A Market Research

Team B Statistics + Computer Support

services; the best that could be managed was a periodic catalogue of available reports which produced disappointingly few orders.

Suppliers, whether of field research or of desk research were another problem which had to be handled. The trouble with desk research sources is that they seldom give you precisely the information you want in precisely the form you want it; and data from one source seldom ties up with data from another source. So a considerable amount of editing and adjustment is needed in order to make it readily usable by customers in the group, some of whom are inexpert in the interpretation of published statistics. The trouble with field researchers is that frequently they are more interested in the intricacies of their own techniques than in the use that is made of the results. So they tend to produce long – and for the researcher fascinating – reports which the layman finds indigestible and confusing. Tell me what it *means,* he pleads, before interring it unread in his files.

For the Department both of these problems boil down largely to a question of communications, in which it has been by no means flawless itself in the past. Effective communication demands first of all that enough time is spent with the customer requiring information to understand the problem or opportunity on which he is contemplating action; and to identify the key points on which additional information can be collected that will help him to plan that action and monitor its progress. It demands secondly, when special studies or special analysis of syndicated research are required, that the research contractors are fully apprised of the problem, so that they can make the research as relevant as possible. It demands thirdly that reports emanating from the department are user-friendly, that is to say, recognise the level of interest, sophistication and attention span of the prospective reader. By and large the more senior the reader and the more indirect (though often decisive) his concern with the subject matter, the shorter the summary report he will require. Contrariwise a marketing manager, directly responsible for planning some new project or product will want to see a full report – though his appetite may baulk at digesting many pages of computer print-out. All of this takes time, manpower and no mean skill. Shortage of skilled manpower in the past has sometimes forced the department to publish long and only partially relevant research company reports – doing the reputation of research very little good.

Rapid availability of information is another problem for the department – given customers' habit (not confined to information needs) of demanding by next week, if not tomorrow, information that it would normally take three months to collect and analyse. Sometimes the demand is unreasonable and more time can be negotiated. Often, however, a management decision genuinely has to be made at very short notice; in such cases partial information in time is far better than complete information too late to be used.

The problems of a service department in a service industry can never be completely solved; if perfection were possible, it would certainly cost too much. But progressive improvement, in step with or slightly ahead of customer demand, is a condition of survival. In MID, the speed and direction of such improvement is dependent first and foremost on the calibre of people in the department – which in its turn is dependent on convincing management, at a time of constraint on total group manpower, that investment in high calibre people in the area of information collection and analysis will pay dividends. Conviction is assisted by an emphasis on quality rather than quantity and by the increased productivity that results from this. Though the department's policy continues to require that all field research is contracted out to independent research companies, more specialist researchers are being recruited from outside the bank to complement the bankers turned researchers; this helps in the selection and briefing of research agencies, contributing to progressive product improvement. At the same time it is being recognised that a banker with a feeling and talent for research may build a rewarding career as a research expert and need not necessarily be transferred back to branch duties after two or three years secondment to the information department.

This gives more scope for building constructive relationships with customers in the group – assisted on their side by increasing sophistication in the specification of information needs and in the use of data. Domestic Banking Division, still the major customer, has appointed an 'information strategist', who performs a very effective liaison function between MID and the domestic planning and marketing departments; the recruitment of an outside expert to head the bank's advertising department has greatly increased the demand for consumer attitude research for campaign planning and monitoring purposes, as well as ensuring its effective use; and as corporate planning becomes more sophisticated, segmented and directive, the planners' appetite for market information and forecasts has grown.

It is now possible, also, to adopt a more proactive policy in approaching other departments and subsidiaries in the group, who have either preferred to go their own way or to dispense entirely with a formal input of market information. Sometimes their needs are so specialised that the central department has little to contribute. But often a knowledge of sources and of research techniques, together with a growing databank available for re-processing can be helpful in increasing the relevance or reducing the cost of actionable information for a new customer in the group. This permissive 'perhaps we can help you' approach has widened the department's in-house market, so increasing its value to the group. Further in the future, there is the possibility of using the bank's information-gathering resources as a customer tool, either for business development or for revenue-generating purposes.

Speed of response has been helped – and will be helped even more in the future – by the use of the computer. The Economists, the Market Research Section and the Commercial Information Section have all been equipped with micro-computers, giving them both processing capacity, and access to external databanks as well as to the bank's mainframe computer. It is now possible to systematise regularly updated reports, storing back data on word processors; and to carry out rapid searches for special information requirements, once the needs and possible sources have been clearly defined.

As every researcher knows, an adequate lead time is likely to increase the quality of any research study; and regularly repeated studies give much more insight into a changing market or customer segment than one-off blockbusters. So the department is working with customers on the pre-planning of annual research and information programmes – not excluding the probability of some emergency requirements, but seeking to establish a predictable structure into which the emergencies can be fitted. This also helps, of course, with the budgeting of financial and manpower requirements.

Another direction in which progress is being made is the encouragement of synergy through regular meetings between the heads of the various sections in the department. The thinking behind this apart from the stimulating personal effect of exchanging information and ideas, is that research contributes more to the solution of business problems by a combination of data from different sources – combining qualitative with quantitative studies against a background of desk research – than by a single all-inclusive study. The idea of a combined operation, focused on a defined problem or market segment, needs to be encouraged both within the department and among its customers.

Appendices

Uses and abuses of statistics

Introduction

Many people regard statistics either with awe or with disdain. such attitudes often stem, like many other ailments, from poor feeding. Everyone who uses statistics to aid an argument has an overriding duty to make certain that their content, presentation, source and purpose is as adequate and as appropriate as possible to the needs of his readers. Data should never be served raw. Obviously no single set of data will be equally suitable for all the uses to which it may be put, any more than even the most precise single set of accounts can answer all the questions a manager may ask about a business. To make your statistics more digestible to your readers there are some worthwhile guidelines; but you should be prepared to discard them whenever you have a good reason to do so; they are not rules but *guidelines*. This brief section is not trying to teach you statistics. If you want to learn that science the Institute of Statisticians can help and can examine you. Rather, this appendix summarises many years of writing, and even more of reading, reports; and many years of studying how figures can best be presented.

There are a number of aspects to consider. For what purpose are the data being quoted? How precise need the figures be? (Not how accurate; that is a different subject and is discussed later.) What standards are there – theoretical or derived in some other way – against which data can be judged? Are graphs useful? Is there a 'right' way to lay out a table of numbers? And so on.

Purpose

Sometimes figures are included in a report simply because the author wants to show everyone that he has 'done the work', and because in any case, the figures 'ought to be recorded somewhere'. If this is your reason at least be polite enough to put the data in an appendix – do not clutter up the main report with them. Better, leave them in the filing cabinet and merely indicate their availability in the report.

For example, if the accounts of a company over a number of years are being analysed, then separate small tables, dealing, say, with liquidity relationships, or sales to stocks ratios, should be used (see Table 6).

Table 6. Sales and stock cover over five years

	Stock	Sales	Stock cover*
5 years ago	297	1,978	7.81
4	360	2,314	8.09
3	414	1,762	12.22
2	349	2,018	8.99
Last year	308	2,133	7.51

* Year end stock divided by sales in previous twelve months multiplied by fifty-two

There are aspects of Table 6, however, that are unsatisfactory and which are discussed below. Readers are invited to draw up their own versions of the simplest way of illustrating the changes in stock cover over the period.

If data are required in the course of a report they should be used in a strictly controlled manner. It is far better to have several small tables than one large one; it is far better to relate tables strictly to the point being made with no redundant or superfluous information included; it is far better to use one table to support or to make one point at a time; better to do these simple things than to put all the data into one table and, in effect, tell your readers to 'sort it out for yourselves'. It is the undoubted responsibility of the author to do the work of sorting, grading, classifying and interpreting the data he uses.

Precision

Too frequently statistical data are given to a much greater level of precision than is needed to support the point being made. It is necessary, though, to draw a distinction here between statistics used for managerial control purposes and decision making, on the one hand, and accounting and 'working data' on the other. The latter group may well need very precise numbers; the former rarely needs more than two digits.

What is precision and what is accuracy? Consider a group of children asked to measure the length of a table. The average measurement given was 5.4913 feet. This is obviously a precise figure, but we cannot say whether it is accurate or not unless we actually know the length of the table. It would be just as precise – that is, to a level of around one in 50,000 – if the children had stated 5.4913 miles as their average. That we 'know' to be inaccurate.

Obviously figures we use should be as accurate as necessary: 'around three or four' may be quite accurate enough, but not if a different decision would be reached if the figure *were* three rather than four. Equally obviously figures we use should only be as precise as necessary: 'five and a half feet' would be quite precise enough for the average of the children's measurements.

Can you now improve Table 6?

Standards

If your doctor told you your hæmoglobin count was a bit below ten would you be happy, worried, or dead? The answer, as it happens, depends on your sex. Most women could be happy; while many men might be a little worried. But most people would not know how to react because they would not know what standard to use as a basis for their judgment.

So, too, in presenting data in a banking context. Beware of assuming that your readers will know the appropriate standard. Better to add just a line to give the 'expected' value than to risk the reader missing the whole point of the table.

But what is an 'expected' value? There are three possibilities. First, one derived from general experience. Often this will be the 'average' of previous measurements, but may not always be very precisely quantified: for example, 'Brighter than the brightest star', or as is implied in a statement such as 'You have put too much salt in', or 'It is a rather high rate of interest.' Second, one given by law or laid down by some authority. For example, 'Average contents forty-eight matches', or '70 per cent proof', or 'A reserve assets ratio of 12.5 per cent.' Third, one based on theory, which of course in practice will usually be based on, or derived from, numerous observations. For example, the expected price of a fixed-interest security, or of a conversion loan stock, or the speed at which an object falls to the ground.

Of course it is essential to use the correct standard of whichever type is appropriate; using the wrong one is worse than not using one at all.

Setting out a table

There are a few simple 'rules' which can help make statistics more digestible when presented in a table. They do not have to be followed slavishly; indeed they cannot be, because sometimes they are contradictory. But when you break them, do so consciously, trading off the specific advantage you foresee against the general experience the rules embody.

To start with, figures which are 'expected' to be similar should appear beneath one another. There are two reasons for this. First, if a series of numbers is read across the page, your eye sees the least significant digit of one number followed by the most significant digit of the next. So there is a see-saw effect to the importance of the numbers your eye scans. Second, it is easier to see changes when the numbers are underneath each other. Try writing out a few 3 digit numbers; each, say, one third bigger than its predecessor. This 'rule', then, implies that with time-series data the years (or months or weeks) should go down the page and not across. (Yes, it is true that such a layout will take up more space sometimes than running across the page, but that is a small price to pay for giving readers an easier task in understanding the figures.)

Another good rule is to not use numbers with more than two, or possibly three, digits. Not of course in your calculations, but in statistics presented to management. it is unusual, to say the least, for managers to take decisions based on figures that differ by only 1 per cent or thereabouts. So a table like, for example, Table 7, is much easier to understand than one like Table 8, even though in Table 7 the actual earnings are 'wrong' in the sense that the result of multiplying £57 million by 1.2 per cent is 684 and not 700. The sacrifice of not being able to check the author's arithmetic (not a great sacrifice, since if you cannot trust his arithmetic should you trust anything?) is much more than offset by the greater ease of being able to grasp the pattern of the figures. Try yourself to re-arrange data you deal with in this way and you will quickly realise the benefits. Note that in Table 7 suitable units have been chosen, and that in the earnings columns this has meant using three digits rather than two, but that the third is zero. Again, try for yourself the effect of entering the third digit and see what difference if any, it makes. The budget column is, of course, the 'standard'.

Graphs and other pictures

Graphs, pie-charts and other pictures can be excellent devices for showing simple relationships between two, or possibly three, measures. Note that

Table 7.

	Loans (£m)	Margin (%)	Earnings in £000 Actual	Budget
Last year	82	1.2	980	950
2 years ago	65	1.3	870	900
3	71	1.2	880	880
4	66	1.3	850	830
5	57	1.2	700	760

Table 8.

	Last year	2 years ago	3 years ago	4 years ago	5 years ago
Loans	£82,231,522	£64,892,464	£71,055,367	£65,698,223	£57,311,576
Margin	1.193%	1.337%	1.244%	1.297%	1.215%
Earnings	£981,022	£867,612	£883,929	£852,106	£696,336

it is the relationship that needs to be simple, not the measures themselves. For example, a graph showing both a set of observations and a theoretical prediction based on a very complex theory will, if the 'fit' is good, show a simple relationship.

But the very simplicity of graphs and other pictorial representations can lead to difficulties. Graphs which have 'unusual' scales can give a quite false impression. Compare the visual effect of the same data drawn to two different scales, as illustrated, for example, in Fig. 6.

Fig. 6.

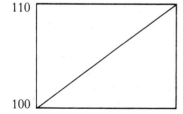 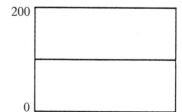

Using pie-charts to illustrate change poses a possible ambiguity: is it the area, or is it the radius that is the proper dimension to reflect the true change in the total? In Fig. 7, for example, it is obvious that the *shares* represented in A and B for factors 1, 2 and 3 have changed and that the total has as well. But has the total doubled in size – in proportion to the two radii or quadrupled in size – in proportion the two areas? It is rare, but not unknown, for a graphical method to be better than a well-produced table. Bearing in mind the ways in which ambiguities or even misleading impressions can arise from using such techniques, it is as well to take special care.

Fig. 7.

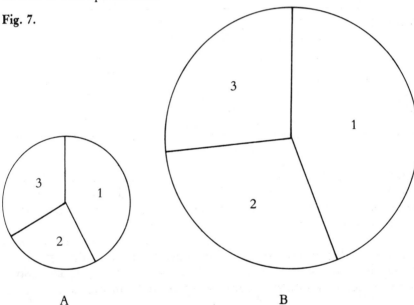

A   B

Summary
Fitness of purpose is the keynote in using statistical data. Different purposes require different techniques. But perhaps the overriding requirement is that each and every presenter of statistics should be aware of the needs of his customers; not an inappropriate attitude to propound in a book on marketing. Beware the trap of assuming your readers will have appropriate 'standards' or benchmarks clearly in their minds; it is better to remind them what the standards are than to risk misleading them.

Business models

Introduction

Models are a representation of the real world, made to a level of accuracy and precision relevant to their purpose. Some models are made to very high standards indeed, perhaps out of sheer pride or enjoyment in their creation, perhaps because they are to be used to test ideas that in the real world will become very expensive (for example, wind tunnel models of new aircraft). The same principles apply to business models, which can range in complexity from the economic system models we read about (the Treasury model or the London Business School model, for example) to very simple types whose greatest use perhaps is purely as an aid to thinking about a particular problem. This latter kind may well be couched wholly in logical terms and have no arithmetical capabilities at all.

Of course, no model can be as 'real' as the real thing – any more than a model train can carry people. (If they do, then they are small trains and not models.) Indeed some models used in forecasting may be virtually unreal all the time, in the sense that actions are taken to avoid their forecasts. But here we will discuss simpler models, and indicate some areas in which they are useful.

Sensitivities

One of the most interesting uses of business models is in predicting the effect of given changes in various elements in the model. To take a very simple example, consider a loan from a bank. By how much should the lending rate rise to offset a given rise in the cost of money? (Here, 'to offset' means that total profit from the loan will stay constant.) Obviously, aside from agreeing what measure of the 'cost of money' to take, the answer depends on what proportion of total cost of money costs represent. For a loan of several million pounds the relationship will be near to 1:1, so that the lending rate should move almost in step with money costs to leave absolute profit unchanged.

But in small loans the inevitable administration and other non-money costs will be a significant proportion of total costs and will lead to a dampening of the effect of changes in money costs. The 'model' could be written as

Revenue = Profit + Administration costs + Money costs

and to take an arithmetical example or two, suppose $P = £10$, $A = £10$, $M = £80$, then revenue will be £100; i.e.

$$100 = 10 + 10 + 80.$$

Now suppose there is a 12.5 per cent increase in the cost of money. By how much must R rise if P is to stay at £10? Well, we know A will stay constant because we *defined* it as 'non-money' costs, so we will have $R = 10 + 10 + 90$ (i.e. 110) and so R must rise by 10 per cent to offset a 12.5 per cent rise in the cost of money. Readers should consider other arithmetical examples such as administration costs of £20 or £1, and also changes other than 12.5 per cent in the cost of money. It will then be possible to draw graphs showing a whole family of lines if the resulting change in R is plotted against given changes in M, with one line for each value of A. And, of course, you will now be able to estimate the required change in R for *any* change in M once you know the value of A. (Just to check for a given change in M, what change in R is required to keep $P = 10$ when $A = 0$? This is what is called a limiting case, since A cannot be negative and is therefore at its lowest limit.) Readers will already be arguing that in real life other factors need to be taken into account. For example, there will probably be *some* extra administration costs when interest rate changes have to be applied to an existing loan. So we cannot say that A will stay constant. But any such *increase* in A will occur if rates go *down* just as much as if they go up. So we cannot say A is linked to M, but would have to complicate the model in some other way. This process of gradually making the model more and more like the real world is typical of the modeller's art. But it is not always easy.

A more complex model can be illustrated by the following (it is part of a model developed by the marketing group at Williams & Glyn's Bank, and we are grateful to the bank for permission to use it here.) It concerns the revenue which might be expected from the personal current accounts of the bank for various tariffs of charges, and is a good example of how predictions may never be right because people may decide to change the way they use their current accounts as a result of any change in the tariff. And while it is true that market research might be able to estimate the likely size of any such change in use, the cost of the research was judged to be more than the extra precision was worth. The extract from the model is

$$R_j = F + N_{aj}. \ C_a + N_{uj}. \ C_u + T_j.t - a.B_j$$

This somewhat frightening equation simply says that tariff revenue from the jth account (a mathematical way of saying for any given account) is equal to the sum of five elements. The first is a fixed charge, F, which because there is no suffix, j, will be the same for all accounts. The second is a charge related to the number of automated items, N_{aj} passed through this account, multiplied by a charge for automated items, C_a. The third is the same as the second but is based on the number of unautomated items, N_{uj} for this jth account and a charge C_u which we can make equal to or different from C_a, the charge for each automated item. Then the fourth element in this revenue model is a turnover charge where T is the total debit turnover and t the rate of charge. In practice, both F and t were set at zero, in other words there was no fixed charge per year on an account and there was no turnover charge for Williams & Glyn's personal customers. But both concepts were included in the model and possible values investigated. The final element is the allowance given on the average credit balance B_j on this account at the rate a, where a might be, for example, 5 per cent or 10 per cent per annum, or indeed any other value. Since this allowance is notional (that is, it can be used only to offset charges that would otherwise be incurred) the model also contained a 'constraint' that caused R_j to be given the value NIL whenever $a.B_j$ was greater than the total of the first four elements.

We can now ask this model about sensitivities. For this we would program a computer with this model and tell it to print as an output the total value of R_j for all values of F, C_a, C_u, t and a that we have set. Then, of course, if we change C_a by, say, 1p we will know how many thousands of pounds difference this single change will make to total revenue (provided that we have also given the computer all the values of N_a, N_u, T and B for every account). In practice, those values would probably be available for only a sample of accounts and the total suitably adjusted, but this would be a fully acceptable approach. And in practice, the computer would probably print only the total revenue and not the detail for each account.

Again, students are urged to do the simple arithmetic to calculate R for a few accounts, setting the charging factors F, C_a, C_u, t and a at say 0, 8p, 15p, 0 and 10 per cent per annum and choosing values for N_a, N_u,

T and *B* to represent their view of how, say, typical students, housewives and businessmen use their personal accounts.

A well-known example of a model is, of course, a business budget and the budgetary control system which goes with it. Data have to be collected and analysed, and then certain predictions can be made. But it is unusual for the relationships which exist among parts of the business (and which therefore should be reflected in their budgets) to be stated explicitly. A budget is usually merely a frozen image, so to speak, of the organisation at one moment of time. But flexible budgets are better models because variations between the original budget and the real-world performance can be better understood, and proper adjustments made, as they arise.

Flow models

Some models have time as an essential ingredient. Consider a very simple model of a market into which a new sweetener is to be introduced which has zero calories, like saccharin, but which does not have the aftertaste some people believe saccharin has. The market consists of people who use saccharin, those who use sugar, and those who use neither and possibly some who use both (ignored in Fig. 8). The question is, 'From which group, or groups, will the users of the new product be drawn?' Diagrammatically, it can be presented as in Fig. 8. opposite.

The likely flows of users of the new product (along the lines *a, b* and *c*) can be estimated by market research. But why bother? The reason, of course, is because the *promotional* appeal will be different to each group. There are three audiences and each needs a separate message. For example, present saccharin users will need no more than reassurance about the calorie value but will have to be persuaded about the lack of aftertaste; for sugar users the message may well need to feature the slimming aspect more; and so on. In this example we have perhaps been over-simple; but the point is that such an approach can greatly assist at the thinking and planning stage.

A better-known model of this type is a network, in which various activities, some of which must precede others but not all, can be shown diagrammatically in a way which highlights the logical time relationships of all the activities. Networks have been widely adopted and have proved their value in many industries, for example in the construction of a major building, ship or refinery. They are also of use in planning the launch of a new product or service. Indeed, a network is virtually essential in

Fig. 8.

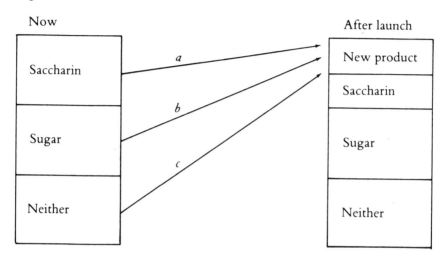

any situation which has too many elements to carry in one's head, all of which must come together on time for a successful outcome, especially if there are substages each of which must be completed on time if the project as a whole is not to be delayed. (The PERT concept referred to in Chapter 9 is a very sophisticated example of such a network.)

As a simple example of a network consider Sunday lunch. It is important to have everything ready at the same time, and to do this some activities must be carried out in parallel with others. On the other hand, you cannot carve the meat until it has been cooked. So a simple meal network could look like that in Fig. 9 overleaf, with five separate routes to start along and four routes which lead to lunch being ready.

It will be immediately obvious that the lapse of time between some of these 'events' is very different from that between others. For example, only fifteen minutes need elapse between preparing the cabbage and serving it; but, if the meat is to be tender, several hours must elapse between taking it from the deep freeze and even starting to cook it. So an obvious development would be to add times to the diagram; and this is exactly what most users of networks do. But networks have a use as an aid to structural thinking even when no times are included.

Fig. 9.

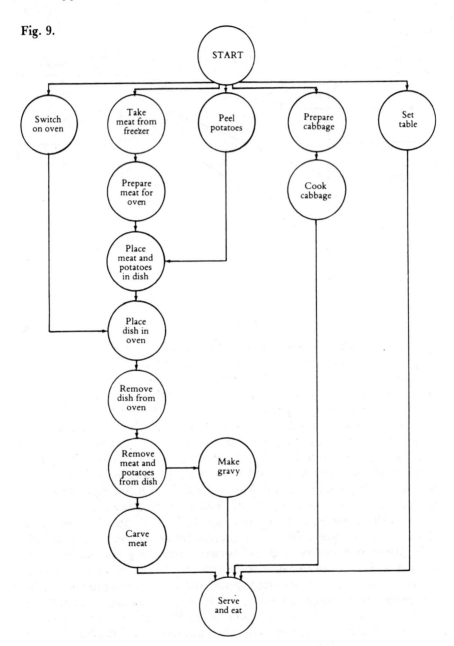

Decision trees

This type of model, as its name suggests, is designed to show up all the possible decisions which are (theoretically) available. (Often, however, it would not be very practical to show them all.)

The likelihood of any given outcome of a series of decisions can be estimated if probabilities can be assigned to each intermediate step. Consider a very simple example of deciding whether to go out with a particular set of friends this evening, as represented in Fig. 10 overleaf.

Now, if each Yes/No split is a 50:50 chance then you can see that there is only one chance in eight (12.5 per cent) that you will go out and an 87.5 per cent chance that you will be staying at home to revise. Of course, most decision trees are much more complex than this, both in having many more decisions to be taken and in each decision having more than two possible outcomes. Moreover, a typical situation to be modelled in this way will contain costs and pay-offs. For example, 'Shall I spend £1,000 and go abroad to try and sell to this overseas customer?' with the probability of making a sale – any sale – being, say 70 per cent if you do but only 40 per cent if you do not. If we now add in the idea that the size of the sale will probably be different in both cases, and the make-up – and therefore profitability of the sale – will also be different, we already have a tree of some complexity. If we modify all these outcomes by whether competitors behave in one way or another it becomes obvious that, without some device to structure our thinking, it will be very difficult indeed to be even fairly sure that all the possibilities have been considered, let alone that the optimum decision has been made. Just how you establish the probabilities (which we assumed to be 50 per cent in every case in the example above) is a topic which we can barely touch on here. In some cases previous experience will be available as a guide; where no guidance is available it is possible to insert guesses and see what changes in them produce a different 'most likely' outcome.

We are thus again considering 'sensitivities', and can see that this concept is a very useful one in marketing management, indeed in management of any kind.

Fig. 10.

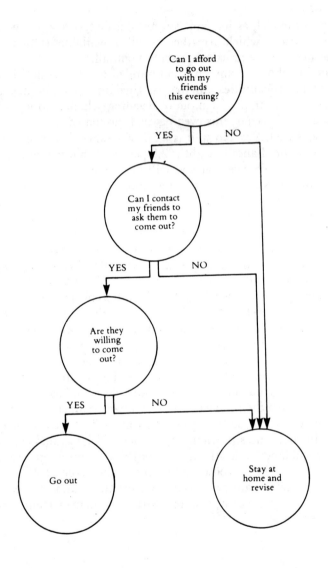

Communicating

A topic as broad as 'communicating' cannot be covered adequately in a mere appendix. After all, some people study the subject for a lifetime and many books have been written about both the science and the art of communication. Nevertheless, telling other people is so central to marketing that we decided to set down some of the more basic principles we have learnt during our combined half-century or more of experience. And the first must be that even these basic principles can be ignored at times.

Brevity is a virute – and we have more to say about it later – but it can be carried too far. One of our secretaries, many years ago, asked to write to decline a sales approach, typed 'Dear Sir, No, Yours faithfully'. One the other hand, when, just after the war, the Ministry of Transport was giving consideration to digging an underpass in London from one side of the Strand to the other opposite Charing Cross railway station, they received, so the story goes, a market research report which said simply '15.8 seconds'. They were happy with this because they had worked out that, using the proposed underpass, pedestrians would take about forty seconds to get from one side of the road to the other. Very sensibly they asked a famous market research company to observe the mass of commuters and time them crossing the Strand. The result, an average of nearly sixteen seconds, convinced them that no one in a hurry to catch his train home would bother to use the underpass. But that such brevity is acceptable is rare. (Of course the market research report probably included some lengthy appendices, but these must have been largely ignored.)

To return to the more general scene, good communication can be judged against four criteria: clarity, credence, relevance and action. There are things to be said about each.

Clarity
Roget's Thesaurus links 'clarity' with ideas embodied in words like 'elegance', 'simplicity' and 'intelligibility'. We would add 'brevity' wherever possible. Learning to be clear in one's communications need not be a slow process. It is important to start with a sharply focused idea of the

structure of your message, and to announce it in advance – just as we have announced that the structure of this section would be based on the four elements of clarity, credence, relevance and action. It is a good idea, too, to summarise from time to time just whereabouts in the argument one has reached, though in brief reports this obviously is unnecessary.

Clarity will be enhanced if more than one 'channel of communication' can be used. Pictures as well as words; tables as well as prose; listening as well as looking, are all improvements. Face-to-face communication can involve facial expressions, gestures and interruptions, all of which can aid communication. Indeed, the instant feedback in face-to-face situations is a very important aspect since it enables the 'transmitter' to judge whether the 'receiver' is 'tuned in' or not. Thus, written communications are not as good as telephone conversations, which are not as good as face-to-face dialogue, in making sure one is being correctly understood; but the written form does of course have other benefits; it is a record, for example.

In writing it is useful to keep sentences short. It is useful to avoid long words. It can be useful to use jargon; i.e. expressions which are clearly understood by experts but not necessarily by others. And it can be helpful to keep to a familiar pattern of reporting or presenting information. Above all, it is worthwhile to keep clearly in mind just who will be the reader that you are seeking to influence, persuade or inspire.

Credence

Roget links 'credence' with 'believability', with 'reasonable' and with 'expected', among other words. It is the idea of expectation which is most relevant for us. If your readers have a frame of reference against which to set the new information then its significance and its credibility can be more readily assessed. An obvious exemple is to be found in management accounting where the budget is the framework against which to set the period's actual results.

Where no such framework exists you must provide one, unless you are certain that normal business experience will be sufficient: but the responsibility is yours. So err on the right side and state clearly what you would have expected as well as giving the latest information. Remember your boss will be even busier than you are, and you should do everything possible to allow him to understand *and judge* what you are telling him. Much too often matters which are of great importance to a subordinate, and which may be one of only two or three projects which he is handling are of much less importance – and one of dozens of responsibilities – to his manager. Good reports, oral or written, recognise this fact and start with a friendly reminder of the previous position.

So far, then, we have suggested that a report should be brief whenever possible, clearly and simply presented always, and contain sufficient points of reference to allow its significance and credibility to be properly assessed.

Relevance

This third aspect has to be considered in two dimensions: not only the obvious one, of excluding extraneous matter while including information necessary for the decisions required, but also time. Roget again: 'relevance' is associated with 'fitness for purpose' and 'in context'.

It is never easy to decide on the first dimension. What is necessary to one member of your target audience may well appear superfluous to another. But appendices can properly be used to meet this point. What is important is that matter relevant to the decision to be made should not be omitted. Models can help in this, by revealing the structure of the problem and the possible solutions. Moreover, as outlined in Appendix II, models will often reveal the sensitivity of any proposed solution to variations in the assumptions made. Obviously more attention should then be given to those factors which have high sensitivities: those with the greatest likely impact on the correctness of the action put forward.

Similarly, networks which include estimates of the costs and times required to accomplish the various intermediate tasks can help to ensure that proper authorisations are obtained at the right moments in the development of a project.

Action

Every report made, oral or written, should have a purpose. At one extreme it may simply be to reassure its audience that all is well, or simply to go towards the building of a data base on which future decisions will draw. In these cases you can expect them to be heard or read, their relevance and accuracy assessed, and then they will be 'filed away'. But at the other extreme they will call for action of a more influential and more immediate kind.

With such 'action now' reports it is essential that they contain a firm recommendation as to what that action should be, and by when the decision to take it should be made. Roget's Thesaurus links 'action' to 'battle' and to 'energy', and it is certainly true that it is often necessary to fight with vigour for the decisions you want. So make is as easy as possible for those who decide. Keep reports of this kind short, with the key elements of the problem defined, with the possible options outlined, and the recommended solution clearly stated, costed and timed. Put less-immediately needed information into appendices.

And end with the polite question, 'Do you agree, please?' That way you are likely to get decisions faster; and in a rapidly changing world that could be a real competitive gain.

Reading List

In the past few years many marketing textbooks have been published either as new works or as new editions of established books. To prepare a list of recommended further reading, of a length appropriate to students of The Institute of Bankers examination, demands great selectivity. We approached this task, as marketing people often do, by carrying out some market research, and we are grateful to those successful students, and to the marketing and training staffs in many major banks, who kindly replied to our short questionnaire.

To their replies and experience we have added our own to produce the list below. What struck us about the replies to our market research however, was the wide range of books students had found useful. Our list should therefore be regarded as a guide to further reading and not as a comprehensive one. In addition, articles about marketing are becoming more common in bank journals, a trend we welcome, and these too should be read.

Finally, the series of Model Answers which The Institute of Bankers has published must *not*, according to our survey results, be ignored.

Among the many textbooks now available the first six received broad support.

1   *Bank Strategic Management and Marketing*
    Channon D. F., John Wiley & Sons Ltd

2   *Insights in Bank Marketing*
    Cheese J., MCB University Press

3   *Principles of Marketing*
    Kotler, Prentice Hall

4   *Marketing Plans – How to prepare them, How to use them*
    McDonald M. H. D., Heineman

5 *The 1982 Gilbart Lectures*
Naylor G. C., The Institute of Bankers

6 *Marketing for Bankers*
Pezzulo M. A., American Bankers Association

The following more specialised books were also mentioned with enthusiasm.

7 *Marketing Communications*
Coulson-Thomas F., Heineman

8 *The Marketing Research Process*
Crimp M., Prentice Hall